Signal

YEARS OF TRIUMPH
1940-42

Signal

YEARS OF TRIUMPH
1940-42

**HITLER'S
WARTIME
PICTURE
MAGAZINE**

EDITED BY S. L. MAYER

PRENTICE-HALL, INC.
Englewood Cliffs, N.J.

A Bison Book

Signal: **Years of Triumph 1940-42**
Edited by S. L. Mayer

This book was prepared and produced by
Bison Books Limited, London, England

First U.S. Edition published by Prentice-Hall, Inc., 1978

Copyright © 1978 by Bison Books, London, England

Printed by Dai Nippon, Tokyo, Japan

ISBN 0-13-810010-1

Library of Congress Catalog Card Number: 77-082134

INTRODUCTION
by S. L. Mayer

Signal, Hitler's Wartime Picture Magazine, was the largest selling magazine in Europe during World War II. Published fortnightly in as many as 20 languages it had a phenomenal sale of 2½ million copies at its peak in 1943. Its English language edition, initially produced for consumption in the United States and the Republic of Ireland, was largely sold in the occupied Channel Islands of Jersey, Guernsey, Alderney and Sark once the Americans entered the war and communication with Ireland became difficult for Nazi Germany. This facsimile edition is based on *Signal* as produced for the Channel Islands from *Signal*'s editorial office in Paris.

Signal: Years of Triumph follows the extraordinary success of *Signal: Hitler's Wartime Picture Magazine*, the first English language facsimile edition of the magazine, which was published in 1976. Like the original magazine, the *Signal* book surprised both its publishers and editor in the enormous interest the modern public has taken in its portrayal of the Nazis' view of themselves and Europe under their domination. In one sense the first *Signal* book sold over 100,000 copies thus far for the same reason that the original magazine was popular even among those peoples who were conquered by Germany. Its articles are fascinating; its layout, imitated later by *Life Magazine* and *Paris-Match* to some degree, is exciting and up-to-date even though the first issue appeared in 1940. Above all, its interest today lies in the fact that *Signal* is an important social document of Hitlerian Europe. It is for that reason that this second *Signal* book is offered to the public now.

Hitler greets the arrival of Mussolini on one of his increasingly frequent visits to Germany during the war.

Above: Troops of the Afrika Korps disembark from their Ju-52 transport in Libya.
Above right: Wehrmacht troops construct a makeshift bridge during the summer of 1941 in their rapid approach to Leningrad.

Signal: Years of Triumph, unlike its predecessor, concentrates on the years 1940–42. These were Hitler's glory years. In less than three months, in the spring of 1940 when the first issues of *Signal* appeared, Hitler's armies overran most of Western Europe. First, Denmark fell in less than a day. As the Wehrmacht proceeded to overwhelm Norway, Nazi spearheads invaded Holland, Belgium and France on May 10, 1940. The Netherlands fell in five days after a hopeless and bitter struggle. The bulk of the French Army and the British Expeditionary Force were quickly trapped in the Dunkirk pocket. Belgium capitulated, and despite the miracle of Dunkirk, France lay open to the German legions. When the French capitulation was signed on June 22, Hitler had achieved a unique triumph, which was portrayed pictorially in the pages of *Signal*. Although the Battle of Britain was scarcely a Nazi triumph, neither was it a defeat. Bombing raids continued ceaselessly over British cities and factories, and Britain was rendered incapable of launching any major counter-offensive in Europe. Emboldened by his swift triumph, Hitler launched a new offensive against Greece to aid his hapless Italian ally in the spring of 1941, and the Balkans quickly fell under the Nazi heel. At the same time General Erwin Rommel was sent to the Western Desert to help the Italians' faltering fight against the British when he formed the Afrika Korps. For another year the Desert War went well for the Axis as Hitler's armies launched their final blitzkreig in Operation Barbarossa: the invasion of Soviet Russia. By December 1941 the Wehrmacht stood at the gates of Moscow and Leningrad, and its offensive, though halted during the winter of 1941–42, began to roll once again during the summer of 1942 until the German Sixth Army entered Stalingrad that autumn. From the North Cape to Crete, from the Atlantic to the Volga, Germany stood triumphantly as the master of Europe.

Signal recorded these triumphs colorfully and vividly. German setbacks, such as those over Britain in September 1940 and before Moscow in December 1941, were glossed over. There was little doubt in the minds of the Propaganda Company, which oversaw the editorial line of the magazine, that the war would soon be over and that Britain would be eventually forced to sign an ignominious peace. These were the glory years of *Signal* and the Third Reich. As doubts began to grow in 1942, after America entered the war and the Russian victory proved harder to achieve, *Signal* became a less effective instrument of Goebbels' propaganda. *Signal: Years of Triumph* concerns itself with the dreams of glory and the promise of ultimate victory that Germany embraced during the first years of World War II.

Belgium 2 Fr. / Bohemia-Moravia 2.50 Kr. / Bulgaria 8 Leva / Denmark 50 Øre / Finland 4.50 Mk. / France 4 Fr. / Greece 8 Drs. / Iran 3 Rials / Italy 2 Lire / Luxemburg 25 Pf. Netherlands 20 Cents / Norway 45 Øre / Portugal 2 Esc. / Rumania 16 Lei / Sweden 53 Øre / Switzerland 45 Cts. / Slovakia 2.50 Ks. / Spain 1.50 Pts. / Turkey 12 Kurus / Hungary 36 Fillér

Signal

Up to date seven ships have been sunk in the Atlantic

by this one German plane. On the tail of their machine, the crew of the Ju 88 paint the silhouettes of the ships sunk showing where they were hit   PK Krempl

BLITZKRIEG -NORTH

The first issues of *Signal* were distributed in early April 1940 just prior to the attacks on Denmark and Norway. Photographers of the PK, the Propaganda Company, were sent with the troops to record the first moves in Germany's greatest year of triumph, which carried their arms from the North Cape to the Pyrenees. The 'first party member', as *Signal* called him, was not quite the first after all, but undoubtedly he was the most important and the guiding force behind the attacks to the north and subsequently to the west. Hitler as well as his propaganda minister, Paul Joseph Goebbels, recognized not only the necessity of winning the war but publicizing Germany's victories to the full. The first pages of this section explain how and why this was done, and the brilliance of *Signal*'s reportage and design is clear from the very first issues of the magazine. Propaganda must be based largely on truth in order to be effective, and it was certainly true that Britain planned a pre-emptive strike on Norway to prevent the shipment of iron ore from Sweden through the northern Norwegian ports from entering Germany. In the face of the planned British assault, Hitler moved swiftly and daringly to seize the key ports and thereby secure the supply of this vital mineral without which his war effort would have eventually ground to a halt. Using Rhine barges and other, less-than-seaworthy craft, the Kriegsmarine crept into Norway literally under the guns of the Royal Navy to capture Narvik and the principal Norwegian ports. This was not to say that their subsequent task of pacifying the entire country was easy. Quite the contrary, as partisans aided the pitifully small Norwegian Army of 13,000 to resist the German take-over of their country for over a month. But Norwegian resistance, unlike the Danish, which scarcely existed, was fierce and necessarily short-lived. Germany hoped that her fellow-'Aryans' would welcome their arrival, and this was hardly the case in Norway or Denmark. *Signal*'s task in Operation Weserübung, as the strike north was called, was two-fold. First, with *Signal* quickly appearing in all the Scandinavian languages, it was meant to cow the conquered populations and convince neighboring Sweden that a similar fate would befall her if she failed to cooperate with the New Order. Secondly, it was meant to convince English-speaking readers as well as still-neutral states like Holland and Belgium that they too would suffer if they tried to resist the Third Reich. In its first issues *Signal* was a weapon of appeasement. The 'phony war' on the Western Front, which had been declared in September 1939 and practically speaking was not waged, was the continuation of appeasement by other means. *Signal*'s propaganda offensive had a similar effect. Britain and France dropped leaflets instead of bombs, and, incidentally, botched their ill-starred effort to retake Narvik during the Norwegian campaign, largely because they feared what all-out war could bring—the devastation of their cities, the mass slaughter of their urban populations, and, to men like Daladier, Chamberlain and Reynaud, the fall of their governments if they dared to actually fight a war which had already been declared against what some thought was the wrong foe. The underlying thrust of Nazi propaganda, even after the Molotov-Ribbentrop Pact, was that Germany was fighting for a New Europe which would exclude Communist Russia. Thus, the coverage of the Norwegian campaign by *Signal* was meant to soften up the will of the West for the next stage in Hitler's military strategy, the conquest of the Low Countries and France, launched even before the fighting in Norway had stopped. Norway and Denmark fell in *Signal*'s first month of publication. Its second month was accompanied by the invasion of Holland and France, an auspicious beginning to *Signal*'s and Germany's first year of triumph.

P.K.

How is the
German war bulletin made?

N. C. O. to the camera man: "*The best spot for you would be out there on that little hill to the left. You can film the entire battle from there.*"

All German war reports, war pictures and war articles bear the initials "P. K." These letters stand for *Propaganda Kompanie* or Propaganda Company. Since the outbreak of war, every report from the front, in words and in pictures, bears these initials and thus establishes their authenticity. Such reports do not emanate from editorial offices or club chairs, nor are any of the illustrations taken from archives. No. All of them are a living and vivid part of the war itself from day to day. Their authors are not war correspondents or press photographers in the accepted sense of the words. They are like their comrades, soldiers of fighting units and at the same time, soldier war correspondents. In other words, they are units of a P. K. company.

The development in technical science and the consequent change in the methods of waging war has removed the distinction between front and home. This distinction, which was in the last war the cause of fatal discord, no longer exists; for the whole nation is taking part in the struggle, everyone in his or her particular place. Thus the people of Germany are not only geographically, but also mentally and morally united in the defence of their country. In the present decisive struggle therefore the war correspondent is not there to satisfy the morbid curiosity of a certain class of citizens, but he has a far higher task to fulfil. His task is to bring the battle before the eyes of the workers and farmers, housewives and scientists, employees and officials, in fact all who are doing their duty at home. Only in this way can they feel a true comradeship with the soldiers who are fighting the great fight.

By thus sharing the struggle with the soldiers the whole nation becomes united by a closer bond and inspired with an inexorable and consistent determination to offer every physical and mental resistance. It is obvious that the soldier himself is better suited than any other to relate to those at home his experiences at the front and in fighting. It is not possible to describe what our soldiers have gone through without having oneself marched for miles and miles across the pathless plains of Poland, without having passed hours fraught with danger inside tanks, whilst breaches were being boldly hammered in the enemy lines, without having accompanied patrols in the forefield on the western front, without having passed in submarines in between the depth charges of enemy destroyers around the British Isles, or having flown in bombers over Warsaw, or in reconnaissance machines, reckless of pursuit planes and anti-aircraft guns over the Shetlands. The job is no longer done, as formerly, by a war correspondent visiting "the front" when all is quiet, and then at a desk at home or beside a warm stove behind the lines writing up highly imaginative reports in extravagant language about his "experiences". It is essential for a German war correspondent nowadays to be a soldier.

This war correspondent, of course, has with him his professional equipment. Nevertheless experience has shown, that the cleverest journalist and the most experienced broadcaster are not equal to their task, unless they posses a soldierly spirit and knowledge of military matters. It is also necessary for a war correspondent to have a good knowledge of those small details, which in their entirety go to determine the spiritual life and conduct of a people.

Thus it is necessary that a German war correspondent today be a man of a soldierly character and have a thorough grasp of his profession; this is therefore the method of selecting our war correspondents, who are accordingly taken from among the best newspaper men, the most fluent broadcasters and most reliable photographers, and news reel men. Only those are selected who have already proved themselves to be good soldiers, or those who are at least qualified for this soldierly task. Military drill and instruction schools complete their training, and furnish a guarantee that the "P. K. companies", into which these war correspondents are detailed, will be well up to doing their work.

A further difference between the German war correspondents of today and those of former times is that they receive their orders from very different quarters. Formerly the war correspondent was the employee of a publisher, who paid him a salary for the fulfilment of his duties. Nowadays the war correspondent is a servant of the state, and has not to fulfil duties towards a single publisher but towards the whole German people. He does not work for money, but is a soldier like the rest of his comrades and receives the same rate of pay. The reports, photographs etc., which he produces at the risk of his own life, are not the monopoly of a single publisher. Instead of that a central distribution department sees that they are published according to their suitability, old professional connections between correspondent and publisher being taken into consideration.

A number of reports are even put at the disposal of the newspaper and the press of neutral countries. When we review the work of hine months done by the P. K. companies in this war we see that these war correspondents of the German armed forces know how to perform their tasks, and how to fulfil their duty. The high proportion of casualties in the P. K. companies proves that our soldier war correspondents have not hesitated to sacrifice

Here is how the weekly news reel is made: *The camera is trained on the men who man the heavy gun which at the moment is being pushed up the hill in order to take part in the battle. The soft buzz of the camera is drowned by the shouts of the soldiers, the rat-tat-tat of machine guns and the noise of battle*

their lives. Furthermore many members of the P. K. companies have received decorations.

Scarcely had our troops crossed the Polish frontier last September when, as was to be anticipated, the Western Powers began their campaign of atrocity propaganda. Simultaneously with the occupation of Tschenstochau these Powers circulated in the whole world the lying report, that the German barbarians and heathens had desecrated and destroyed the black Madonna of Hellen Berge, which was sacred in the eyes of every Pole. Seldom has it been possible to disprove such a dangerous piece of atrocity propaganda so quickly as in this case. Detachments of a P. K. company had entered Tschenstochau with the troops who stormed the place. Thus while fighting was still going on in the streets, not only was the picture photographed and thus shown to be undamaged, but also gramophone records were made of a conversation with the Prior of the monastery of Hellen Berge, in which this Polish priest thanked the German military authorities for the protection afforded by the troops to the monastery and the holy relic in his charge. It was therefore possible to bring the Berlin newspaper correspondents of neutral countries the incontrovertible proof that this picture was undamaged, and thus once and for all to show up the incredibility and intrigues of this questionable propaganda. It was also possible to do this on the very day, on which the lying report of the "destruction of the black Madonna of Tschenstochau" had been spread by the broadcasting stations and press of our enemies.

During the first days of last September a war correspondent detachment of a P. K. company was attached to the tank units operating at the head of the von Kluge army, which was preparing by means of an advance

across the Tucheler Heide and the Brahe to cut off the divisions of the Polish army in the north of the Corridor from the main body of the army which was operating to the south of the Vistula. Regardless of the danger, this P. K. detachment advanced with an élan which did them every credit, into the territory occupied by the Poles, in spite of all the obstacles in the advanced positions. This P. K. detachment was the first German unit to cross the Corridor and entered Danzig at the head of the German forces amidst the ovations of the people. Different members of this P. K. company and the leader of the detachment received the Iron Cross as a reward for this daring exploit, which must distinguish them both as soldiers and journalists. When the Narev was to be crossed on both sides of Pultusk it was decided to include a war correspondent detachment from a P. K. company. While the leader of this detachment was actually making reconnaissances necessary for the undertaking, those left in charge of the transport vehicles at the northern exit of Pultusk could see, that several soldiers of an infantry regiment, waiting in readiness near-by, had got into a Polish mined area and been severely wounded by the explosion of mines. Without further ado six war correspondents made their way into the mined area, in order to liberate their wounded comrades from their dangerous positions. The P. K. men had to go backwards and forwards several times, and five of them were killed by exploding mines, whilst rescuing the last of their comrades who had been severely wounded.

On September 14 a war correspondent, who was driving in a car from Kontun to Gredke, fell in with a Polish patrol. In the surprise of the moment the patrol surrendered without resistance, and they were all made prisoners. One of the patrol, who spoke German, disclosed the fact that there were more Poles ambushed in a wood near-by. The war correspondent then cocked his pistol and proceeded to the edge of the wood indicated, leaving his driver behind to guard the prisoners. When he had come to within a few paces of the wood, there was a shot, which however missed him. The return shot of the German hit the Pole in the forehead, and thereupon twenty-eight Poles surrendered, being terrified at their opponent's accuracy of aim. The war correspondent and his driver, who had taken thirty-one Poles prisoner, received the Iron Cross of the second class.

We should be going too far beyond the scope of this article, if we tried to enumerate in detail all the deeds of self-sacrifice and soldierly devotion to duty by which the German war correspondents have distinguished themselves, and we shall reserve this for a later occasion. In this article the examples already cited will suffice to prove what is quite evident, namely, that the German war correspondents are not merely editors, photographers, broadcasters and newsreel men, but soldiers. For this reason alone these men have won the entire confidence of the combatant units. For their comrades

The wireless reporter crouches in the mud-hole *among the soldiers who man the bomb throwers, and speaks into the microphone. His spoken words are accompanied by the terse commands of the officers and interrupted now and then by the bursting of enemy shells in the rear of the position*

Three or four leaps, *and the party has worked its way to enemy barbed-wire barricades. With lightning speed one of the men places the fuse under the barricade which soon flies into the air with a deafening roar. The men lie face down on the ground and one of them is the news reporter*

in the units to which they are attached know by experience that the war correspondents do not merely show themselves now and again to disappear when things are getting dangerous, but that they remain at their side, whether they are doing out-post duty in the forefield, are lying in the bunkers, or are in rest billets.

The war correspondents of the air force and the navy belong to the combatant units just as is the case in the army. The fact, that these service units are smaller in number, makes it a military necessity for the men to stick more closely together. Mine sweepers, U-boats, or even fighter planes cannet be hampered by unqualified people. In this case it is quite indispensable for the war correspondent not only to be qualified for his reporting work, but also for military tasks; he must in every way prove himself to be a fully reliable comrade in his small fighting uitn for better or for worse.

The front line reporter *follows at the heels of a skirmishing party. He goes through the barbed-wire barricade just demolished by the explosion, and faces all the danger of battle, a comrade among comrades*

NORWAY
before April 9th

BY ALFRED GERIGK

"The Royal British Consulate in Trondheim has the honor to announce that it has become necessary, in the interest of well-regulated trade traffic, to subject to detailed examination all books and records of firms carrying on trade with the Royal British Government." Mr. Rayn, captain in His Majesty's navy and the current British Consul in Trondheim, paused thoughtfully. "Put that into better phrasing and follow it up at once with the announcement that consular officials will appear shortly to inspect the books. It is to be sent to all shipping lines, lumber and paper firms, as well as export trade." He glanced expectantly at his colleague.

World War Memories

John Craig shook his head doubtfully. "That will bring us more trouble than results, Captain."

"You know yourself what Mr. Paus's instructions are. It is clear that we must find out where commercial relations with Germany still exist, and the only way to do that is to inspect the books."

"We'll only get 'no' for an answer, and that might be very embarrassing in the light of future developments."

Captain Rayn made a gesture of annoyance. "Just recall the many examples during the world war. Even then Mr. Paus's instructions were absolutely clear on this subject." He paged through his papers. "Take this declaration, for instance: 'We hereby swear that no cordage, packing-string etc., received by us from Great Britain, shall either directly or indirectly, whole or piece-wise, nor as wrapping for merchandise, fall into the hands of those nations now at war with Great Britain.' Imagine — they signed statements like that in the world war, and we are still a long way off from anything of that sort."

"But that was after one and a half years of war. By that time they were pliable. This war has not been on even half a year. The whole thing is premature."

Captain Rayn was not fond of contradiction, but since he still felt somewhat uncertain in his new position as consul, he was only too willing to depend at times on the judgment of Craig, his right hand . . . After short consideration, he said, "You think it would be better to sound them out first? Perhaps you're right. Try to pump Halvorsen Tryggve first; then talk to Christensen and Johannsen. If you handle them right you may persuade them to sound out other firms."

View of the Harbour

Trondheim is the third largest city in Norway and one of her most important harbours. Since the outbreak of the war it has become one of the most significant Norwegian centers for the agents of the British Government. Captain Rayn took over the consulate as early as September, supported by a dozen newly appointed agents and officials. New office rooms were rented, with an excellent view over the harbour, so that all ship movements could be observed with ease. Contacts, social and otherwise, were established. It was not difficult to approach those families which were closely connected with England through marriage, not to mention those which had made money on England during the world war. In the state wine monopoly and in insurance circles there are men who are in constant touch with all classes of population. Given the right kind of treatment, they make excellent agents, voluntary or involuntary, for England's 'cause'. Luncheon in the Hotel Britannia, a cosy chat in the pompous, old-fashioned restaurant or the Palm Garden, and enough information about shipping, trade and public opinion has been gleaned to last several days . . .

"And a report to Mr. Paus in the meantime?" asked Craig.

"Yes indeed—as soon as possible. He seems to be very impatient."

*

Mr. Paus was fond of stepping out into his bay window—almost a small conservatory, with its abundance of green plants—to take a look at the weather. The snow lay deep on the terrace between the gaily painted wooden pillars, and on the street, where shovellers were kept busy constantly trying to keep the street passable for auto traffic . . . Mr. Paus's scholarly face with the gold-rimmed spectacles had become markedly nervous within the past few months, in spite of the outward calm and control so characteristic of him.

He regarded the war as his big opportunity, and particularly these last few days in January were significant for his future. He could no longer afford to spend much time on the weather, snow conditions and the like. As he stepped into his car before his home in Dagaliveien, Slemdal, he thought of the strenuous day ahead of him at the embassy . . .

Thomas Coats, second Baron of Glentanar, had arrived from London. Because of his family connections—consisting in the main of a Norwegian marriage—he had been singled out to get the Anglo-Norwegian trade relations under way. Mr. Paus, commercial attaché in the British Embassy, would soon have opportunity enough to justify his reputation as a great expert in Norwegian affairs. And this is just what occupied him as he drove toward the city . . . The butler with the wine-ruddy face greeted him with his customary dignity—war had done nothing to ruffle his calm visage. Mr. Paus went through the large entry hall and passed by the throne room on the second floor, where the empty throne stood, flanked by the portraits of Edward VII and George VI. (This is a custom observed by all British legations.)

The conference which had been arranged to prepare Lord Glentanar for his role in the trade negotiations was held in the office of the chargé d'affaires.

Mr. Paus spoke in the short, concise manner for which his reports were well-known—and much esteemed. "We began working on public opinion even before the war started. 1933 marked the elimination of the German language from the curriculum of the public schools. In 1934 the importation of German films into Norway was reduced by one-half. In 1935 German language lessons over the wireless were discontinued. Of course this all sounds like what the Germans call 'Kulturpolitik', but it was necessary. The whole situation was very different from world war days. Strong interest in Germany and German affairs, political cliques which sympathized with the Nazis, and then the embarrassing effect of the Danish aversion to a Scandinavian block—all those points had to be overcome."

Lord Glentanar wanted data for his negotiations "How are shipping conditions?" he asked abruptly.

Mr. Paus, as usual, had his figures at his finger tips, and was ready for the question. "Almost one-fifth of all the tankers in the world belong to Norway. By the end of December we had chartered one and a half million tons from Norway and I have been promised another quarter of a million tons for January and February."

"But the Norwegians refused to comply with our demand that the whole fleet either be chartered to England or put out of service."

The Black List

The scholarly face of Mr. Paus relaxed in a quiet smile. "When we introduced the black lists here during the world war there were wild protests. But by 1916 we had the Norwegian government where we wanted it and they acknowledged the lists. In fact, the government itself imparted the news to the firms which were placed on the black list, and the ministry of finance accredited the declarations made by certain companies in which they pledged themselves to discontinue their trade with Germany. A little patience is needed, that's all."

"But what about the export law?"

"Inconvenient, of course. . . . 'All purchases are cancelled if goods are not called for within fourteen days of issuance of order.' . . . After all, the government has to keep face here. A little pressure from London would expedite matters, however."

"And ore shipments? Narvik is important to the Germans nowadays."

Mr. Paus smiled. "The official figures are false. German ore imports from Narvik in January of last year were three times as high as this year, while English ore shipments out of Narvik have doubled in the same lenght of time." He handed the papers over to Lord Glentanar.

But Lord Glentanar was unreceptive to nature's beauties at this moment. "During the consultation," he said hesitantly, "you made a remark which caught my attention. Pressure from London was necessary, you said, to expedite matters. Did you mean a general change here, or one specific intention?"

Mr. Paus reddened slightly. He too spoke hesitantly, choosing his words with care. "Oslo had always been a convenient shelf for unsuccessful diplomats, Sir Thomas. No harm could be done here. Which is nothing against Sir Cecil Dormer, but after all when a man is transferred from Siam to Oslo, after the tropics have got him, so to speak, is it likely that he would still possess enough energy for this war?" Mr. Paus glanced covertly at Lord Glentanar's face before he went on. "Oslo has changed, however, and has now become one of the most important spots in Europe. From here the German barrier can be attacked . . . But Sir Cecil Dormer has been here six years now, just waiting for the day when he'll be pensioned off. And over there?" He made a gesture in the direction of the French embassy, nestled in a snow-covered park farther down the hill. "The son of the ambassador has set Oslo completely on its ear with his 'scandals' — and the atmosphere in the embassy is just what one would expect, as a result."

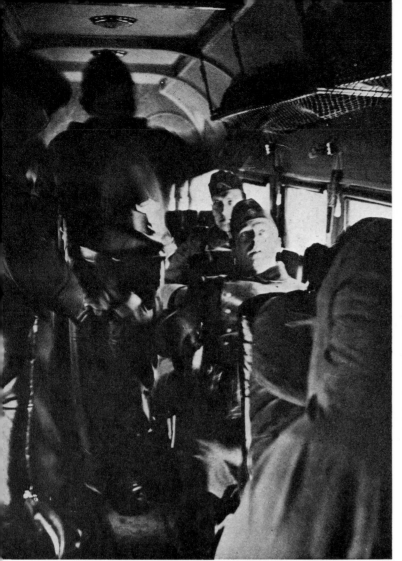

On the way
TO NORWAY

In the transport plane
German infantry on the flight to Norway. Troops of all types are being brought day and night not only by troop-ships, but also by large transport planes to their positions

Landing on Norwegian territory
Soldiers, arms, ammunition, provisions and baggage are unloaded and the plane departs again. Fresh air-transports arrive and land ...

On an aerodrome somewhere in Norway:
German infantry which has been landed ready to advance

**Lorries are loaded
with baggage and a guard placed over them**

*The infantrymen clamber into the other vehicles
of the column, and drive off, while planes
continually come and go*

The provisions are brought with the troops

*The German troops in Norway provision them-
selves. It is only, when they are in a difficult
country, and the provisions do not last, that
they make requisitions and pay with vouchers*

In the "Drying Turret"

*Parachutes, which have got wet
are made serviceable again by
being hung up to dry in a high
room, which is well heated and
ventilated. They can then be folded
again according to regulations*

Full steam ahead through the Skagerrak: There is an incessant stream of German reinforcements

War-ships and troop-ships bring German fighting forces to north

Photographed from a German diving fighter bombing plane:

The gigantic primeval panorama of the coast of northern Norway. A huge range of mountains covered with everlasting snow and ice rises out of the Atlantic. The German fighters thunder their way to Norway over a labyrinth of steep walls and narrow fjords, of glaciers and rocky ridges. Their goal is Tromsö

Diving fighters

over fjords

← **High above the clouds . . .**

The detachment rushes towards its goal, with the order to bomb the large Tromsö power-station. The pilots gaze feverishly through the openings in the clouds, and suddenly recognize two masts, the transmitting-towers of the Tromsö wireless station. The goal is almost reached

The first bombs are released:

Pitch black clouds of powder, and showers of earth and snow spur up into the sky. The next bomb hits its mark. The engine-house collapses, and the main pipe has been hit. An enormous column of water shoots up towards the sky like a gigantic fountain. The Tromsö transmitter, which up to the last moment had been carrying on its agitation in the service of England is severed from its source of current

Airplanes versus battleship

The English cruiser 'Effingham' (9770 tons) which was so badly damaged by bombs from German battle planes near Bodö that it had to be beached, and finally capsized

In Norway

In Northern Norway,

since April 9 German mountaineer troops and marines under the leadership of Lieutenant-General Dietl are engaged in a bitter struggle for Narvick. The Air Force supplies them with arms, ammunition and rations. Reinforcements also, continue to land with parachute

THE GOAL IS REACHED

A narrow peninsula, topped by a lighthouse, extends its point out into the sea. Wreathed by white sands, southern Norway stretches out peacefully below the airplane

Transportations of German reinforcements to Norway go on unceasingly

Protected by the German naval and air forces against all enemy attempts to attack, new German transport-ships continue to arrive in a steady stream to Norwegian ports, bringing troops, ammunition, arms, provisions and vehicles

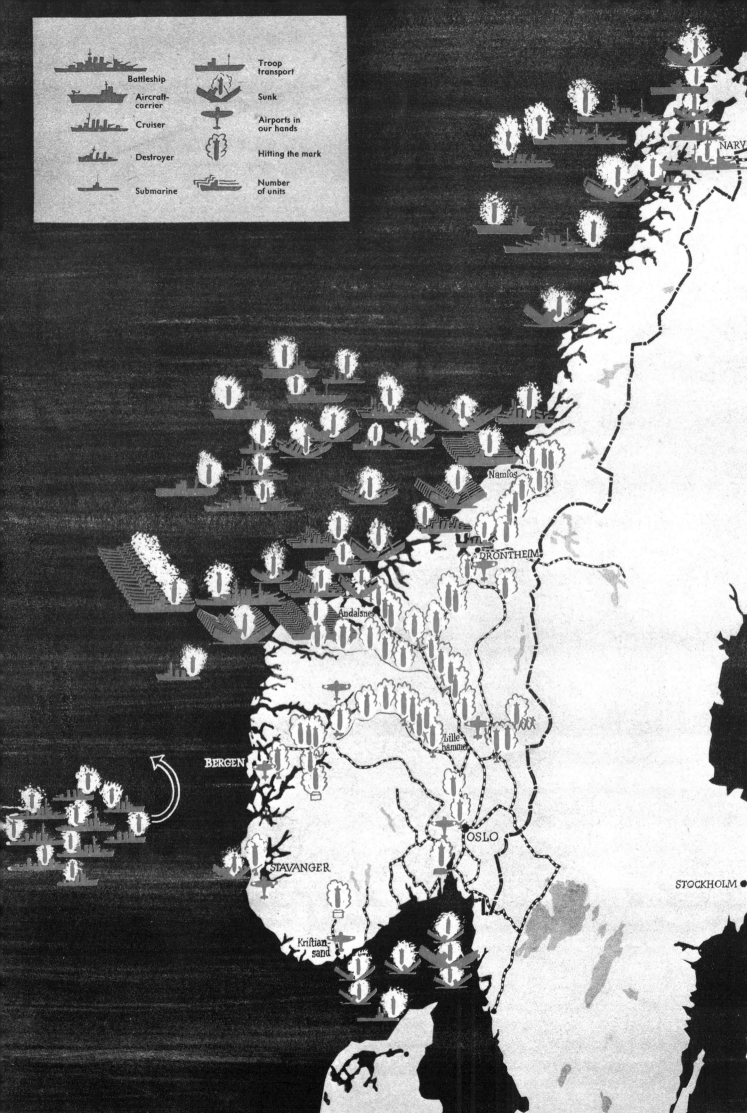

Battleship
Aircraft-carrier
Cruiser
Destroyer
Submarine

Troop transport
Sunk
Airports in our hands
Hitting the mark
Number of units

NARVIK

Namsos

DRONTHEIM

Andalsnes

Lillehammer

BERGEN

STAVANGER

OSLO

STOCKHOLM

Kristiansand

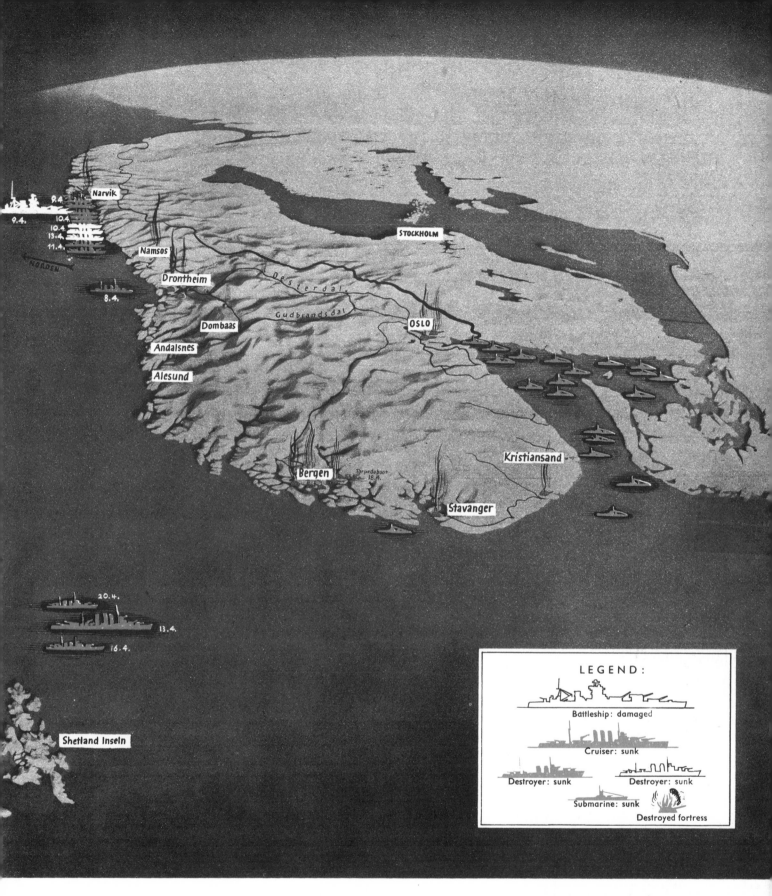

Narvik

9.4.
10.4.
10.4.
13.4.
11.4.

NORDEN

Namsos

Drontheim

8.4.

Oesterdal

STOCKHOLM

Dombaas

Andalsnes

Gudbrandsdal

OSLO

Alesund

Bergen

Torpedoboot
18.4.

Kristiansand

Stavanger

20.4.

13.4.

16.4.

Shetland Inseln

LEGEND:

Battleship: damaged

Cruiser: sunk

Destroyer: sunk   Destroyer: sunk

Submarine: sunk
                        Destroyed fortress

History on maps

Military operations in Norway from April 9 to May 9

What the German air forces accomplished in Norway between April 9 and May 9

The map on the left gives a conception of the success achieved by the German air force, which had a two-fold task to fill in Norway: 1. the destruction of communications between the Norwegian and allied troops and their reinforcements during land operations, and 2. to disturb the landing and transportation of allied troop detachments, which was to take place under the protection of the British fleet. As a matter of fact, the German air forces destroyed aerodromes and anti-aircraft, roads, railways and marching columns in the entire territory. The success of the German airforce in its attacks on allied troop transports and the British navy have given historical proof that not even a strong navy can carry out its tasks if it encounters a superior airforce. This superior airforce sank 30 units in 30 days and badly damaged 99 units.

What the German navy accomplished in Norway from April 9 to May 9

This map, which like all the others, was drawn in collaboration with the High Command of the German army, gives a view of the success achieved by the German navy. It vanquished 11 coast fortifications and destroyed 31 enemy units. Although the British navy, supported as it was by French naval forces, had the advantage of numbers, the German navy not only supplied the convoys for German troop transports to Norway and assisted in effecting the landing, but succeeded in leaving the fjords with the majority of its units inspite of English attempts at blockade, in order to be ready for the next start. German naval forces maintained steadily their 9 hour advantage, and — long after the first moment of surprise had lost its effect — escorted further German troops to Norway.

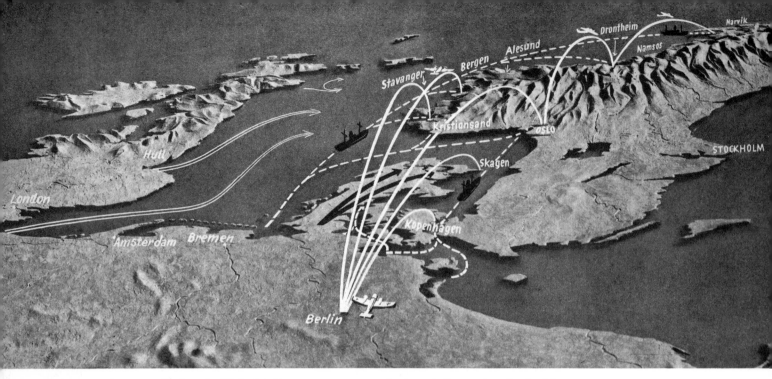

1. The dash to Norway

The first task which faced the German army was to occupy all entrances to Norway and put them into defence position in lightning time, before the arrival of the English. There were scarcely nine hours time for this. Naval convoys and transport planes land the first German troops in Oslo, Stavanger, Bergen, Alesund, Trondheim, Namsos, and Narvik. After arranging for the defence of the harbour they begin gradually to feel their way inland

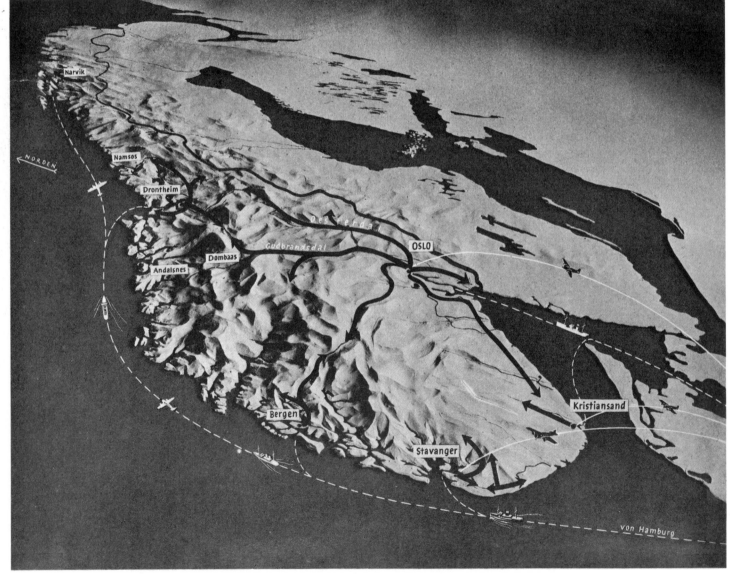

2. Two weeks later

Supported by the auxiliary troops brought in a steady stream by the navy and air forces, the German landing troops were able to force their way into the Norwegian hinterland. In spite of most unfavorable weather conditions and heavy British attacks, the troops occupying Narvik held the place against all odds. The tank and infantry columns in South Norway in the meantime steadily worked their way into the center of the country. The march through the Gudbrandsdal and Oesterdal was carried out with great speed

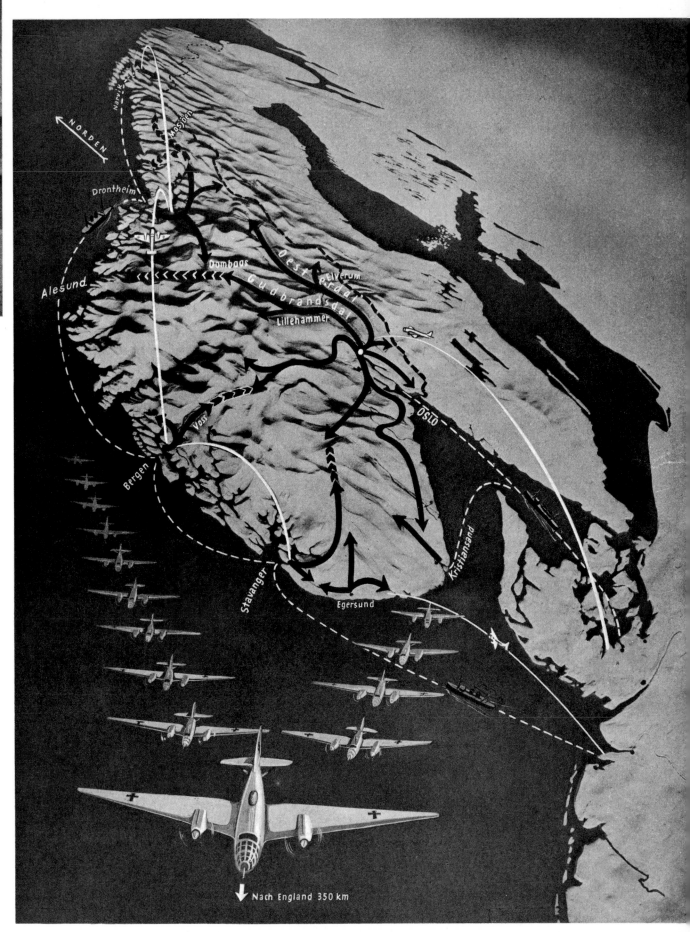

3. The last phase:

Detachments from Oslo, Stavanger, Bergen, Alesund, Trondheim and Lillehammer are united. British landing troops leave the country in wild haste. Norwegian troops, left suddenly without support and cut off from reinforcements, surrender. Protected by the army and anti-aircraft, Norwegian aerodromes are being repaired. While British transport ships return to England, followed persistently by German air forces, the new air base for attack against England nears its completion. 30 days after the beginning of the operations, this air base reached from the German North Sea coast all the way to Narvik

BLITZKRIEG -WEST

The sudden attack on the Dutch, Belgian and French frontiers in the early morning hours of 10 May 1940 came as a shock and surprise to the Western Allies and the neutral states of the Low Countries despite the warnings sounded by the intelligence services of a number of states as well as a number of diplomats and even the occasional wink from German military officials. Nevertheless public opinion had been sufficiently prepared softened in the Western democracies by German propaganda to fear the worst. Nazi weaponry contributed to the atmosphere of fear, with the parachute assault over Holland and the screaming Stukas over France. The campaigns lived up to all that Hitler expected of it and more, and *Signal* was quick to seize the theme of total victory. Although the occasional nod was given to the role that Italian forces played in the defeat of France, the fact that Mussolini was not invited to the capitulation at Compiègne even after he had asked if he would come was indicative of Germany's cavalier treatment of their now humiliated ally. Essentially victory in the West belonged to Hitler. But even he did not expect such an easy victory over French arms which, on paper at least, looked formidable. Above all it was their own lack of will which defeated them, and the capture of the Maginot Line by the Germans at the end of the Battle of France happened as quickly and easily as *Signal* portrayed it. Inevitably *Signal* sought to discover the reasons for the French defeat and found them in fact and fantasy. Aryan racial superiority was Germany's principal fantasy, and the ill-disguised smugness shown in the photographs of captured African troops who fought with the French was one of the few examples of overtly racist propaganda exploited in the pages of *Signal*. German propaganda reveled in Britain's withdrawal from Dunkirk, although *Signal* took a rather softer line toward their British foes because Hitler still hoped to 'do a deal' with the United Kingdom after France fell. Besides, the British were fellow Aryans. Churchill, who took over as Prime Minister the day that the western blitzkrieg began, was initially viewed as another Chamberlain, eager for appeasement. The full force of Churchill's oratory and determination never to negotiate with Hitler and never to surrender was slow to take effect in the Reich. Indeed the power and speed to the victory in the West gave *Signal* the opportunity of gloating over every detail of the campaign for months after it was over, and this chapter is drawn from contemporary material distributed while the battle was on as well as material drawn from issues which appeared in the following months. There was little good news for *Signal* to report during the late summer and early fall while the Battle of Britain was going on. *Signal* was faced with its first editorial problem which continued throughout its publishing life. How could a propaganda journal, instituted to glamorize German victory, continue to create reader interest when there were no victories to report?

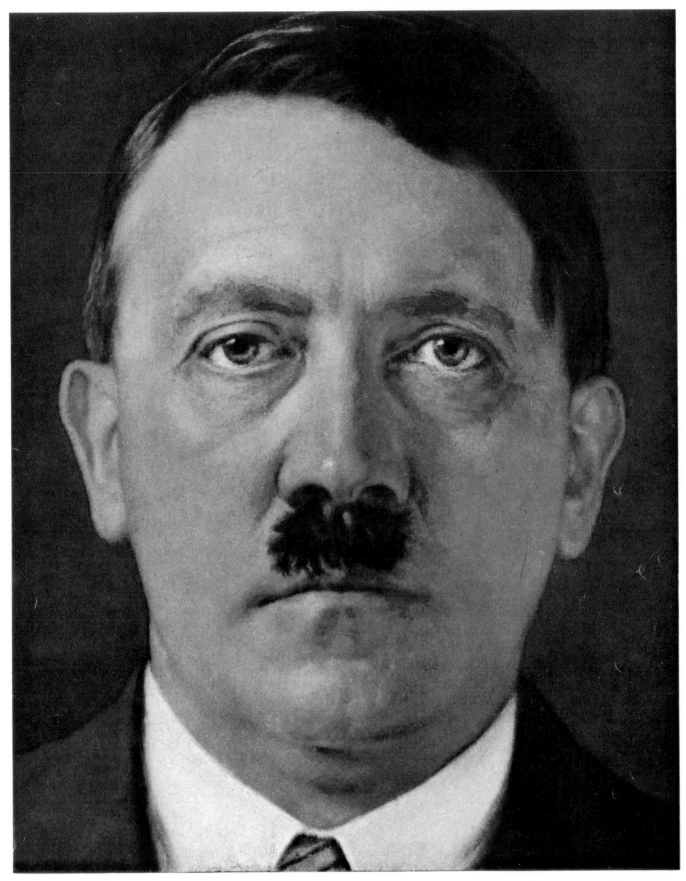

The First Party Member

Adolf Hitler, born on 20th April 1889 in Braunau on the Inn, was the son of an Austrian customs official. He enlisted in 1914 as a volunteer in the 16th Bavarian Infantry Reserve Regiment "List", served for 4 years at the front, was twice wounded, was awarded the Iron Cross of the First Class, left the Army with the rank of lance-corporal and in 1919 became a member of the "German Workers' Party." It counted at that time six members. And so the new member, Adolf Hitler, was Number 7.

Nobody at that time could dream that Adolf Hitler would from these beginnings create the movement known as the "National Socialist German Workers' Party" which numbers millions, that he would rise to be the Leader of a nation of 80 millions, the founder of Greater Germany, the Commander-in-Chief in the battles which have been fought during this war and the creator of a new order in Europe. In the cash-box of the "German Workers' Party", an association with indeterminate aims, there was at that time the sum of seven marks, fifty pfennigs. There was nothing but firm trust and goodwill. The new party member was an unknown lance-corporal with the experiences of his bitter youth. He was compelled to earn as a workman the money for his intended studies in architecture. Nothing distinguished him from the others, bu he was the future leader

"Well—the war has at last begun"

Paris

Henri de Kerillis, who was a flying officer in the Great War and is now one of the trusted journalists of the French General Staff, had finished writing a leader for the Epoque. He read his conclusive words over again, as they were to appear the next morning in the paper: — "If Germany should succeed in gaining a firm footing in Holland after now having made herself master of South Norway and Denmark, then she would be in possession of a very formidable base for air raids half round the B-itish isles. She would further be able to use this base for disputing the supremacy of the English fleet in the North Sea, and also for severe and repeated bombardments, for the purpose of bringing about a moral collapse of the English people.

Are not these words hint enough? Henri de Kerillis knows still more about the plans of the general staff. For it had been confided in him that British and French troops could be in Holland and Belgium in record time, because the final preparations had been made a few days before. But that was information which might only be published at the right moment. It must for the time suffice to mention that, if the Germans got hold of Holland, it would then have to be regarded as a zone of danger for the Allies.

The fatal 9th May was a mild spring evening in Paris, and the café terraces and main boulevards were crowded with people. The newspaper sellers were shouting out the evening news, but although the war had been going on for eight months people were far from being in the same state of excitement as during the first days. Had it not been for the great prevalence of uniforms among the passers-by and those sitting in the cafés and bars, and also for the shop windows plastered over with paper and the sand bags in front of the cellar windows which reminded one of war, no one would have noticed the difference from peace-time in the spring atmosphere of Paris.

It was at this hour of the evening that the Norwegian Minister of Foreign Affairs, Koht, had gathered a number of French journalists around him in one of the large hotels. It was easy to detect in his broad face, which with the brushed up hair suggested that of a yokel, the dejection caused by his flight from Norway and the disappointing negotiations in London. "I could never describe to you", he said to the press representatives, "the feeling of grief felt by the Norwegians, when they heard that the English and French troops had been re-embarked." He paused and then added with constrained optimism: "But since being in London and Paris I now have the hope that the French and English Governments will do all they can to support the co-operation between, the Norwegian and the Franco-British forces.

The people were pouring out of the theaters and cinemas into the darkened streets of Paris, and tediously groping their way in the moonless night to the underground and home.

Towards midnight the French Embassy in Brussels rang up the Quai d'Orsay:— "The Germans are apparently about to march into Belgium. A night meeting of the Belgian cabinet has been called. Will report further in the course of the night."

During the night the members of the French cabinet were hastily summoned to Premier Reynaud, he and Daladier, the Minister for National Defence, having already conferred with the Supreme Council for National Defence. Reynaud stated the result briefly: — "Gamelin reports that our troops were ready for our own action the night before, and our armies therefore ready to march in, although the Germans have again deprived us of the advantage of being first in the field. The co-operation of the Dutch and Belgian staffs has been guaranteed long ago. Gamelin is in touch with General Gort, in order to assure simultaneous action on the part of the British army. Gamelin's daily orders to the army are ready. The language is calm and confident". He handed a few typed duplicates round.

Daladier began to speak: — "By order of the Ministries for National Defence the War and Air Ministries are immediately cancelling all leave. All officers on leave have to join their units to-morrow."

"How about leave for the farmers?" asked Tellier, Minister for Agriculture. For he had just declared in an interview that the food supply of France was guaranteed, since he had got his way with the Ministries for National Defence.

Daladier shrugged his shoulders and answered: — "No exception can be made, Tellier, we can only consider the army."

"If there is to be no leave for the farmers, then there will be no spring sowing." answered Tellier.

"You can come to an agreement to-morrow, Gentlemen." Reynaud broke in, for he does not like such discussion of details. "There are more important matters, such as changes in the Government. You know that, when the new Government came in, it had only a majority of one in the *Chambre*. We now require a national coalition Government, and the Conservatives must come into the cabinet."

"Together with the Socialists?"

Daladier broke in again in support of Reynaud: — "Yes, together with the Socialists" adding, "if you take my advice, you will even appoint the Conservative ministers to be members of the Supreme War Council, for they must be offered something."

"I had even thought of making all the under-secretaries of state resign so as to have posts vacant." "But for God's sake leave us the specialists for aeroplane production, for evacuation and other such matters."

Reynaud's secretary appeared at this moment with the news: — "The Belgian cabinet has decided to call upon England and France for help. The German troops have crossed the Dutch and Belgian frontiers."

The discussion was suddenly interrupted by the prolonged howling of the sirens: — "Air raid alarm". The members of the cabinet looked at one another: "It's getting serious. Is that an air raid alarm? Any way the first for months." "The tenth since the outbreak of the war, if I am not mistaken."

Paris was awakened from its peaceful spring sleep, and every one was startled by the shock: "Is that an air raid alarm?" Watches were consulted. It was not quite five o'clock. "Was it then only a trial?" But the sirens continued howling. Lightly clad figures hastend in the darkness down into the anti-aircraft cellars, with only a cloak or blanket thrown over them. But we so often have air raid alarms, some of them said, and it was never serious. Let us go out on to the balcony. There were soon lightly clad figures at the windows and on the balconies, and the humming of the engines began to be heard. The sky was swept by the quivering search lights and two aeroplanes could be seen flying in the direction of Vincennes.

There could be seen the flashes of bursting anti-air-craft shells around the shining planes accompanied by the screams and groans of people, who, in their curiosity to see, had been wounded by falling splinters of the anti-air-craft shells.

At 6,20 the sirens howled again, the danger being past. But at this moment a terrific explosion was heard in the far distance. "The aerodrome of Pontoise has been bombed by the Germans," was shortly after reported to Head Quarters. This was followed by the report: "The Aerodromes of Lille, Lyon, Annemasse, Metz, Amiens bombed. The air raid on Lyon is continuing". Reports then followed in quick succession. Paris then went to bed again cursing. An hour and a half later the sirens were again heard in Paris, and people again fled into the anti-air-craft cellars, which had been laughed at when they were built; in the case of better class houses there were even couches, easy chairs and stocks of drinks in them. "What is the meaning of two air-raid alarms in one night" was the question angrily asked by every one when they returned home, and they put the wireless on. "German troops have crossed the Belgian and Dutch frontiers", the wireless bawled out. The Belgian and Dutch Governments have called in the assistance of England and France. All who are on leave are to return at once to their regiments. The public are to wear their gas masks if they have any ... The terrified Parisians were overwhelmed by endless orders.

Early in the morning officers of all ranks and regiments were hastening to the railway stations. Early in the morning placards announced that the railway lines to the north and east were closed for traffic, as they were required for the army. Early in the morning there were Placards calling upon the public to leave the city and to remain in the country wherever possible. Early in the morning the Dutch and Belgian legations called upon all their nationals to report at once for military duty. In front of the banks and shops there were long queues of people, who wanted to draw money from the bank, or make purchases. For the first time since September

Whilst the English cabinets were wasting time with discussions German parachutemen were landing in the morning of the 10. May 3.5 kilometers from Rotterdam. A German landing party (left) getting into touch with their comrades

people were seen wearing gasmasks, and saying to one another: — "The war has actually begun on the 250th day of the war.

London

In the evening of the May 9th a discussion went on for three quarters of an hour at No. 10 Downing Street as to whether it would be possible, after the disaster in Norway, to form a cabinet including all parties. Late in the evening Lord Halifax telephoned to the Prime Minister:

"Telephone calls to the Hague are not possible. The Dutch Government has apparently stopped all telephone calls." "Stopped all telephone calls"? The decision is premature for our purpose". "Should the Germans ..."

Soon after, there was a whole series of telephone calls. "Report from Brussels: Night meeting of the Belgian cabinet. Reports from Paris, reports from General Gort, the Commander in Chief of the British Expeditionary Force in France: German air raids on the aerodromes of the expeditionary force."

The Prime Minister called a meeting of the war cabinet. The First Lord of the Admirality, Winston Churchill, appeared, just shaved, and wearing as usual his dark blue white spotted bow: "You will win the race, Churchill," Chamberlain said to him with a languid smile. "The Labour Party is mad to see you Prime Minister."

With a condescending movement of his hand Churchill replied: "That is unimportant at the moment, but what is going on in Holland?"

"Apparently the Germans are marching in".

"Then we are again too late? I will immediately summon the Ministers of National Defence and the Staffs".

The siren began to howl. Air raid alarm over London. It was only short, and London is used to air raid alarm. But it was not long before reports arrived: Enemy planes over the mouth of the Thames and the county of Kent. Four bombings and the anti-aircraft batteries in action.

Then came the final report: German troops have entered Holland and Belgium. A call from the Hague: The Dutch Government will officially call for the help of Great Britain, and is confident that the arrangements already made will be carried out. The Ministers for Foreign Affairs and the Colonies will arrive to-morrow by air.

When the Londoners looked out of their windows early in the morning, they were amazed at the unaccustomed sight. For all along the horizon the huge silver grey inflated sausage shaped barrage balloons were swaying in the sky. "What is the matter". They put the radio on, but could only hear the usual morning program, when towards eight o'clock there was an interruption and the following announcement was made: German troops and air force units have invaded Belgium and Holland last night. The Dutch and Belgian Governments have requested the British Government for assistance, this assistance will of course be given without delay. There is a special meeting of the war cabinet at eight o'clock". A little later: "The Home Office states that particular attention is to be paid to the doings of secret agents in England. All foreigners, even when not enemy subjects, may henceforth be interned in case of suspicion". And a few minutes later: "Hallo, hallo!, the sentries in the streets of London have been ordered to fire ball cartridge at once, if their orders are not followed. All Whitsuntide leave is cancelled, also Coronation leave. Munition factories will continue to work throughout the holidays without stopping".

Sir Dudley Pound, the first Sea Lord, who was just leaving after the Cabinet meeting, realized that he must say something encouraging, while taking the few steps from the exit of No. 10, Downing Street to the car, in which his own minister, who was about to be his Prime Minister, was awaiting him. He jerked his head on which he had just put his naval cap, and turning to the journalists said: "Well if you want my opinion, the war has at last begun".

The floating island

Well camouflaged with reeds and bog-rush the Pioneer Company paddles silently in its rubber boat towards its goal. The object is to form a bridge-head on the enemy side of the river. The hand grenades are ready to be picked up and thrown ... During the fighting in Belgium and the North of France, the rubber boat was one of the most indispensable means of transportation for the advancing German Infantry

M. g. to the front
It will be quickly sending its steel greetings to the enemy

Infantry creeping forward

Zzzzz ... with eyes like a lynx,
it is possible at any minute to light on the enemy

General Christiansen

looking at portraits of Dutch Generals in the Dutch Ministry of Transport

German-Dutch co-operation in the occupied area

In connection with reconstruction work in Holland the Führer has appointed Dr. Seyss-Inquart, Reich Commissioner in the occupied areas of the Netherlands. Dr. Seyss-Inquart had been Deputy Governor-General of the occupied districts of Poland, and before that Reich Statthalter of the East Marches (Austria). One of the first things he did was to establish a fund for reconstruction work, in order to help the Dutch people to recover from the losses caused them by the war. General Christiansen, the famous airfighter and leader of the National-Socialist Flying Corps has been appointed Commander-in-Chief of the forces in the Netherlands.

German and Dutch Officers

discussing the carrying out of measures decreed by the Commander-in-Chief

**Reich Commissioner
Dr. Seyss - Inquart,**

whose official residence is in The Hague, receiving a report from one of his collaborators on work in the occupied areas

Heavy firing at an armoured fortification in the Maginot Line —

Somewhere in France: the end of a defended town ...

The enemy had converted this town into a fortification, and one morning the German advance was held up; for every house was a fortified position bristling with machine-guns and cram-full of men pouring a murderous fire into the streets. Then amidst the howling of sirens, swarms of dive-bombers suddenly swooped down from the sky, dropping in all directions death-bringing bombs of every calibre. Roofs and walls were torn to pieces and the resistance of the enemy broken. Flames burst forth from the empty window frames, debris piled up in great mounds, and the roads became blocked with charred beams. The Germans had beaten the enemy and taken possession of the town. The illustration overleaf shows evidently that the war only roared along the strongly defended retreat-highways of the enemy. Homesteads in the vicinity of these roads remained absolutely undamaged

Here the German troops broke their way trough:

An armoured turret in the area of the Maginot Line Extension was smashed by German guns. The fire from this turret dominated a wide stretch of the foreground

In 25 Seconds

ACROSS THE UPPER RHINE AGAINST THE

MAGINOT LINE

Dawn somewhere on the Upper Rhine: *Major Gantke, a specialist in attacking boats, issues the last instructions to his Engineers*

Anybody who in peace time had practised bridge construction across the Upper Rhine as a pioneer, acquired the reputation of being somebody above the ordinary; the river flows very fast, anchors do not hold, pontoons are carried away or overturn. Many a man has been injured here and many have lost their lives, but many a life-saving medal has also been won. Today, however, the bank on the other side of the river is heavily fortified. One fortification next to the other, one obstacle behind another. Mine-fields and field positions traverse the impenetrable undergrowth. Armoured cupolas dominate the river and their loop-holes cover a wide field of fire on the flanks. Anybody wishing to cross the river in the face of a determined enemy must prepare himself for the worst! The jungle on our side of the Rhine comes to life. The rain is pouring down. Th night is as black as pitch. Things could not be better for the sappers, the rain smothers every sound. Heavy pontoons are dragged through the darkness to a spot close to the river. Neat, shallow assault boats twist their way to a point behind the dam. Innumerable men lie down in readiness; tomorrow, in the early morning, they are to cross the river. A strategical crossing, a frontal attack against a strong enemy, but so important that it must be successful under all circumstances, the object of which is to storm and to break the Maginot Line. It has already been encircled widely from the North. As a result of this attack, the enemy inside the great encircling ring will be broken up into smaller groups, which can easily be overpowered separately.

Close to the banks of the Rhine *and well camouflaged against air and other observation, the attacking boats are distributed in readiness over a distance of one and a half km*

Colonel Th., who has a fresh and spirited method of training, and who has just gone over in extraordinarily vivid fashion a similar crossing of the Elbe with his officers, is responsible, as regimental commander, for the crossing. Then there is another Silesian here too, whose name will tomorrow be mentioned in the Army Report and become familiar to the whole world, Major Gantke. Once a soldier, always a soldier. He and his twelve brothers and sisters come from a small farm near Liegnitz. He is among the Engineers a specialist in all kinds of difficult accomplishments pertaining to flame-throwers an other apparatus connected with this arm. His seven brothers were soldiers during the Great War and still are in so

At precisely 10 a. m.

the artillery begin to fire at the French fortifications along the Rhine and at the same moment the camouflage is torn from the boats

Phot. PK Grimm

While the artillery fire is still roaring and the boats are still on land the powerful engines are tried out

Whilst the thunder of the shells falling on the French fortifications on the other side of the 200 metre wide Rhine drowns every other noise, explosive charges blow up our own barbed wire entanglements. The way to the river bank has been cleared for the attacking boats

far as they are alive and capable of service. Major Gantke's face and left arm are uninjured, but for the most part the remainder of his body has suffered damage; his left leg has no artery and he has lost a number of ribs. Until 1930 the wound in his chest was still open and it was not until a general learned during manœuvres that Gantke was obliged to sew a new bandage into his jacket every morning, in order to prevent the blood coming through, that energetic treatment was ordered and carried out. When, during the period of our small army, Major Gantke once applied for a position in the police, he was refused on account of his injuries. But this man, born in 1893, will today be the first on the other side of the river . . .

It rains all night and is still raining in the morning. A heavy mist lies on the water. Everything has been

A minute later the attacking boats push their way through the blown up wire entanglements. The men are now working under fire from the French bank, but the bullets are flying too high

Meanwhile a raging inferno has been let loose on the French side by our heavy artillery. Six men jump into each of the boats, which lie at a distance from each other, flatten themselves against the thin steel sides, the engines start throbbing and . . .

. . . clearing the waves and shooting up spray the boats speed across the full, rushing river. It is here 200 metres wide. No boat takes more than one minute to cross. 10.09 a. m. and the boats are on the other side

The first assault troops have landed. Smoke bombs cover the river from the enemy's view. The boats rush back in order to fetch reinforcements

Major Gantke is the first across the river. Standing up in the stern of the boat, he steers it across to the other bank in 25 seconds. He makes the crossing 50 times during the attack

prepared in the best possible manner for this crossing, one of the boldest ever undertaken in the history of warfare, the success of which is essential.

It is a task which even the most experienced pioneer would undertake with a feeling that it was highly probable that he would not come out of the venture alive. In the morning, in broad daylight, the guns suddenly begin to roar; the light artillery is aiming its direct fire across the 200 yards of water against the cupolas and the loop-holes and also at the neighbouring sandbag positions. Any of the enemy making a rush out of the fortifications and installing themsel-

A machine-gun points from the up-tilted bows of the attacking boat in order to quell the enemy fire from emplacements which have not yet been destroyed

ves in these field positions may possibly be of more danger to the crossing than a loop-hole with which one is perfectly familiar, because one has lain opposite it so long.

The fortifications cannot withstand the fire for long. The armour-piercing shells split the concrete from the positions and wrench them apart. The armoured plate is now a tangled mass, greyish white clouds of dust rise from the powdered concrete, shells explode with a roar in the undergrowth, the infernal din of the preparatory fire thunders across the river. At 10.9 a.m. Major Gantke is standing ready with his first boat in front of the dam. He jumps in, takes his men on board, streaks across the river together with about thirty other boats to the right and left of him. He is fired at by machine guns and artillery, but his speed is so great that the bullets and

The boats reach land, the artillery moves its fire further back and the assault troops leap from the boats. At places where it is necessary to save time, the boats dash at full speed against the sloping banks of the river, and remain lying there (see picture on right)

Whilst the attacking boats continue to flash one side of the Rhine to the other and have succeeded within four minutes in landing a whole company to form a bridge head, the assault troops are beginning a flank attack on the first fortification of the Maginot Line. The loop-holes in the fortifications now open a heavy fire . . .

. . . but within an hour the sinister monsters, which for many years had glared menacingly across the river, have lost their terror. They have been destroyed and on the evening of the very same day an immense military bridge has been thrown across the Upper Rhine and battalions, regiments and divisions are marching across it to the attack on the Maginot Line (picture below)

shells almost all fall behind the boat; the French have not aimed sufficiently far in front.

The Major is the first man to reach the other side. He leaps out of the boat, positions his infantry men in front of the fortification, throws a few smoke bombs to protect his other boats from view, jumps into his boat once more and at hectic speed repeatedly crosses the river with fresh troops.

One fortification after another is captured during the severe fighting and shortly afterwards the engagement spreads deeper into the woods. The crossing has been accomplished. Major Gantke with his well-trained specialists requires only 25 seconds to cross the river. A man who is no longer young, who has no artery in his left leg, who wears two life-saving medals and who was refused by the police because he was apparently too damaged in body, has forced the breach, thanks to his experience in the hard school of the engineers and his indomitable fighting spirit. The instinct of this experienced soldier has led him to choose the right spot for the first landing beyond the field of fire. The artillery fire has soon ceased, the French observer has obviously retired quickly. This dare-devil attack in the middle of the morning, and carried out so openly too, was probably too much for him.

Whole companies have now been set across the river and they in their turn are followed by battalions. And now the troops stream through the breach, one unit after another, as so often in this most strange of all wars, and penetrate fan-wise into the country occupied by the enemy.

Meanwhile the heavy pontoons have been advanced across the dam and been converted speedily into ferries by the engineers. There are ferries of every imaginable kind; only the expert could distinguish between them and give them their correct name. The powerful engines in the boats made of thin steel begin to throb and push the ferries together until they form a daring bridge across the swiftly flowing river. The anchor line is stretched at a point 80 yards upstream beyond the bridge, the warning line is 120 yards upstream beyond the bridge, every ferry has two anchors and every anchor 25 yards of chain before the rope, otherwise the river would carry away everything with it.

The first prisoners are now being brought in. They had thought that no Germans would come in this rain, and in broad daylight too.

By 11 a.m. the engineers have begun to build the bridge, and 12.25 a.m. the bridge is already beginning to take shape. Major Gantke brings up one ferry after another. At 17.45 the last ferry has been brought into position and by 21.30 the bridge is complete.

Now the tide begins to roll across the bridge. One gun follows another. Battalion after battalion marches across. At a distance of scarcely 2 miles powerful fortifications in the second line are still resisting fiercely. But the army has been provided with a bridge and is now pouring through the breach. All night long the troops pass without intermittence across the bridge. All the next morning, until noon. The sun breaks through the clouds. The Upper Rhine has suffered a frontal attack and been mastered. The Maginot Line has also been smashed at this point. All resistance is useless now.

The nooses which have just been cast are tightening.

In a few days time endless columns of prisoners will cross this bridge.

Major Gantke packs up his equipment and, quiet and modest as he had come, he returns whence he came.

And now
for the Maginot Line!

A cupola of armour plate offers a desperate resistance. It is attacked with all the means at the disposal of the engineers. A smoke bomb first does its work

The man with the explosive charge waits under good cover until the smoke has settled in front of the fortification . . .

. . . and then he leaps forward

The flame throwers and the machine guns (below) lie close behind him and cover his advance

The man with the flame thrower creeps forward towards the fortification, which is now enveloped in fog . . .

The flame thrower is brought into action

The loophole from which an unpleasant fire from the flank is being directed, is approached from the side. The flame thrower is brought into position out of the range of fire and directs his flames against the loophole

The first flame reached the mark. Burning heat and intolerable fumes penetrate into the interior of the forti-fication, but the men inside, fighting with determination, do not slacken their fire. Well then, we must get nearer!

Illustration on the left: this is the view obtained by the machinegunner who is covering the flame throwers while they are at their work

The detachment has gone forward under the now diminishing fire from the loop-hole and completely covered it with the flame thrower. The camouflage on the fortification is now ablaze

The loop-hole is silenced. *The gun behind it has been withdrawn and the slit is closed. At the same moment in which the flame thrower dismounts his apparatus . . .*

The end is near

. . . engineers leap forward with an explosive charge and blow up the loop-hole

When explosive charges are not at hand. the pioneers are nevertheless not at a loss. One sandbag after another is brought up and the loophole obstructed

Even when all the loopholes of a fortified position have been silenced, the enemy may still be esconced in the fort, which is often 30 or more metres deep, and may attempt a sortie. A specially concentrated charge splits open the fort, whereupon the last few men usually came out with up-raised arms. (Right) In this way the fortified positions are successively captured. until the signal "Halt!" announces the armistice

The German air patrols advance over ńo man's land far into the enemy country

Quick fighter planes guard them in their flight over the enemy positions, and keep the enemy quick fighters at a distance; these reconnaissance machines then advance further alone. making use of every means of cover in the sky, and generally succeeding in flying without being observed right up to the prescribed targets. Their return over the fortresses of the Maginot Line, and the flying stations of the French quick fighters is again guarded by our own quick fighters who fly out to meet them

Booty of the reconnaissance machine:
A photograph from the Maginot Line with bunkers and holes caused by German shells

Before the No Man's Land

"Day by day we experience the same thing again and again",
writes our special reporter Kenneweg as text for this sketch of Hans Liska. "At a great altitude and always just under the clouds the heavy reconnaissance machines, underneath and beside them formed in twos and threes the little silvery quick fighters: and thus they disappear on the other side of no man's land. Then the quick fighters come back. We count them: 1, 2, 3 ... 8, 9. They are all there, and then we know that the reconnaissance machines have got through. A few hours later we see them, but now in inverted order: First the quick fighters alone advancing from Germany towards the west and disappearing in the blue sky far off. Then one hears again the sound of the engines. Thousands of eyes from the forefield search the sky, and then one sees them again and counts again 1, 2, 3 ... 8 and 9 ... 12, 13. They are all there. "Have you seen them, old chap?" ask those on the ground. "They are back again" and they smile at one another.

The soldier in the forefield has a special liking for his comrades in the air; he knows the individual types of machines, and their tasks, and he knows also how important it is for him and for them to be successful. We shall soon get to know them closely for we are leaving the forefield, and the bunker zone in a few days to be attached to the flying stations and anti-aircraft batteries of the air defence zone.

We have to-day entrusted to the military post a result of our work during the last fourteen days, that is to say, films, drawings and sketches of the "land that belongs to no one", out of the forefield, out of the chief fighting line, and out of the bunker zone. Our report from the air defence zone will soon follow.

No man's land

Forbach, a district and industrial town in Lorraine, since 1918 in possession of the French. Population = zero

The windows were smashed, furniture broken into pieces, books and papers torn up and thrown into the street, this work of destruction having been committed by the French on their retreat. This was the condition in which our reporters found the place when visiting it with a patrol

Silence on the wine road, German frontier place, known for its wine gate, which was also called "The gate of peace". Number of inhabitants = zero

Amidst the ruins of this town which had been senselessly destroyed by the fire of the enemy there is a German m.g. position for covering the advance of a patrol

Street battle in Forbach

By our artist in accordance with statements made to him by the German officer who led the action. A German patrol, which had been attacked by the surprise fire of the enemy out of several houses of this town in no man's land, succeeded in defeating the enemy who was in superior numbers and in making prisoners

May in PARIS

This all happened in Paris in May of this year, about eight months after France declared war on Germany

"The motor buses now only continue to run to Neuilly, St. Cloud and St. Denis".

The crowd waiting at the stopping places for the omnibus began to get impatient, and one could hear shouts of:—"Palais de Justice?" "Quai d'Orsay?" "Market?" The policeman, who had been answering such questions a hundred times since the early morning, shook his head and said:—"Take the Métro. The omnibuses now only run to the suburbs." He then turned towards the dirty, old-fashioned motor car, covered with dust and crammed with luggage, which was just stopping beside the kerb, and answered the questions of the driver who had a harassed look in his eyes. This was one of the many cars containing refugees who did not know where to go. The people waiting at the stopping places, and who were still grumbling in a hoarse voice, moved on to the underground station on the other side of the road. Several of them were carrying those old-fashioned trunks, which the thrifty Frenchman takes great care of for years, and has with him when he travels. Now and again one could hear a sarcastic question such as:—"You are going away, Monsieur?" "Only to relatives near Bordeaux." "My sister has already sent her children into the country. But we are stopping here, for I am an official and must; you know what I mean."

The sun was shining through the haze on to the Place de l'Etoile on the 16th May, when Paris learned to its consternation that they had now also requisitioned the motor buses. It was a mild pleasant spring morning like the rest of May 1940. The fresh green trees in the avenues of the Bois de Boulogne were shining in the sunlight, and in the Champs Elysées Paris was trying to keep smiling. One could see elegant women with their hair charmingly done in the new way, that is to say brushed up and arranged in a knot or quite short at the neck. They were either wearing the new sunny colours, as they are called by the creators of fashion, and which are a kind of goldish yellow, chamois and tobacco colours, or coral or russet with pale-blue. This was the bright picture on the boulevards and on the terraces of the large cafés.

It was only just a week since people could think, in peace and quiet and with any degree of pleasure, of fashion, of walks or engagements; just a week since the 10th May when Paris was aroused in the night by an air raid and the fire of the anti-aircraft guns, and when it was announced on the wireless, that the Germans had marched into Holland and Belgium. Just a week since all men who were on leave had to return to the front. But the scene

Capitulation in Flanders

at Etoile was no longer in harmony with this last remnant of gaiety. For in the place of the large elegant cars which a week ago were driving round the Arc de Triomphe, the road was now filled with old cars and carts covered with dust. These were cram-full of refugees and household utensils. One could see in the faces of the occupants that they were worn out with fatigue and were disagreeably surprised at the display of elegance still to be seen here. There were cyclists covered with dirt and their clothes in tatters sitting exhausted on the benches along the boulevards, their luggage being tied on to their cycles; these were refugees from Belgium and Northern France. "Just the same as in August 1914", the elder people said who could remember those days:—"The Germans were already in Meaux." "In Meaux?" A third one heard the words and the rumour was soon spread: Rheims captured, Meaux threatened.

Churchill, who had rushed over to Paris by air in order to inspire the Allies with energy, was overwhelming the French Premier with reproaches in his residence. "The Germans have crossed the Meuse, are on the west bank, and have broken through the French lines at Sedan; what has been happening to your Meuse army? How about the fortresses on the Belgian frontier?" Reynaud answered very bitterly:—"Since 1934 my cry has been for mechanized troops, but our philosopher Gamelin, was against this. The situation is even worse, for the Meuse army has proved a failure, badly trained troops having been employed at the most dangerous spots. But we have made a change in the Army Staff and Giraud is taking over command." "But how are we going to hold up the German advance to the west?" "Gamelin wants to retreat to

the Marne." "That is to say the armies are to be separated? Out of the question."

This excited argument continued for two hours.

Opposite the Concorde Bridge people were trying to crowd into the entrance of the *Chambre*, but the police forming the cordon kept shouting out that all the seats were full. Reynaud proceeded quickly into the *Chambre* and mounted the speaker's platform. In a suppressed voice and in short, terse sentences he said:—"We have hard weeks and months before us, men and methods must change . . . There can be only one punishment for neglect of duty, and that is death.

In the lobbies one could hear such remarks as:—"Jacobite methods are necessary." What is the old Jacobite song?" The words occurred to them: "Conquer or die. He who fails suffers death. Our country is in danger." The appropriateness of these words to the present occasion rendered them breathless.

There were dense crowds practically besieging the loud speakers in front of the cinemas and cafés. The people in these crowds looked at one another and were pale as death, when the following mysterious warning, which almost sounded like a threat, was given:— "Supplies of drinking water are to be immediately stored in an air-tight place under lock and key. If any impurities get into the drinking water, colouring matter will be added to it as a warning . . . Such discoloured or suspicious-looking water is not to be drunk." What was the meaning of this warning? Did it mean that the water would be poisoned? The report spread through Paris, and the Government itself made the people lose their heads, and even increased the panic, by giving out such warnings. "Parachutists have landed on the Place de la Concorde." This cry caused people to get very excited, and there was a cordon of policemen placed around the square and the following statement was issued to calm the crowds:—"It is only a meteorological balloon for experimental purposes which has landed, and there is no need for anxiety." All the same the rumour spread further. On the 18th May the inhabitants of Paris were greatly disturbed by mysterious news in the morning papers, and appeals were made to the public to maintain self-discipline:—"Don't become desperate . . . stop the panic-mongers . . . help to strengthen the morale of the nation . . ." The police announced that no one was to leave Paris without an official identity card, and the chief of police announced that dancing was prohibited, that there was to be the greatest possible economizing of food stuffs, and that plundering would be punished with death. Then, most important of all was Gamelin's order of the day:—"All bodies of troops which cannot advance must hold their positions to the very end . . . death or victory."

What can have happened? There is no broadcasting. At all events the general uneasiness was increased by this silence and by the fact that none of the French wireless stations were transmitting on the 18th May in the morning, but those listening in to the foreign stations heard:—"The Germans have occupied Brussels, Louvain and Malines. The enemy is in Maubeuge and Dinant. The French tank divisions have been beaten." All this caused a public panic.

Gamelin, the Commander-in-Chief, was sitting in the Palais des Invalides. For years he had been working out his plans of defence in these huge unadorned rooms, that almost resembled those of a monastery. The desk, at which he worked from eight in the morning to seven o'clock in the evening, and the huge table were covered with a heap of maps. The walls were brightly distempered and covered with maps and strategical plans . . . Was that all going to come to an end? The Commander-in-Chief was an indefatigable worker, working days and days without a break, and years and years without leave. Was all this laborious work not enough to prove him to be a great general? The lines of defence had been broken through, the Meuse abandoned and the Ninth Army annihilated. Would this be his last orders of the day and his last words to the Army?

Pétain

Reynaud received the aged Field Marshal Pétain in the Palais Matignon and said to him:—"Two weeks ago I refused you the plenipotentiary powers which you demanded, and the result was that you would not enter the Government. Now you can have the fullest powers you desire, for the only way out is a dictatorship."

Marshal Pétain had just arrived from Madrid, and it is reported that he was always against this war. He nodded to the Premier as if he were tired and said:—"France recalls her children just before the catastrophe."

The premier blinked and jerked his head back uneasily, with a hasty movement; these nervous symptoms of his had been increasing with the excitement of the past few days. He gave the Field Marshal a hasty survey of what was being done:—"The *Garde mobile* has been called out, volunteer corps have been organized for combating the parachutists. Mandel has been made Minister of the Interior with plenipotentiary powers, and all foreigners have been interned." A strange procession was passing down the Boulevard de Courcelles, and on the right and left of it were heavily armed policemen in their black uniforms. Between the latter were men of every age, of every class of society and of every nationality, men in worker's smocks, their faces full of wrinkles and with a wild look in their dark eyes: Spanish Reds to whom the French Government had given shelter during the Civil War, German Jews, German refugees, and foreign film stars who the day before had been acting.

A few streets further on there was a procession of women likewise accompanied by policemen, these were also suspicious foreigners. During the night searches had been carried out in different houses and people arbitrarily arrested if they were known to the police as foreigners. People were standing on the edge of the pavement angrily watching the procession. The men were conducted through the Avenue des Ternes to the Port de Champerret, and the women to the large race-courses in Neuilly and Levallois, both of which have been made into concentration camps. Growds of women had assembled in front of the entrances crying out:—"Down with the traitors! Hang them, shoot them!" Every batch was received as it arrived with fresh insults and abuse.

From early in the morning there had been unusual excitement in Levallois-Perret, for it had been reported that two parachutists had landed in the suburbs, and for hours a mad search went on until it was found out that the occupants of a French kite balloon, who had had an accident, had saved themselves by jumping out over this part of the city in a parachute.

The outward appearance of the city had changed, and one could read such notices as: "Temporarily shut because away from home." Everywhere there were white placards on the shutters which had been let down in front of the shop windows, announcing that the owners had fled. In the interior of the city the doors had been locked and the goods behind them packed up ready to be sent away. The jewellers' shops in the Rue de la Paix and the Rue Royale had long ago put their valuable stocks in the safes of the banks in the south of France. At the Madeleine one could no longer see the flower-sellers with their bunches of bright spring blossoms, for who could be expected to decorate the abandoned apartments of the refugees with flowers? The stream of refugees along the streets continued to get more dense. Coming from and going to the railway stations there were peasants, carts loaded up with furniture, and children on the top of piles of chairs, tables and mattresses; the procession was incessant. The anti-aircraft cellars were placed at the temporary disposal of the refugees. The police no longer knew where to accommodate these hundreds of thousands of people. About five o'clock in the afternoon the sirens began to howl. The streets emptied very quickly and the doorways of the houses and the Métro stations were used as provisional shelters.

In the anti-aircraft cellar of the *Chambre* the deputies crowded around the president, Herriot and Louis Marin, who nine days ago had been nominated Minister, that is to say since the advance of the Germans into France.

"How is the change in the Cabinet proceeding?" Hereupon Herriot shook his head and said:—"When the air-raid is over I am going to the Premier." Half an hour later the siren gave the "all clear" signal, the anti-aircraft guns not having had to do any firing this time.

Later on Reynaud broadcast the following:—"The situation is serious, and France expects deeds, not words. Marshal Pétain, the victor of Verdun, has entered the Cabinet, and I have taken over the War Office."

Rumours began to spread all over Paris to the effect that Gamelin had been dismissed, the French army on the northern front had collapsed and that Gamelin had committed suicide.

In the Elysée

In normal times we should see motor-cars proceeding on joyrides people going for a wav-, and young people making their way to the railway stations on a spring Sunday in the Champs d'Elysées. But on the 20th May of this year, although it fell on a Sunday, the bright spring morning could not put to flight the gloom hovering over the city. Everywhere the black uniformed constables were patrolling in pairs armed with revolvers and carbines, and in the side streets the police had their armoured cars.

Two heavy cars coming from the Place de la Concorde turned into the Rue de l'Elysée; their occupants looked fatigued and outworn. Only one of them looked youthful and fresh and this was the eldest, General Weygand. The sentries stood at attention and saluted as he passed. His youthful appearance was more marked as he left the car, saluted and proceeded to the entrance of the building.

This was for General Weygand a triumph in a crisis, for he was being recalled at seventy-three years of age, after having been too old at sixty-eight. It had become necessary to recall this orthodox Catholic, who had been nicknamed the "Jesuit General", and his opponent Pétain had to do this after having refused, while Minister of War, to prolong the age limit for Weygand. The scene was enacted in the conference room of President Lebrun, formerly the music-room of Madame de Pompadour, and the pictures of the French kings seemed to be looking down from the walls upon this conference which was taking place in an hour fatal for France.

Reynaud gave the cue by saying: "The General has accepted." "On conditions, Mr. President." The General had just reached Paris by air early in the morning, and had only been able to get a very general idea of the position of affairs at the front, during a short visit to the General Staff Headquarters. The picture he gave was gloomy.

"It is perhaps too late to save the situation: the best troops have been sent to Belgium and are threatened with encirclement. The Meuse army has been destroyed and General Corap dismessed too late. There is a complete ignorance of the possibilities of defence in the Meuse sector. The Germans are on this side of the Sambre and Oise. St. Quentin and Le Cateau have been lost. There is danger of the Germans breaking through in the west."

"What can we do to stop them? Gamelin wanted to withdraw to the Marne."

Weygand nodded and said:—"Yes, that is Gamelin's old theory of defence. By all means there must be a withdrawal, because this affords the only possibility of starting an offensive, and it is necessary to rally the troops."

He pointed to the map and continued:—"We must hold the line between the Somme, Aisne and Meuse, at least until the reserves come up. What are the transport conditions? What is the position in regard to reserves? What railway lines are still intact? Those are all matters of which I am ignorant. But I shall hold this line, from this position the counterattacks must be made.

Weygand's face with the little toothbrush moustache, the sharply formed nose, and the tightly compressed lips had become stern; it was solely the deep wrinkles in the corner of his eyes which indicated the age of the man who on his removal from the service announced: — "On no account will I die before I am seventy-five years of age."

Reynaud who was sitting beside him looking uneasy and harassed said: — "How about keeping in contact with the English?" Weygand shrugged his shoulders and said: — "We have probably lost the contact for the time being, and it is too late to establish it after the collapse of Corap's army. I am not able to change the consequences which bad strategy has brought about. As regards the future, that depends upon the success of our counter-offensive. Moreover I have no idea of the extent of the catastrophe." General Weygand knew that he was required and he also knew that the myth surrounding him made his position impregnable. The rumours concerning his origin and career added to his importance. For he was reported to have been born in Brussels, and to have been the illegitimate son of Maximilian of Habsburg, who was executed in Mexico, and of a lady from the district of the Saar, further that he had become a Frenchman by choice and had been a confidant of Marshal Foch.

The President made a weary gesture and asked: —"What are your conditions?"

"War material, tanks, ammunition. That is to say a twelve hours day for munition factories, and further no day off on Sundays."

"That has already been ordered", Reynaud broke in.

The General nodded and observed "That is to say, military law, and courts martial for workers in munition factories. Further parliamentary control must be abolished, and there must be no more postponements." He paused and then added: — "You must get rid of the military critics, they are too clever and their outspokennes is fatal; in fact the German General Staff can read between the lines of their articles all that we intend to do. The telegrams sent by the English and Americans everywhere in the world are even more outspoken." Did General Weygand know what he was saying? Did he know that his demands amounted to the burial of a political system?

Within an hour the people of Paris read in the papers and on the walls and placards everywhere, that there would be work on Sundays and that no munition worker might stay away from work without an excuse.

About the same time the *Garde mobile* was stationed everywhere, at the Cours de Vincennes, the Port des Lilas, the Avenue de St. Quentin, the Boulevard Nation, and the Rue du Président Wilson in order to stop the influx of refugees into Paris, and one could hear the command: —

"Halt! About turn! Entrance prohibited!" and in answer to frantic questions the reply was: —"Go back by Le Raincy and Le Bourget! or "Go back by Stains and Ormesson to the Rouen road."

The refugees resisted the orders and shouted insultingly from their carts drawn by oxen and cram-full of household articles, poultry and children, with calves and goats tied to them: —"We want to go to the south. What are we to do in Rouen?"

The policemen shook their heads, and were again the pleasant persuasive constables directing streams of motor-cars with a movement of the little finger, or with a turn of the head in the midst of the densest traffic. They were then successful and the carts turned about. It was a question whether thay would proceed to the north or to Rouen; probably they intended to take the next turning to the south again. The police, however, had done their duty.

Crowds had collected before the cafés and bars at the street corners to read such notices as — "Burgleries in Boulogne". — "Armed burglers arrested at Montparnasse". "Shops plundered in the Boulevard des Capucines". Highway robberies at Montparnasse". And every time the local defence organization was the scape goat for such higway robberies.

Advance guard action

The enemy has established itself in a farmyard just a few meters ahead and is keeping the road under fire. A German infantry-gun is put into position. Ten shots tear the air and walls tumble, a cloud of dust and rock soars high. The enemy is silenced! The march can proceed

The pride of the Italian Air Force: *the heavy bombers. Squadrons of three-engined bombers at their base aerodrome drawn up for their final inspection prior to active service*

Italy's Air Force

Heavy bomber
The bomber SM 79 which is heavily armed with machine guns *is the creation of the famous aeroplane constructor A. Marchetti and on account of its radius of operation and carrying capacity proved of great value in the Civil War in Spain and in the Abyssinian War.*

Fast bomber
The fast twin-engined bomber, the Fiat B.R. 20 *which is also employed for long distance air attacks*

Hydro-aeroplane bomber
This is the very reliable Cant Z 507, *a three-engined seaplane produced by the Monfalcone Works, a fast bombing and longrange reconnaissance plane for the war in the Mediterranean*

Fast fighter
Italy has developed two kinds of fast fighters: *the fast pursuit planes and the especially nimble fighters. The fast type is represented both by the Macchi C 200 with the Fiat engine and...*

Handy fighter
the compact Fiat G 50 which is often used in driving of enemy air-craft

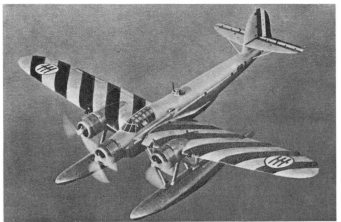

Torpedo-carrying seaplane
The winged brother of the submarine: *the torpedo-carrying seaplane. The torpedo-carrying fighter roars across the surface of the water close towards the enemy vessel*

The Italian Army

Ready to fight — Prepared for war

The Italians are a young nation. Although the Roman Empire lays claim to being the oldest in Europe, Italy is a new state. This probably explains the spirit of the Italian army. A youthful spirit pervades this great machine, a latent power can be felt in its fever for action. The standard of motorization is high. The doctrine of Italian military science, which endorses

"The force of our arms is undoubtedly great, but greater still is the firmness of our hearts"

These were Mussolini's words at one of the great parades on one of the traditional national holidays showing the force and efficiency of the Italian army. Beside Mussolini the Crown Prince: Fascism hand in hand with the Crown, fighting for the right to live of the Italian people

Badoglio in conversation: —

An attentive listener

Pietro Badoglio, Chief of the General Staff, and Duke of Addis Ababa, is not only a splendid narrator but also an attentive listener

Badoglio cuts in

Whenever the conversation touches the sphere in which he is the first expert of the nation, he likes to take part in the debate

The narrator on the defence

A fighting method upon which he frowns, and for which he is temperamentally unfitted: long discussions

. . . and attacking

Just as he defeated the enemy in battle, so he now puts an end to objections thanks to his exact military knowledge

132 militia battalions of blackshirts

132 militia battalions were incorporated in the Italian army, one blackshirt legion for each infantry division. Thus the greyish green regiments of the army and the legions of blackshirts form from henceforth one single bulwark

mobile warfare and frowns upon a "war of nerves" or of defense, appeals to the youthful spirit of the nation. But on the other hand—Rome was a world empire 2000 years ago. So this vigorous, potent young army has the advantages of a glorious national history, and the experience gathered in 2000 years. It also knows the value of organization, and every young Italian soldier today considers himself the apostle of Roman civilization, just as his ancestors did 2000 years ago. Graziano, 20th century Scipio Africanus, not only conquered Libya, but immediately began its colonization. His soldiers built military roads through the deserts, founded cities and reclaimed sand-buried oases. The "Cittadino soldato", the soldierly citizen, has been molded by today's training into a type which also existed

The Song of Victory

flows from his lips. The great victories that Italy gained in Libya, Abyssinia. Spain, and Albania

2000 years ago. The Italian army has two problems to solve. The first is in the Mediterranean, the European Mediterranean area. The second, and more complicated, is on the "fourth coast", the African side of the Mediterranean. From the first day of his rise to power, Mussolini has equipped, organized and trained his armies for these tasks. The Italian army has already proved itself equal to the burden on four battlefields: Graziani's conquest of the Fezzan and the Senussi oases of Kufra were the first feelers extended on African soil, which incidentally still bears the columns, fortresses, temple ruins and graves of ancient Rome. Then came Abyssinia, a colonial war won by Badoglio in record time, another triumph of mature organizing ability and youthful enterprise. Then Spain and Albania . . . new victories which brought new experience. It may well be said that the Spanish war formed the Italian army as we know it today. The mixed divisions of General Roatta, second in command of the Italian General Staff, were here put to the test for the first time. The air force too had excellent opportunity to try out

new types of machines in Spain — planes which now play the most important role in the Italian Air Force. This is Italy's army! Rich in experience — spendidly equipped and burning for action, highly alert to its great aims in Europe and abroad. Not a neutral army, but one belonging to a non-combatant power, ready to fight.

"The pilot Mussolini has created one of the strongest airforces of the world," *said General Pricolo, Secretary of State in the Ministry of Air a short time ago before the Fascist parliament. The efficiency and experience of our pilots, the genius of our inventors and engineers are materials of which Italy will never run short*

Ubaldo Soddu
Secretary of State in the Ministry of War, which Mussolini personally directs

Rudolfo Graziani
the conqueror of the Fezzan and Harar, the Scipio Africanus of the 20th century, chief of the General Staff of the Italian army

Mario Roatta
head of the Intelligence Department in the Abyssinian War, commander in Spain, now vice-chief of the General Staff

Tested in Spain
The small two-men tanks, the employment of which decided many battles in the Spanish War

Stood the test in Abyssinia and Albania
Every Italian infantry division has besides the usual infantry, machine-gun and motorized troops also an artillery regiment

The last resistance is broken!

On the beach at Dunkirk: loaded guns, tanks ready to move off, coastal forts, these are all put out of action, deserted by their crews and demolished by the force of German arms

Tanks versus warship

English warships and transport vessels were fired on and damaged by tanks unexpectedly arriving on the scene

On England's threshold

Pictures of the great battle of annihilation

This is what was left

As yet huge quantities of war materials were abandoned by the British in their hurried flight

It would not . . .
*explodde. An unexploded shell on
the embankment near a French fort*

At the last moment
*The British attempted to make an improvised
jetty to their ships by driving long rows of lorries
into the water at low tide. But all in vain!*

Direct hits
*A large unit of German fighting planes
carried out an attack off Dunkirk, during
which 18 warships and 49 transport stea-
mers were either sunk or severely damaged
by bombs*

The last phase of the great annihilating battle in the West once more
demonstrates the irresistible power
of the combined German arms. The
English had desperately attempted to
hold the French coast lying opposite
their island. They were unsuccessful.
Protected by the French, they desperately attempted to reach their island
and safety. This also was a failure.
The élite of the British Expeditionary
Force was annihilated and vast quantities of war materials fell into German hands.
The German army stands on England's
threshold.

Many thousands . . .
*The remnants of the British army defeated
at Dunkirk, which were unable to reach
the ship, were captured by the Germans.
Endless columns march towards the collec-
ting buses behind the front*

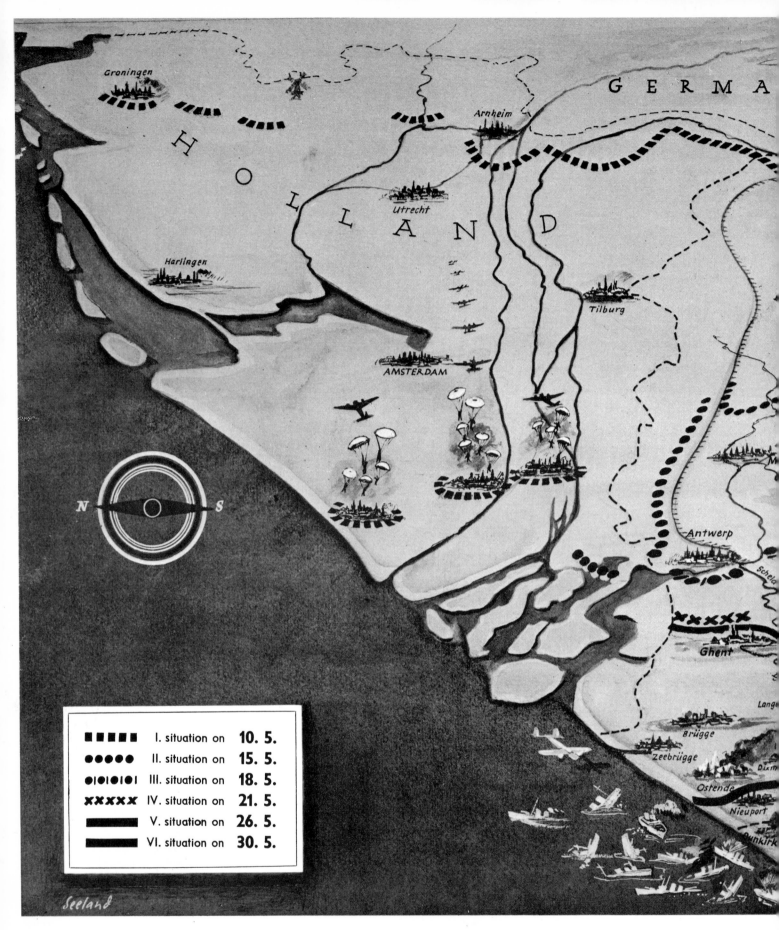

▪▪▪▪▪	I. situation on	**10. 5.**
●●●●●	II. situation on	**15. 5.**
◑▮◐▮◑▮	III. situation on	**18. 5.**
✗✗✗✗✗	IV. situation on	**21. 5.**
▬▬▬▬▬	V. situation on	**26. 5.**
▬▬▬▬▬	VI. situation on	**30. 5.**

Seeland

The Campaign in the West from May 10 to June 4, 1940

On May 10, the German army in the West advanced on a very wide front to the attack across the German western frontier, in order to forstall the intended allied push towards the Ruhr district. From the very first day the air force screens the land army, destroys the enemy planes and land bases, smashes the infantry and tank concentrations of the enemy in their preparations for counter-attacks and provides the German Command by means of aerial observation, with a continuous record of the situation. Specially selected units of the air force, employing the very latest means of warfare, occupy the most impregnable forts of the enemy, parachute and landing troops occupy aerodromes in the rear of the enemy and guard important means of communication. Holland capitulated on May 15. By this date all the fortresses on the frontier and all the fortified positions in North and South Belgium have been penetrated and enemy tank units annihilated, while between Dinant and Sedan the Meuse has been reached. Soon afterwards the strongly reinforced frontier fortifications which are defended by the Ninth French Army are overrun by mechanized and infantry divisions on a front of 60 miles. The air force once more plays a decisive part.

On May 13, the attack penetrates as far as the upper

Oise. The same day sees the fall of Antwerp. Brussels, Louvain and Malines are in the hands of the Germans. The Ninth French Army is completely annihilated and its Commander-in-Chief, General Giraud, is taken prisoner. The German divisions pour through the breach they have made and reach the Channel coast near Abbeville. In this way the allied armies operating in the north of Belgium and in Northern France are encircled.

On May 21, the German mobile units are able to move up along the Channel coast, with no need for any protection from the rear, as in the meantime a strong German defensive front has been formed. The enclosed armies were repulsed and the circle around them continually drawn closer. Boulogne falls.

On May 26 Calais also falls. On the same day it was possible to carry out a deep thrust into the enemy front as far as a spot just before Ypres and the next day a similar movement was successful in the north. The situation of the Belgian army, which now has no other task than that of covering the retreat of the British Expeditionary Force, is hopeless. King Leopold capitulates. Now the British had to make a stand, in order to cover the retreat of their own troops to the coast and to the ships. But the German air force dominates the Channel and bombs the British warships, transport vessels and the Channel ports. Only small units are able to save even their very lives. At first the French cover the retreat of their allies and attempt to hold Dunkirk. But on May 30 the bulk of the German divisions is free for new tasks. Altogether more than 1,2 million prisoners have fallen into German hands, besides limitless amounts of war materials, the equipment of between 75 and 80 divisions. France's and Britain's finest troops are annihilated. England is now separated from France and exposed to a direct German attack. One June 4, this battle of annihilation came to an end with the fall of Dunkirk.

A damned near hit. Lucky that we got our heads out of the way quickly enough . . .

Church parade less than a thousand yards from the enemy lines: A soldier, who is a parson in private life, is preaching to his comrades in the church of an evacuated village

The barracks of the German soldier at the front: The big bunker

The big bunker works of the western front are built several storeys deep into the earth. The foundations are held fast by heavy iron bearers, and the cement walls which are several meters thick are reinforced with iron. Only the turrets are outwardly visible; their armoured cupolas protrude from the earth and their machine guns and cannon barrels are directed against the enemy through narrow loop holes which can be closed. The ammunition is brought up by means of a lift out of the store, which is underneath the fighting emplacement. The working rooms for the men, the cantine, the recreation room with library and wireless are one storey deeper. The command headquarters are in the middle of the bunker, and remains in continuing communication with the neighbouring bunkers, and with regimental headquarters by means of the telephone exchange, which is next door to it. In the deepest storey are the dormitories, lavatories, sick room, and separated from these the kitchen and store rooms for victualling the occupants. The big bunkers have their own power and lighting plants, and are thus independent of what is going on outside. All rooms are continually supplied with fresh air by ventilation and gas filters make it impossible for poison gases to penetrate into these rooms. The separate works have subterranean communications with one another, these communications being supplied with electric vehicles running on rails. The communication tunnels can be closed by steel bulkheads

After heavy bombardments and air attacks, a German assault-detachment penetrates into the enemy town

The men warily advance in short rushes through the grey-black veil of smoke from the explosions, through collapsing masonry and the smoke from burning houses. Desperate resistance is still offered from a few cellars. It is overcome. Only very seldom is the assault detachment compelled to take cover from the fire of enemy machine guns

...somewhere in France...

"Here is the front line!"
The Infantry get into communication with their Air Force comrades. White cloths spread out on the ground indicate to the German airmen where the front line of their own troops is situated

... and a press photographer was also present

An anti-tank gun arrives and is brought into position . . .

It is part of the vanguard, situated well forward, of an advancing infantry regiment and is allotted the duty of guarding against enemy tank attacks. Any moment may bring a surprise. The gun stops in front of a village on the edge of the quiet street

Suddenly a burst of fire shatters the stillness

at the next crossing an enemy tank, which until then had been under cover, advances from behind a house. Quick as a flash the guns in the tower are directed against the Germans, but . . .

. . . before the first enemy shell has left the gun,

the German anti-tank gun officer has realised the danger and given the order to fire. The anti-tank gun takes up its position. — The very first shell registers a direct hit! A cloud of smoke rises from the colossus of steel

Tank Nr. 12173 on fire!

Put out of action by shell fire, it lies there motionless, one more wreck on the German army's road to victory. The regiment can continue its advance

A camouflaged fortified position

A harmless house

situated on a hill which dominated the line of advance for a great distance. When the German vanguard approached it, they were met by furious machine gun fire from all the windows. A field gun was brought into position. At the first direct hit the walls of the house were demolished. An ordinary fortification was made visible. A short time later an experienced assault-detachment put it out of action

At the Arc de Triomphe

For many hours the noise is heard of the divisions as they march along the roadway. The regimental marches echo across the square. Lieutenant-general v. Briesen (on the right), takes the salute. With his right hand, which was wounded by a Polish bullet in the battle of Kutno, he greets with happy feelings of pride his troops

The kind of prisoners taken in France

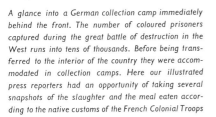

A glance into a German collection camp immediately behind the front. The number of coloured prisoners captured during the great battle of destruction in the West runs into tens of thousands. Before being transferred to the interior of the country they were accommodated in collection camps. Here our illustrated press reporters had an opportunity of taking several snapshots of the slaughter and the meal eaten according to the native customs of the French Colonial Troops

THE NEW ORDER

Signal increasingly turned its attentions to political indoctrination and cultural news once the first flush of victory in Europe had subsided. One of the principal purposes of *Signal* was to convince subject peoples that the war was not only won, but over. Consequently the European populations under the swastika or at least its influence, as in Spain, Switzerland and Sweden, had to be convinced that the victorious Reich was the legitimate center of culture and the recipient of the mantle of European civilization. This preposterous thesis nevertheless won its adherents. Life in Germany was, in the main, peaceful and prosperous in 1940–41. Shortages were few and rationing had scarcely begun, while in Britain the economy was obliged to institute severe austerity. The worlds of fashion and film, café and night club were seemingly untouched by the war. Apart from the Jews and a few political dissidents, the midnight visit from the Gestapo and the rigor of the concentration camp was unknown, at least until after the attack on Russia in June 1941 brought a rush of anti-Nazi activity from Communist elements throughout Europe. Nevertheless the soulless face of the Third Reich shone through the pages of *Signal* to those who wanted to see it. Nazi art, like its proletarian counterpart in the Soviet Union, was retrospective and, *au fond*, decadent and mechanical. Films of the Third Reich were flippant at best and repulsive at worst, with certain brilliant exceptions in such films as *Die Goldene Stadt*, an all-color panorama of Prague, and *Die Grosse Liebe*, a moving drama of two lovers caught in the maelstrom of war. But *Signal* portrayed the highly structured society of Nazi Germany in the sort of detail that even Germany's many critics would have been unable to do. The rigidity of National Socialism, praised by *Signal*, indicated that the Nazi Party penetrated German life from the national level down to every street and house. Red tape and bureaucratic muddle was rife, even in such a simple manner as getting married. The underlying implication of this fact was that petty corruption was the only practical way to circumvent the problem. The thrust of post-blitzkrieg propaganda was aimed at the same goal as Nazi Germany itself, already swollen with recently acquired territory. It was a policy of absorption of peoples into the New Order and acclimatizing them to eventual, if grudging, acceptance of it. Admittedly the attempt to draw Franco's Spain into the Nazi orbit with something less than a success, but Vichy France was most obliging, and *Signal* was right in assuming that numerous foreign workers came to Germany of their own volition to find jobs there. Many others, of course, were forced to work in Nazi war plants, and *Signal* pretended that they were equally willing to work for the Reich. *Signal*'s view of the Home Front in 1940–41 was the ideal of a United Europe under the swastika which was supposed to last for a thousand years. It endured for a rather shorter period of time, and the cracks in the Nazi edifice were already beginning to show in 1942, Hitler's final year of triumph.

0.9

Signal

Belgium Fr. 2.— / Bohemia-Moravia Kr. 2.50 / Bulgaria Leva 10.— / Denmark 50 Öre / Estonia 40 Sent / Finland Mk. 4.50 / Greece Drs. 11.— / Italy Lire 2.— / Latvia 50 Sant. / Lithuania 60 Cent / Luxemburg Fr. 2.— / Netherlands 20 Cents / Norway 45 Öre / Portugal Esc. 2.50 / Rumania Lei 16.— / Sweden 50 Öre / Switzerland 45 Cts. / Slovakia Ks. 2.50 / Spain Pts. 1.25 / Turkey Kuruş 15.— / Hungary 36 Fillér / U.S.A. 10 Cents

After the victory in France:

The entry into Berlin

■ MINERAL COAL
|||| LIGNITE

The quantity of coal in Europe, estimated to a depth of 2200 yards, amounts to 779,718 million tons of pit coal and 108,856 million tons of lignite. Of this, Germany alone, before the commencement of the conflict with Czechoslovakia possessed 288,865 million tons of pit coal and 56,758 million tons of lignite. As a result of the extension of her zone of influence after the victorious conclusion of the campaign in Poland and her occupation of Holland, Belgium and Northern France, these extraordinary figures have risen to a remarkable degree. At the present moment Germany possesses approximately 483,014 million tons of pit coal and 88,091 million tons of lignite, all of which is at the disposal of German industry

Where are the coal-fields of the continent?

Coal deposits in the German sphere of influence

In our world of inherited concepts England was the country for heavy industries, the master of coal and iron. We will now gradually have to become accustomed to new ideas. Several years have already passed since the rise in the German iron industry increased our steel production to a level which is 50 % greater than the English and French combined, so that now the position is that England's predominance in the coal market has been shattered.

The war, the successes of the German army and the military events in the East and in the West have fundamentally altered the relative positions in the mining of coal. Poland was the first step; Eastern Upper Silesia and the Cracow and Olsa basins increased the coal output of the Reich by approximately 50—60 million tons annually. Then came Holland and Belgium, whose coal mines are now at Germany's disposal to cover the needs of her system of war economy. Holland will mean an annual increase of 14 million tons and Belgium an increase of as much as 30 million tons. As for France, almost 70 % of her annual coal output of 48 million tons was supplied by the départements Pas de Calais and Nord, i. e., the precise districts where the great battle was fought, which was lost by France. Between 30 and 35 million tons of coal annually will

be at the disposal of the German economic system for the duration of the war.

If we add this output to that of Eastern Upper Silesia, Holland, Belgium, the Protectorate and, of course, to our home coal production, we arrive at an annual total of approximately 320 million tons— 40 % more than the total output in England last year. England, once King of Coal, has been dethroned, the German economic area, together with the districts at Germany's disposal for the period of war, has gained a long lead in the output of coal. Apart from Germany, and the occupied areas, there are no other countries on the Continent worthy of mention, which produce coal; to complete the picture, the fact must also be mentioned that Germany totals today approximately 80 to 85 % of the world's output of lignite. England has suffered a defeat on one of the most important fronts of the economic war, a defeat which is irreparable.

The English mining industry is, moreover, in a serious situation with regard to a most important technical matter. The supply of pit-props, which were for the most part imported from Scandinavia, has almost ceased for England. But mining cannot be carried on without pit-props; wood is just as important to the mining industry as is his daily bread to the miner. England cannot change over to iron supports in the galleries from one day to the next,

especially as she is already feeling the lack of iron. On the other hand, it is difficult to cover the requirements in pit-props from other countries, e. g. Canada, if only on account of the lack of shipping. England's coal production then is already on the decrease and it is difficult to see how England can possibly escape out of this tight corner. The most important coal deposits on the European Continent reach in two belts from Eastern Upper Silesia, and the neighbouring area of Bohemia and Moravia, across Western Silesia to Saxony and then, after a break, through the Sarre basin across into Lorraine. The more important belt lies further to the North and reaches from the Ruhr district, where the richest coal deposits are found, across the Belgian coal area, to the North of which there lies a secondary deposit, the Dutch coal mining zone, as far as the region in the North of France and almost up to the Channel coast. Not a single link in this chain is today under control of the enemy! Germany has incorporated all this in the area under her influence for as long as the war lasts and has thus complemented her own coal mining industry by tangible control of all the important coal areas in the central zone of the European Continent. Whatever coal is found elsewhere in Europe is negligible by comparison.

New power
for Europe

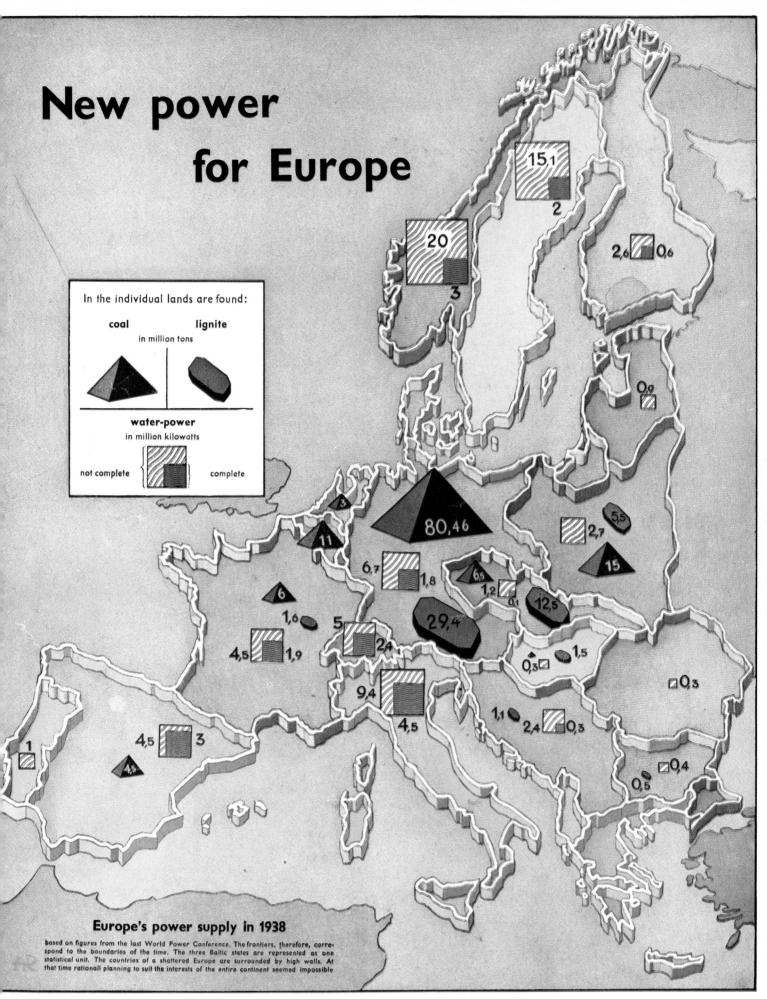

In the individual lands are found:

coal   **lignite**
in million tons

water-power
in million kilowatts

not complete   complete

Europe's power supply in 1938

based on figures from the last World Power Conference. The frontiers, therefore, correspond to the boundaries of the time. The three Baltic states are represented as one statistical unit. The countries of a shattered Europe are surrounded by high walls. At that time rational planning to suit the interests of the entire continent seemed impossible

Are Europe's sources of power inexhaustible?

Yes and no.—No, if Europe continues to waste coal, one of its most precious mineral treasures, by over-exploitation of the mines.—Yes, if Europe at length recognizes the demand of the times to employ the ever self-renewing sources of water-power to the last drop, and turn them into electricity so as to make coal free for other more important purposes. The water-power of Scandinavia and the Alps are the chief reservoirs from which Europe could obtain an enormous amount of electric energy. It would necessitate tremendous operations to develop them, but it would be an untold blessing for the coming generations of Europe

An October day in France

The 23rd October 1940 was marked by the friendly meeting between the Führer and the Caudillo on the frontier between Spain and France. The place and the hour were in accordance with the total revolution in Europe. Placing his trust in the Führer and the Duce, Generalissimo Franco (picture above) some years before had begun the struggle for Spain's independence. The trust he then had was not deceived. Spain today sets her seal upon the alliance with the Axis. (The Spanish Minister for Foreign Affairs, Serrano Suñer and the German Ambassador in Madrid, Herr von Stohrer, are seen in the illustration below on the right.)

O n the third day of the Führer's journey in France, on 24th October, 1940 about noon, a four-engined Condor plane set off from an aerodrome near the Bay of Biscay on a short flight towards the North. The Führer's special train had already left Hendaye before dawn and would soon reach the day's destination, Montoire-sur-le-Loir. The German Minister for Foreign Affairs, Herr von Ribbentrop, who this morning had held a second important conversation with the Spanish Minister for Foreign Affairs, Serrano Suñer, followed the Führer by plane in order to arrive in time for the reception of the Head of the French State.

Fourteen months previously, at precisely the same hour, on 24th August 1939, this identical aeroplane, flown by its famous pilot, with its accustomed speed and reliability, had headed across the plains of Western Russia in the direction of Moscow, where the Foreign Minister that very night on behalf of the Führer signed the pact between Germany and Russia in Stalin's presence. The proud Condor had then still been painted pale cream and the swastika had been emblazoned on a gleaming red field. Today, however, like the machines of the Luftwaffe which fly out after their prey across the glistening expanse of the Atlantic on our left, it is painted field-grey and the cross is in black.

Politics on a grand scale in the midst of war, a diplomatic journey through the war area, unknown to the enemy, seen by the troops of occupation and the indigenous population here and there just for a moment as though by flash-light, that was the nature of the Führer's journey in France in October 1940, of which the flight, lasting barely an hour from the Bay of Biscay to the Loire, through ragged clouds beneath the sky of Southern France, formed a small part.

What had taken place since the afternoon of the discussion?

The incomparable panorama of the Basque landscape had appeared in almost tangible clarity after the rainy morning of 23rd October. Yonder, on the other bank of the Bidassoa, at the bottom of the foot-hills of the Pyrenees, lying in deep

Four months after the Armistice of Compiègne, the Führer of victorious Germany and Marshall Pétain, the Head of the State of France now arising from her most disastrous defeat, shook hands. The Germans and Frenchmen who on the afternoon of 24th October were the witnesses of this unique event on the tiny station of Montoire-sur-le-Loir, gained the profound impression of a break with a centuries-old continental tradition. The Marshal afterwards said: "I voluntary accepted the Führer's invitation. I was not submitted to any dictate or pressure on his part. Collaboration between our two countries has been planned. I have accepted the principle underlying it." (In the centre of the picture, the German Minister for Foreign Affairs, Herr von Ribbentrop.)

blue shade, nestled the small Spanish town of Irun. During General Franco's War of Independence it had been the centre of fierce conflicts. In the spring of this year it became the Mecca of all those wishing to flee from France at the last moment, until suddenly the first motor-cyclists belonging to the Black Guards on active service came roaring down the road from Bordeaux through Biarritz to Hendaye and hoisted the swastika flag on the French side of the bridge of Irun.

Today, 23rd October, it flutters more proudly even than before, when the special train of the Caudillo crosses the railway bridge and after another few hundred yards draws up in the station at Hendaye. On the front platform of the electric train, a Spanish General, recognizable by the red sash against the field-brown uniform, such as is also worn by the Caudillo, raises his gloved hand in salute. The guard of honour of German soldiers in field-grey stands motionless on the platform in front of the Führer's train, whilst the Spanish colours, red, gold, red, and the flaming red of the Swastika banner flutter overhead.

And now the Führer, who with his suite had been awaiting the foreign Head of State, welcomes the Caudillo with a hearty handshake. The Spanish national anthem is played and the Caudillo salutes the battalion colours with outstretched

Pierre Laval, Marshal Pétain's deputy and now also his Minister for Foreign Affairs, was received by the Führer on 22nd October in the presence of the German Minister for Foreign Affairs, Herr von Ribbentrop. As a protagonist of a European system unfettered by England, he is a champion of collaboration between Germany and France

A little stroll

*over Berlin's famous street of beautiful
shops and café-houses and finally . . .*

On
Kurfürsten-
damm
at

. . . a little refreshment

*in one of the sidewalk cafés, where one
goes to see and be seen — this is one
of the Berliners' favourite pastimes*

How is this possible?

TOLD BY A GERMAN WORKER

This picture was taken long before the Great War. That is my father, at that time a mechanic in a machine factory. The girl beside my mother is my sister Hanna, the younger one is called Bertha and I am the boy with the whip ...

In 1933 I suddenly got work

This is our house. How did we manage it? It was not easy. But to call it a miracle would be saying too much. I was able to take up a loan and am now paying interest instead of rent. Since the middle of 1933 I have had good earnings. Up to 1937 I earned 300 marks a month, from then on until today it has been 346 marks — and then came the wage-limit law. Father has his labour-pension and the disability insurance, 130 marks together. The house as it stands is worth 20.000 marks. But of course it was cheaper for us because we all worked on its construction, father especially. Wiring, plumbing, painting, papering — all his work. In the meantime ...

How time flies! That was Christmas 1929. One-and-a half rooms in the Ackerstrasse, Berlin's slum section. Lots of worries. Skilled worker without work. My boy Rolf was scarcely two years old. There was not much under the Christmas tree, but my wife sang a carol ... Things are going to be alright again.

Children are always happy. In the summer of 1930 my wife did laundry work at home, and when she did the rinsing in the backyard, little Rolf tried to help her. I was on the dole, sold cigarette-pictures and spectacle cases, repaired cigarette-lighters — oh well, the less said about it the better.

...the family has grown: little Erich is here now. This picture shows us on our Sunday morning walk. My wife — that is not the same worried face of 1929, is it? And I myself — feel like a new man since I have work and know what I am working for. There is a fine team spirit in the family too, you really ought to ...

On the day of the opennig *of the Bayreuth Festival, the Führer declared before the Reichstag: "It has never been my intention to wage wars, but rather to build up a state with a new social order and the finest possible standard of culture. Every year that this war drags on is keeping me away from this work."*

This is how the "House of German Art" in Munich will look *when the annexe which is planned (illustration, left) is completed. Even during the war year 1940, Greater Germany did not abandon the celebrated German Art Exhibition which has become a most valuable tradition, and was the fourth to be held in this house*

"A Socialist State of the highest Culture..."

From Adolf Hitler's speech
in the Reichstag on July 19, 1940

Every year thousands of people from all over the world did not shrink from crossing one or even two oceans in order to visit the Bayreuth Festival or the great German Art Exhibition. During this year of war. 1940, the doors of this institution of culture were open as usual: it is true that on this occasion it is not "Society" which graces the Bayreuth Festival Theatre and the House of German Art. To compensate for this. wounded soldiers and munition workers are enjoying the tones and colours of sublime art.

"An autograph, please!" *Franz Völker. the opera singer, who sings the part of Erik in the "Flying Dutchman". cannot refuse the wishes of either the strong or the fair sex*

In 1940 as in all previous years *the fanfares to announce the beginning of the performance sounded from the balcony of the Bayreuth Festival Theatre, according to an old Wagner tradition. On this occasion they were blown by soldiers of the Armed Black Guards*

In exactly the same manner *as in the theatre. the air raid precaution accommodation is arranged according to the seats*

The guests of honour *are gathered together in the Ludwig Siebert Hall. A lecture familiarizes them with the opera which they are to hear shortly afterwards*

Frau Winifred Wagner *is delighted with the flowers presented to her by wounded sailors*

The German physiognomy

at the Great German
Art Exhibition of 1941

The Fifth Great German Art Exhibition was ceremoniously opened on July 26th in the House of German Art in Munich. It is the second of these exhibitions since the beginning of war. The guiding principle of German art in wartime is: "When Mars rules, the Muses need not be silent." German culture is unaffected by the war. This year, 746 German artists, of whom a large number are serving, have exhibited 1,347 examples of painting and the graphic and plastic arts. We here show details of two particularly characteristic works of German sculpture: Professor Arno Breker (left) "The Summons", Professor Fritz Klimsch (right) "Anadyomene". Both figures represent the ideal of the German man and the German woman. Breker's work is an especially happy expression of his desire for the noble attitude and severe form. The "Anadyomene" is the beautiful contrast to the manly seriousness of Breker's creations. The doyen of German sculptors has given this Venus who, true to the conception of ancient Greece, rises from the waves, the spiritual traits of the German soul. Two generations of contemporary German art meet here

The Pg.

The Party member, the man one meets everywhere in Germany and recognizes by the badge in the left revers has become a familiar figure in Germany today. He can be the labourer paving the street; he can be the chauffeur driving the car along that street; or he can be the merchant or manufacturer sitting in that car. Social position is of no importance where membership of the Party is concerned. The form of address used by a Party member is "comrade", and "Mr" or

At the local group headquarters of the Party:

Solemn reception of a new member

The right arm is raised in the German greeting, and the oath of loyalty is pronounced: "I solemnly promise to be loyal to my Leader, Adolf Hitler. I promise to respect and obey him and the leaders he has appointed at all times." Then the local group leader hands him his membership book with the words: "In the name of the Leader, remain loyal to the Party"

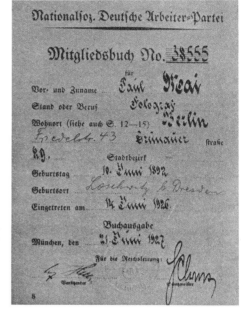

The party membership book

In the bottom left-hand corner is the Leader's signature. The number of the book is 36,555. The member is, therefore, a veteran and holder of the gold Party Badge which was awarded to all Party members below 100,000

any other title is omitted. The salutation is "Heil Hitler", and at the same time the hand is raised according to the ancient German custom. Whoever becomes a member of the Party is not merely joining an organization; he has become a fighter in the German movement of liberation, and that implies much more than paying a subscription and attending meetings. The Party member binds himself to put aside all selfish interests and to devote all his energies to the welfare of the people. In the National Socialist German Workers' Party only the best National Socialists are to be accepted as members in accordance with the decision of the Leader. It is his will that the Party should be a sworn community of political fighters. Every German national of German blood can be admitted. In order to avoid admitting unsuitable members, each application is sent to the block supervisor of the block where the applicant lives. The block supervisor must form a clear and accurate judgement of the applicant before accepting his application. The financial situation and the profession are immaterial, but a good reputation and a firm character are decisive factors. Young members are given the preference on principle.

Number of members up to the assumption of power

1919	6	1929	176,000
1925	27,000	1930	389,000
1926	49,000	1931	806,000
1927	72,000	1932	1,200,000
1928	108,000		

... and a page of pictures showing the various activities of the men and women in the

National Socialist German Workers' Party

The German vocabulary has become larger since 1933. Words have been created to designate ideas previously non-existent. Words already existing have likewise changed their meanings. A "Pimpf", for example, is a lad from 10 to 12 years old in shorts and a brown shirt, with freckles on his face and with an enormous appetite after his spell of duty. The "Pimpf" is a familiar sight everywhere. "Strength through Joy" connotes a holiday trip to the mountains, a production of "Faust" at the municipal theatre or the crowded bus taking you out into the country on a Sunday morning. All these illustrations consequently have their own particular significance, each one vividly represents a side of contemporary life — these pictures are symbols

The People's Car

Everybody knows it and after the war there will be hundred thousands of them on the roads. It was designed at the instructions of the Leader by the German Labour Front for employees and workmen, it costs RM 975.— and can be bought on an easy purchase system with weekly payments of RM 5.—. The car has a marvellous performance. It can keep up an average of 62 m. p. h. along the German arterial motor roads. Petrol consumption is approximately 33 $\frac{1}{2}$ m. p. g.

The "Wilhelm Gustloff" is one of the ships in the "Strength through Joy" fleet. It was launched in May 1937 and since then has taken innumerable comrades of every class on journeys to foreign lands. It is fitted with every comfort and all the luxuries of the modern passenger steamer—theatre, bathing pool, and sports deck. The accommodation, consisting of outer cabins only, is sufficient for 1500 passengers. A trip on this vessel costs only from five to seven marks per day

The House of German Art in Munich

The "German Art Congress" is held in this building every July. The Führer and his staff are the first visitors. Photographs of the opening ceremony and of the procession of the six thousand can then be seen in every newspaper. For weeks on end people stream through the exhibition rooms and by the last day every picture has been sold

Just as in peacetime

A day's racing in Berlin

Europe's most beautiful steeple-chasing track. *This year's great day on the Berlin race track at Karlshorst was a warm Sunday in late autumn. There were eight races on the programme including the "Grand Prix of Karlshorst" with a stake of 65,000 marks, the highest in Germany*

Just as in peacetime, *the spectators thronged the stands and the grass along the course. The fast electric trains left Berlin every three minutes. Programmes and racing papers were sold out ten minutes after the meeting began*

Whose money is on the right horse? *The young lady's tip seems to have been a good one. Her horse is the first to come round the bend into the straight. But the winning post is still a long way off. The two wounded officers favour the stable of the Army School of Riding and Driving. Their horse is Tootish, a fleet chestnut with legs of steel. But its rider broke his collarbone the last time he rode and today he is riding with his arm in a sling. Will he manage it?*

Coming round the bend. *A photograph showing the beauty of racing and riding. The horses' hoofs thunder over the green turf. The jockeys shorten the reins. Now for the last jump!*

Photographs:
Diedrich Kenneweg

He has done it! *Wolf, the jockey, rode the race with one arm. A fall would have been very serious. But he and Tootish won the Grand Prix in spite of everything. The jockey's face as he goes off with the saddle to be weighed-in shows the strain it cost him*

Everything for the nation!

In the following pages the "Signal" gives a description of the political Party in Germany which, founded 21 years ago and from the very outset inspired with the revolutionary spirit, swept the German people along with it and created the most modern socialist state in the world. A description, which will perhaps correct a number of false impressions, of the organization of the National Socialist German Workers' Party, the spirit which gave it birth and the aims towards which it is striving, will therefore be of interest

This is the final and supreme task of the organization of the National Socialist German Workers' Party:
To ensure for the German man a happy and industrious existence, for the German woman a beautiful and worthy life, for German children a bright future

It has unfortunately been concealed from the peoples of Europe ever since the Great War — this would not have suited their politicians — that the drab misery of a nation numbering 60 millions stood beside the cradle of the National Socialist German Workers' Party. Inhuman methods were employed against Germany during the Great War. It seemed as though the Dictate of Versailles were intended to drag out the poverty, the serfdom and the hunger of millions of people for an indeterminate time. Something unprecedented in the world's history was done: the German people was robbed of its honour and branded a nation of slaves. A man came forward to help this people; he resolved to become a politician. The Germans who heard his first speeches will never forget how this man, in contrast to all the politicians of that time, did not try to obtain votes for a group of individuals with interests who called themselves a party, but tried to gain the people for a national movement. He neither flattered nor made promises, he repeated to his listeners the simple, sober, age-old truths which are perhaps rather hard. He said to them: you must be united, you must be industrious, you must be honest, brave and relentless towards yourselves. He said to the Germans that they must first put their own house in order before they could regain their liberty and their honour. It was with these aims that he founded the organization of the National Socialist movement, on a grand scale, magnificent, destined from the very first day to become later on the new and unique organization of the German people.

Germany's position in respect of foreign policy when the National Socialist German Workers' Party was building up its organization:

Believing in the promises of the American President Wilson and in the promises of those governments which, under the cloak of democracy, were relentlessly pursuing a strong-handed policy, the German people laid down its arms after a war that had lasted for four years and during which Ger- *many with her few allies had fought against the whole world. The Dictate of Versailles was intended to enslave Germany for all time. She was robbed of her armaments, her navy and her merchant fleet; the blockade was maintained, with the result that tens of thousands* *of women and children died of hunger in Germany. The reparations demanded were enormous, and no time limit was fixed. The debt was to be perpetuated. It was a "peace" after Clemenceau's own heart. He had said: "There are 20 million Germans too many in the world."*

The international condition of Germany until the Party took over power:

The governmental system which was officially imposed on the Germans by her former enemies with the help of all the means of propaganda at their disposal as one of the conditions of peace brought a large number of parties into being which placed their own selfish interests before the public weal. The advantage of the individual was the *supreme law, and whoever—it was immaterial by what means—acquired power and wealth determined the fate of millions. Such a system was not adapted for the struggle to liberate an impoverished people. Adolf Hitler was the first who recognized the situation. Therefore he assembled courageous men who gloried in action* *and who thought as he did and formed them into an organization which was not only intended to fight against the existing chaos, but which at the same time had the germ of a government in it that could unite all the strength of a nation at work in such a way that the fruits of its labour benefited not individuals but the whole nation*

The National Socialist State

When a German

The Registry Office requires their family-tree, *with the date and place of birth, Aryan descent, and the denomination of brothers, sisters and ancestors*

If the young couple wish, *they can obtain the State marriage loan. After the birth of the fourth child the obligation to repay the loan ceases*

For the wedding reception *special food rations for twelve people are granted during the war*

Since 1933 it has been the chief aim of the German State to establish the family as the primary cell of the nation. The one and a half years that have elapsed since the outbreak of war are sufficient to give an idea of what has been achieved during peace-time. The results are most significant. The war weddings registered up to April 1940 exceeded the normal forecast by 330,000 in 19 different age groups.

Gertrud Müller of Berlin-Falkensee. *She is engaged. Her fiancé, an N. C. O., is stationed somewhere in France. They have decided to marry*

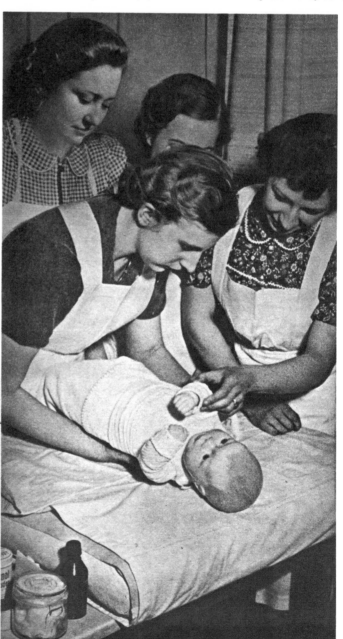

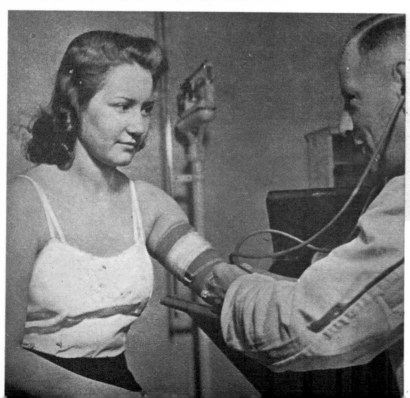

The bride can consult the special doctor *appointed by the Board of Health in order to find out if she is thoroughly healthy*

At Schools for Young Brides *girls learn the care of infants and household management before their marriage*

girl marries...

hand with advice and practical help

purchase of linen and cur- ...s, in fact of everything re-...ed for the household, is ...litated by the local authorities

The living-room in the little home where the young couple will live

The bedroom . . . They had only to add a small sum from their savings to the State marriage loan to pay for every-thing, including the kitchen equipment

The German standard family album *in which the family re-cords are to be entered. It will be handed to every newly-married couple by the registrar*

The man whose name she is going to take. *With his pass and the marriage licence from his unit in his pocket, and his future wife at his side, he has every reason to smile*

What she enjoys most *is buying the linen. Thanks to the prompt regulation of the textile market on the outbreak of war, a large selection and good quality have been assured for years to come*

The happiest moment in her life — *her mother-in-law arrang-es the bridal veil*

The German people's tree of life

The German people classified according to age—Increase of births since 1934—Better marriage prospects for women

A people is like a tree: in the same way it must be firmly and securely rooted in the soil; like the tree, it needs space, light and air in order to grow and thrive. Thus there seems to be some indication of a mysterious connexion in the fact that the diagram of the German people arranged according to age resembles a tree in its outlines. This might be called the German people's tree of life, the lower branches lie wide-spread and thick over the maternal soil: these are the youngest groups upon which the future of the people depends. Towards the top the outline becomes more slender, terminating almost in a point which represents the oldest groups. That at least is how it should be. And it was so in fact on the basis of the figures for 1910, shown in black and white on our illustration. The small notch caused by the war of 1870—71 had been quickly made good. Certainly a decline in births was noticeable with the turn of the century, but this remained within narrow limits and was compensated for by the fall in mortality since the 70's. This normal course of affairs was decidedly upset by the Great War and the post-war years. The census of 1939, shown in our illustration in red, evidences the double effect: the terrible losses of 1914—18 resulted,

Like the outlines of a tree. *That is the appearance of the diagram classifying the German people according to age. It shows the number of persons in each age group as given by the 1939 census. In order to afford a comparison covering the last 30 years, the figures for 1910 are shown in black and white, while those for 1939 appear in red*

according to the figures of 1939, in a considerable reduction in the number of men between the ages of 40 and 60 compared with women, and the great decline in births during the Great War is shown by the reduction in births from 1915 to 1919, that is to say, of those who are now from 21 to 25 years of age. It appeared as if this reduction could be compensated for, because the number of births increased in the years 1920—22. But this hope was vain: from 1923 onwards the number of births declined at an almost regular rate. Now for the first time the economic, and still more, the spiritual burden of the dictate of Versailles was making itself felt to the full extent. It might have been an exaggeration to say that nothing but old people were left. But the excess of older persons above younger persons was and is as undeniable, as serious, and a decline of births means a diminution of national strength.

It is thanks to National Socialism that this truth was recognized. When National Socialism assumed power the decline of births was checked. As early as 1934 there was a considerable increase of births, which have since increased from year to year. This increase was also maintained in 1939 and in the first half of the war year 1940. If in our representation of age groups the branches for the year 1939 appear to be too short, this is not actually the case, but is due to the fact that the census only goes as far as the middle of May, that is to say does not even embrace one-half of 1939. The progress since 1933 is particularly encouraging although the figures of births are not by any means as high as before the Great War. The decline of births caused by those four years of war has taken on serious proportions in recent years because there is a shortage of young persons. This is felt most in those occupations for which long periods of training are necessary. The shortage is acute amongst those from 21 to 25 years of age. On the other hand, the number of younger employees, those between 14 and 18 years of age, who have to attend training schools, is now on the increase. Now, however, the figures will fall for a few years because the age groups of the low years 1926—33 are now coming into this class.

To anyone looking at our tree of life, the difference between left and right, between the male and female sides, will be striking. On the right-hand side the branches reach out further, in the higher age groups there is none of the indentation which is to be seen on the male side. The excess of women can easily be realized from the diagram. In 1919, in the Reich territory of that time, there were no less than 1101 women to 1000 men. That was the direct consequense of the Great War. Nature slowly began to correct this unnatural proportion: according to the 1939 figures there were only 1048 women per 1000 men. Women's marriage prospects have thus considerably improved. In reality, women's prospects of being able to wear a wedding-ring are even better. The figures given above apply to men and women of all ages, from infants-in-arms up to the extremely aged. The prospects are far rosier, at least for women, if the proper age for marriage is considered, i. e. between 20 and 30. Between these ages there are only 979 women for 1000 men. But that is not sufficient: still younger men, those who are now under 20 will have to be still more gallant because for one thousand of them there are only nine hundred and sixty-five girls. Certainly there are remarkable differences in this respect between town and country. Here migration to and from the city plays a considerable and not very desirable part. The proportion remains steadiest in small and medium country towns, approximating to the standard for the Reich. In the country itself, however, a serious shortage of women is evident in the important group between 25 and 40 years of age, only 929 women being available for 1000 men, while large towns show a great surplus of women, namely 1067 women against 1000 men. The prospects of marriage are thus far greater for women in the country than in the city.

Many problems of this kind only appear when details are considered, and on the whole the policy in regard to population since 1933 has given favourable results. The tree of life of the German people is sound to the core, from the root to the tree-top and the outlines of its branches are about to develop, in healthy growth, their harmonically beautiful lines.

Otto Robolsky

RECORDS

Even during the war German athletes break records

Germany was the most successful nation at the last Olympic Games. This fact imposes a duty and this duty is faithfully fulfilled by German athletes. Although naturally most of the crack athletes of an age when it is still possible to break records are wearing field grey, progress has been made and the women, who, often enough among quite different conditions of life imposed by the war, work at their place on the Home Front, are also certainly well in the foreground in this connexion.

On 6th June in Düsseldorf

Anni Kapell of München-Gladbach improved on the German women's 200 metres swimming record

The best German long-distance runner
Max Syring of Wittenberg on 15th June in Jena set up a new 10 000 metres record. He clocked 30 min. 6.8 sec., thus achieving a time which had hitherto only been reached by the Finns Nurmi and Mäki

A strong man "raises" the weight
Hans Clausen of Lübeck on 30th June in Hamburg created a new record for the middle weight class in the two-arm snatch. He managed 116 kg

A policeman from Vienna
was successful in establishing a new world's record. Toni Richter, a featherweight, which means that men of his class are not allowed to weigh more than 9 st. 10 lbs. with both arms jerked 284 lbs. in Vienna. A quite amazing achievement which provides proof of tremendous concentration, strength and conscientious training for many years

Grey — yet bright

A SHORT HISTORY OF UNIFORMS

"Uniform" is a French word derived from the Latin. German military contingents fighting under the French flag were the first to wear uniform clothing.

In the old German Reich all ranks and classes were obliged to provide their own troops for the Emperor when he went to war. Thus it happened at about the beginning of the 16th century that the rich town of Nuremberg contributed to the imperial levy a body of foot-soldiers under Captain Willibald Pirkheimer who were entirely dressed in red cloth. Many writers on manners and customs are of the opinion that the Nuremberg patricians chose this colour from motives of compassion, not wishing the young recruits to be discouraged by the sight of the bloodstains which they might well expect. Actually, however, this red colour was intended as a compliment to the Emperor. The contingent from this free, wealthy town was arrayed in the colour which is the attribute of majesty.

Red and purple are the colours of emperors, kings and rulers in general. In ancient Rome the senators had purple stripes on their white togas and red heels on their sandals. The example set by Nuremberg inspired kings and emperors from then on to dress the special troops entrusted with their protection, the Life Guards, in red coats. This royal red is still to be seen in the peace-time uniforms of the British Guards Regiments.

The well-dressed citizen as a prototype

The colours of uniforms in the last four centuries—uniforms did not become general till the end of the 16th century—were white, blue and red. The French kings preferred white and red, white being the colour of the Bourbon fleur-de-lis. Frederick William of Brandenburg, known as the Great Elector, who fought first with the Swedes, but later had to turn against them, usually dressed his soldiers in blue. In Germany blue was the colour of the free burgess, and by giving his soldiers a good middle-class coat, felt hat, woollen stockings and breeches, the Great Elector raised them far above the hired foot-soldiers, who often, as an observer wrote, appeared with their chests, legs and even the rear part of the body, quite exposed. Thus the troops of the Great Elector were as well turned out as any citizen. As regulation uniform was not yet in general use in the 17th century, the troops in the field wore various badges, the colour of these badges corresponding to the heraldic colours of the houses which they served. Thus the men who fought for Sweden wore blue sashes with golden fringes, the Dutch had the orange colours of the House of Orange from the South of France, while Wallenstein's men fought wearing the red of the German Emperor.

At first, then, a uniform was only of symbolical value. It was intended to enhance the appearance of the soldier and, as it bore the coat of arms or

livery colours of his master, it showed to what house he belonged. The purpose—that is to say the military serviceability—of the uniform was first brought out by George von Frundsberg, a leader of mercenary foot-soldiers, at the Battle of Pavia on 25th February 1525. Frundsberg ordered his soldiers to put on white shirts over their armour. This made his men visible in the faint light of early morning, in mist and in moonlight: it was easier for them to keep together and co-operate. He himself put on a monk's white cowl by which his men could recognize him as their leader. But Frundsberg had another idea at the back of his mind; he hoped that if he should be killed in the Battle of Pavia he would be able to slip through the gates of Heaven more easily in a monk's cowl.

The white fleur-de-lis colour of the Bourbons, in which French infantry were dressed, subsequently became practical from a military point of view, as well as having a symbolic meaning. White infantrymen were easier to recognize in the black gunpowder smoke than soldiers dressed in blue or red.

It was Napoleon, who, riding over the battlefield covered with killed and wounded after the Battle of Eylau, was horrified at the sight of white-clad men lying in their blood in the newly-fallen snow. He therefore gave orders that the infantry should be dressed in blue in future, and the guards in red cloth. As blue dye was difficult to obtain at that time, the carrying out of this order was delayed. Blue dye was expensive, but red, on the other hand, was cheap, because rape-seed, with which the breeches of the French soldiers were dyed red, grew in large quantities in Alsace, which in those days belonged to France.

The Prussian kings kept to the blue cloth which their ancestor, the Great Elector, had chosen for his soldiers. In the time of the great Brandenburger there had been only one regiment dressed in red, the Dorothea Regiment of Life Guards. Red uniforms were cheaper, but in spite of this economy the two great Prussian Kings, Frederick William I, the "Soldier King," and Frederick II, the Great, or "Old Fritz," clung to blue cloth. Blue cloth with a red lining—the red was only visible on the facings—made the figure of a man appear more slender and elegant, and by reason of the symbolical value of the blue colour gave him an appearance corresponding to that of the well-to-do citizen.

The elegance of the Prussian grenadiers

At that time an officer's uniform cost nearly 35 thalers. The uniform of a private soldier came to about 8 thalers. This was a heavy expense, considering that a man was entitled to demand a new uniform every year.

The Prussian uniforms were extremely closely cut. The uniform coat of the soldiers corresponded roughly to the present-day cut of an English morning-coat. The white breeches were modelled closely to the leg and the

calves were encased in tight gaiters. The Soldier-King was accused by his enemies of meanness in giving his soldiers such tight-fitting clothing. The truth was, however, that a Prussian uniform cost twice as much as that of foreign soldiers. The Soldier King did not care about money when he was equipping his soldiers; elegance and distinction were the first consideration.

A grenadier's wardrobe

Just think what it meant to a journeyman of those times, strolling past a recruiting office or a Prussian sentrybox in his shabby linen clothes, to learn that a grenadier's outfit included two pairs of shoes, two pairs of spare soles, two vests, a shirt, a pair of leggings of waxed canvas, two red ties, two hair-ribbons, a hat, a cap, a coat, two pairs of breeches, three pairs of stockings and three pairs of gloves. The regiment also paid for the curled wig, the plait and powder which he needed for the maintenance of his coiffure. It was not the gold braid but the fact that every man had a close-fitting tailor-made uniform that gave the Prussian grenadiers their reputation for elegance.

It was the elegance of these troops more than perhaps their soldierly bearing which gave the other European rulers the idea of imitating the Prussian uniforms.

The urge to imitate is particularly pronounced in military history. A conquered enemy seeks to discover the reason for his opponent's success. He studies the organization of the victorious army. Externals are the easiest to copy and the uniforms of the European nations display a mixture of many strange additions. The Poles contributed the ulanka, a short, waisted tunic, and the Croats (as the first Hussars were called, irrespective of whether they were Croats or not) added the laced Hussar's coat to the uniforms already in existence. The plumes on the helmet have been frequently copied. The Swedes, for instance, stuck wisps of straw in their hats, so that they could recognize each other during the battle.

Soldiers invented the dress-suit

The contributions made by soldiers to the fashions of their times are extraordinarily numerous. The close cut of the Prussian uniforms and the smartness of the contrast between white, blue and red induced the civilian to dress in the same way as the soldier.

It was the experience of soldiers that a buttoned coat was troublesome when they were riding, as it became rucked up round the lower part of the body. So they cut away the troublesome parts of their coats, and this was the origin of the tail-coat. The idea of historians of fashions who supposed that the tail-coat was created by a French courtesan who had such a passion for exposed male hips, is therefore erroneous.

The neck-cloth of the Hussars, the Croats, is the origin of the cravat, and long trousers, which have now been the fashion for nearly 150 years,

Our series of illustrations portrays the story of the uniform. In the upper row of illustrations are to be seen four soldiers at the turn of the 17th century, Dutchmen, Swedes, Brandenburgers and Prussians. Coat and hat are bourgeois. The brims of the hats are upturned because they are troublesome in battle. The sash was attached to it later on. The large Swedish cuffs of the Prussians had shrunk in size by the year 1703 to that of an ornament. The Prussians preferred wearing a tapered cap to a hat with a turned-up brim. The tapered end was supported by a metal frame. The cravat is of starched linen

As a long coat worn by civilians was troublesome for the infantryman in attack or on the march, the Prussians turned it up at the sides (second row, centre). This was the origin of the half round coat, called a cut-away by the English (picture below). The evening dress coat is a cross between the half-round coat, adopted by the English and the Austrians (second row, right) from the Prussians, and the Polish ulanka (second row, left). The French cavalrymen (next to the Polish Uhlans) were the first to wear it. The Polish helmet, the czapka, was a better protection for the head in hand-to-hand fighting with swords, than a felt hat

The Prussian spiked helmet of the 19th century originated from the czapka, the metal stiffening of the grenadiers' caps and the old knight's helmet. The glittering spike was a good target and for this reason disappeared in the Great War first of all under a covering, and a steel helmet finally replaced the leather helmet

The 19th century (third row, left) gives a survey of all kinds of uniforms in vogue up-to-date. Long trousers, formerly only used to protect the parade breeches, were generally introduced: the new battle dress has been evolved from the ulanka, the Hussars' tunic and the single-breasted infantry coat from which the coat-tails have entirely disappeared. The only inconvenient (but smart) thing remaining in the 20th century was the stiff collar, which finally made way everywhere for the turn-down collar. The Bulgarian officer (second from right, third row) is depicted in the service uniform of the Great War, while the British Guardsman next to him still wears the royal red which caused the British such heavy losses in the Boer War

The steel helmet is still in vogue at the present day. The Russian forage cap has been introduced everywhere as a service cap. The service uniform is entirely designed for camouflage and practicality and it is only on the full-dress and parade uniforms that the old colours and symbols, the sashes and the Swedish cuffs, are still conspicuous as picturesque adornments

400 Years of Uniforms in Pictures

Drawing by J. C. Schmitz

1. The Block

(there are 539,774 blocks)
consists of 30 to 40 households. It is the smallest unit coming under the care of the National Socialist German Workers' Party. The block supervisor, a member of the Party, helps the families in his block and aids them in cases of illness, death and economic distress, inspects the housing conditions and forwards inquiries and complaints to the appropriate Party office. In wartime he sees to the distribution of the food cards

2. The Cell

(there are 121,406 cells)
consists of 4 to 6 blocks, i. e. approximately 200 households. The block supervisors are responsible to the cell leader. He sees to the Party notice boards (see drawing), as well as to help given by one neighbour to another where people are aged or ill, welfare work for tiny tots and in wartime also to the cleanliness of the footpaths, the collection of waste paper and scrap material, the removal of garbage and unloading of lorries and the air raid precautions

3. The Local Group

(there are 30,601 local groups)
This consists in large towns of from 1500 to 3000 households, and in country districts, of several parishes. The local group leader organizes the work of the block supervisors and cell leaders. He is also responsible for the street collections in aid of the Winter Welfare Work, the collection on hot-pot day which occurs once a month, Party exhibitions and meetings on a small scale and the sports and school work in his area

4. The District

(there are 890 districts)
This consists of whole towns or in large towns of several areas, and in the country it consists of a number of villages. The district leader applies the orders coming from the provincial headquarters in the appropriate form to his own district. His specialist advisers give their attention for example (see drawing), to beautiful recreation rooms and bright clean workshops in industrial concerns, to the development of small holdings, to the theatre, art exhibitions and special film shows, to health and hygiene, the Press, education, physical exercise, etc.

5. The Province

(there are 43 provinces)
This is the largest unit in Germany. The provincial leader receives his instructions directly from the Führer and in accordance with them carries the great social, cultural, economic and propagandistic projects into operation. The drawing shows: a Strength through Joy seaside resort, a parade at a national celebration, an employees' convalescent home, a convalescent home for mothers, a Hitler Youth political training college, a large-scale settlement belonging to an industrial works, a recently constructed waterway etc.

1. DER BLOCK   2. DIE ZELLE   3. DI

A survey of the marvel of the

Party organization

The organization of the Party originated in the practical requirements of the period of struggle, but from the very commencement it was moulded in accordance with the Party's great state conception, the idea of embracing every individual in order to employ him in furthering the good of the community which naturally also means his own personal well-being. The "Signal's" artist has here attempted to show the widely discussed and much admired basis of this organization. The smallest unit is the block, which is followed according to size by the cell, the local group, the district and the province. The family for the centre of the block, the cell embraces the life one or more streets, the boundaries of the local gro include whole communities, and in towns it co prises a number of areas. In a district, for examp there may be a middle-sized town of about 250,0 inhabitants, in country regions there are a numb of villages or small towns. The province, of cours is of some considerable size and there is more th one province in Germany which is more extensi or has a larger population than some of the smal

DER GAU

SGRUPPE

4. DER KREIS

KDF

European states. The province is the largest administrative unit in the Party organization. The initiative is transmitted directly to the province from the Reich administration. It is here that the political power — as it were — is distributed from the high power electrical network to the districts under the control of the separate provinces. The districts in their turn transform the current according to local requirements and convey it to the local groups. Here the wires once again divide and a "cable" runs to each cell which supplies the street and house groups. In the block, however, the current flows into each separate house, so that in the end every individual in the nation which numbers 80 millions has his "connexion".

The whole network is connected up in such a manner that — to continue the illustration — any short-circuit which may occur is almost automatically registered in the nearest central station and can be reported to the Reich administration. This system of organization in the Party is sufficiently strong and adaptable to cover every conceivable, politically important reaction of a great nation and at the same time it can bring new impulses to bear in every sphere of life. The system brings all the tasks allotted to the Party to their conclusion. Any creative initiative to be introduced in health and hygiene, the training of youth, welfare work on behalf of the working man (as, for example, improvement in working conditions, embellishment of workshops, etc., convalescent homes, holiday and wage questions, etc.) whatever revolutionary idea is to be introduced into the crafts, industry, trade or among the peasantry, all flows through the channels of the Party organization.

Where they marry in Innsbruck!

The Registry Office is in one of the city's most beautiful buildings, the "Goldene Dachl". A former chapel of the Fürstenburg was changed into a wedding room

"When we have children . . .!"

The new stained-glass windows of the late Gothic room illustrate family happiness. The ancient "Goldene Dachl" where modern weddings take place gets its name from the gilded copper roof of the oriel window (picture right). Is a distinctive mark of Innsbruck. The richly decorated bay was added 400 years ago by the Emperor Maximilian I. when he transferred his court to the Fürstenburg, and was made use of as a spectators' box for processions and festivities

Where it is a pleasure to say "yes"!

The "Goldene Dachl" in Innsbruck

Camp Commander

In the Women's Labour Service. All girls perform one year's compulsory service in the Labour Service

Summer uniform

of the League of German Girls of which all girls between the age of 10 and 21 are members

A drummer in the Boy's League

The Boy's League is a sub-formation of the Hitler Youth to which every boy belongs until his 18th year

A boy in the Marine Hitler Youth

which is a special formation of that organization, with a training ship and its own small flotilla

Labour man

in the German Labour Service. All young men spend one year in the German Labour Service

A District Leader in the National-Socialist German Workers' Party

The differences in rank of the political leaders are recognizable by the tabs

A Section Commander in the SS

It is the duty of the SS to protect the Führer and to ensure the internal safety of Germany

Battalion Commander in the SA

Service as a storm-trooper is military and voluntary. Every German can be a member from his eighteenth to his forty-fifth year

Platoon Commander

in the National Socialist Flying Corps. This is a voluntary flying corps whose duty it is to train the youth of Germany in gliding and flying

A Company Commander

in the National Socialist Motor Corps. This motorized unit is a formation which is complementary to the Storm-troopers

The uniforms and badges of the Party

The Party Badge

Worn by all members of the National Socialist German Workers' Party

The Badge of Honour in gold

For the first 100.000 members. It is also awarded by the Führer and is the highest civil order in the Reich

The Blood Award

For participants in the struggles which took place in Munich in November 1923, and for special sacrifices of blood and liberty

The Service Medal in bronze

For ten years' active service in the Party

The Service Medal in silver

For fifteen years' active service in the Party

Greater Germany's war medals.
The Iron Cross, the traditional German medal, is awarded for bravery and conspicuous leadership. A single deed of outstanding personal bravery or one action showing particular qualities of leadership is rewarded by the Knight's Cross to the Iron Cross. The highest grade of this order, which is awarded for conspicuous and repeated acts of gallantry in the face of the enemy, is the Knight's Cross to the Iron Cross with the Oak Leaves with Swords and Diamonds (centre, above). The Knight's Cross to the Distinguished Service Cross with Swords (centre, below) is awarded for distinguished service in the Fighting Forces having a decisive influence upon the conduct of the war. The award without swords is reserved for conspicuous service in the execution of military duties. The Distinguished Service Cross of the First Class with Swords (centre of the picture) is the reward for service under enemy fire of the highest importance in the conduct of the war or for especial merit in the military conduct of the war. It is awarded without swords to men who have done service of decisive influence in the execution of military duties. The Distinguished Service Cross of the Second Class (below, right) is awarded with swords for meritorious service under fire or for merit in the military conduct of the war, and without swords for merit in the execution of war tasks. The Distinguished Service Medal (below, left) is the reward for meritorious activity in the execution of war duties, the work having taken at least six months. The German Cross which was recently created by the Führer and Commander-in-Chief of the Fighting Forces is an award conferred upon members of the Fighting Forces, in gold (above, right) for repeated and conspicuous gallantry or for repeated conspicuous actions showing particular qualities of leadership, and in silver (above, left) for repeated and outstanding merit in the military conduct of the war. *Photograph: Deutscher Verlag*

A few hours of leave in Berlin

During their leave German soldiers often come to Berlin for the first time, where they have a few hours to wait for their connexion. They naturally want to see something of the town. Are they to wander haphazardly through the gigantic city? No, the organization "Strength through Joy" comes to their help. It has had the delightful idea of taking them in genuine historical breaks to see Berlin

Circular tour of Berlin in 1941

The visitors are German soldiers who are strangers to Berlin. The break is taking them on a circular tour of the city and all sorts of sights are shownd and explained to them by expert guides. It is obvious that the soldiers are, of course, also greatly interested in the Berlin girls. Witty remarks are made and smiles and greetings are exchanged. The good mood of the soldiers on leave also helps and a number of girls are boisterously welcomed into the break. Then a halt is made at the Brandenburger Tor so that they can have photographs taken of themselves as a souvenir, and then they make a short halt . . .

. . . in the Tiergarten. And here, among the trees, a pleasant time is spent, the description of which will provide a capital story for their comrades when the soldiers return. And now they buy . . .

. . . a few flowers from a flower seller on the Potsdamer Platz when they thank and take leave of the charming girls who had accompanied them. Then they go to the station, and perhaps one of the girls waves to one or other of them. Addresses and field post numbers had, we may be sure, been exchanged beforehand and carefully noted

Photographs: Voigt

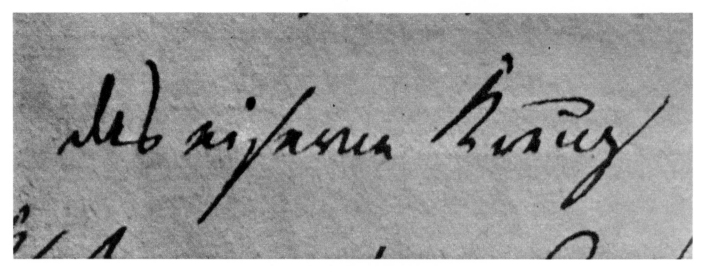

In the handwriting of the founder. *An extract from the first plan of King Frederick William III for the institution of the Iron Cross in 1813*

Times were hard and full of dramatic events, when the Iron Cross—the first decoration to be awarded both to officers and other ranks—was instituted. On 17th March, 1813 King Frederick William III. issued at Breslau his passionate "Appeal to my People". On 10th March the Statute of Institution for the Iron Cross, signed by the King, was published in the "Schlesische Zeitung".

The King had first of all made designs of his own and then commissioned others to do so; it was Karl Friedrich Schinkel, the great Berlin architect, who finally made the design which the King at once authorised. Originally the Cross was intended to be all black; only when it was seen that this dark decoration was hardly visible on dark tunics, did the thrifty King decide to add the silver edge to the cross. Many an experiment was necessary before a way was found of blending the silver edge with the cast-iron part of the cross. By the middle of April 1813 only four crosses had been made, but the method of working had been mastered and by the beginning of May about three hundred were ready. Each cost 2½ talers which was a considerable sum of money for those days.

The Iron Cross, First Class, consisted originally merely of two pieces of black and white ribbon sewn over one another in the shape of a cross; it was not until later that it was likewise made of cast-iron. In addition to the Iron Cross, First and Second Class, the King also instituted a Grand Cross which was awarded in five cases at the end of the Wars of Independence, viz. to Blücher, Bülow, Tauentzien, Yorck, and the Crown Prince of Sweden. The fact that there were only nine awards in the Franco-Prussian War of 1870/71 and only five in the Great War shows how high this decoration is. A special class was created for Prince Blücher; he received for the battle of Belle-Alliance the Grand Cross on a gold radiant star. It was only once again awarded in history, and that 103 years later to Field Marshal von Hindenburg in 1918 for the great battle in France.

The first Iron Cross, Second Class, was awarded to Major von Borcke of the first Pomeranian In-

fantry Regiment in recognition of his brave conduct at the storming of the strong fortress of Lüneburg; the Iron Cross, Second Class, has been awarded about 5,500,000 times between the date of its institution and the end of the Great War. The first Pomeranian Infantry Regiment behaved with such gallantry, that five officers, eight non-commissioned officers, and two private soldiers were the first to receive the Iron Cross. The first Iron Cross,

Karl Friedrich Schinkel
the designer of the Iron Cross of 1813, and the greatest Prussian architect of his day

First Class, was awarded on 17th April, 1813, after the battle of Wanfried to Lieutenant-Colonel von Hellwig, officer commanding the ninth Regiment of Hussars.

It is a strange fact that at the desire of Frederick William the side of the Iron Cross, First Class, on which were engraved the initials, the oak-

leaves, and the date, was regarded as the back. It was not until June 1813 that the King issued an order to the effect that "the underneath side was to be worn upwards".

In addition to those to whom the decoration had been awarded, there was during and after the Wars of Independence also a category of individuals, "having acquired the right". These were those persons to whom for reasons of economy the Cross was not actually presented. After the decease of the wearer of a Cross the decoration was passed on to another soldier who, according to the regimental list, was next entitled to wear it. It was not until 1837 that this order was cancelled and the King himself presented the Iron Cross to all surviving candidates.

On 19th July, 1870, King William I. reintroduced the Iron Cross. The rear side remained the same as the decoration of 1813, but on the front side there was a crown with a "W" in the middle and underneath the date 1870. There were about 1,300 Iron Crosses, First Class, and almost half a million of the Second Class awarded during the Franco-Prussian War.

The second reinstitution was enacted on 5th August, 1914. Soldiers of non-German origin belonging to the armies of the Central Powers received this high decoration for the first time during the Great War. Of 13,400,000 participants in the war 218,000 were awarded the Iron Cross, First Class.

On 2nd September 1939, the Führer and Supreme Commander of the German Fighting Forces reinstituted the Iron Cross, which is already proudly worn on the breast by many of the defenders of the Greater Germany. In addition to the Iron Cross, First and Second Class, and the Grand Cross, Adolf Hitler created the new decoration of the Knights Cross. This decoration is worn round the neck and is awarded not only to officers but also to other ranks. According to the Order of the 8th July, 1940 there has also been instituted the Oak-leaf to the Knight's Cross, consisting of three silver leaves on the ribbon claps. By thus distinguishing the bravest of the brave the Führer has carried on the high tradition of the Iron Cross.

The Iron Cross, Second Class, as submitted for consideration. *A sketch by Karl Friedrich Schinkel, which he was commissioned by the King to make*

The 1813 Iron Cross, Second Class. *The King accepted the simple and artistic form as proposed by Schinkel*

The 1813 Iron Cross, First Class. *The black silk ribbon with white edge was worn on the left breast and the I. C. II. Cl. on a ribbon*

The Grand Cross with radiant star, *also named the "Blücher Star". Field Marshal von Hindenburg was besides Blücher the only holder of this decoration*

The Iron Cross, 1939

Above — The Grand Cross of the Iron Cross. Middle left — The Knight's Cross of the Iron Cross with Oak-leaves. Middle right — The Knight's Cross of the Iron Cross. Below left — The Bar to the Iron Cross, Second Class. Below middle — The Iron Cross, First Class; above it the Bar to the Iron Cross, First Class. Below right — The Iron Cross, Second Class

The home for the child comes first

Germany planning in advance for the future

Germany knows that the foundation on which her future will be built is the large healthy family. And the first need of this family is a home and all that a real home offers—security and comfort in its bright, spacious rooms furnished with practical good taste, fitted up with solid and pleasing household equipment and all those technical gadgets and facilities which are a matter of course in the present century.

A gigantic task

Although much has already been done, a really satisfactory solution to the housing problem can only be hoped for after the war. During the next ten years the German housing programme plans to raise the number of dwellings in existence from 18 million to 24 million, that is by one third. It will work according to the following fundamental principles: 1. Steps are to be taken to provide all those German families who want them with their own homes in the shortest possible time. 2. The size and furnishing of the dwellings are to take into consideration the national aims regarding population policy. 3. The houses are to be built with a minimum expense of material and labour. 4. The rents must be within the people's reach. 5. The organization of the building must be simple. The principles are at first sight so convincing that one is tempted to take them for granted until one recalls the fact that for years they were completely disregarded as a glance at any large European city will prove. Large scale plans and a vast amount of preliminary work are necessary to obviate all those mistakes and miscalculations which later cannot be remedied.

Houses for the millions

By far the greater number of the dwellings planned include a large living-dining-room, a bedroom for the parents, two or three separate two-bed rooms for the children as well as the other rooms indispensable everywhere in Germany today, hall, scullery, bathroom, and lavatory. These general lines control to a large extent the design and manufacture of the household equipment; for similar to the actual building of the house the furnishing must be completely standardized and rationalized if one of the most imperative aims is to be reached, that is, a considerable decrease in the cost of manufacture. That sounds very simple but it is far from the case if people are to be given something better than a "living machine" from which they have no real pleasure. A home must be not only practical but also cosy and comfortable; it is bound up with feeling and feelings in their turn are

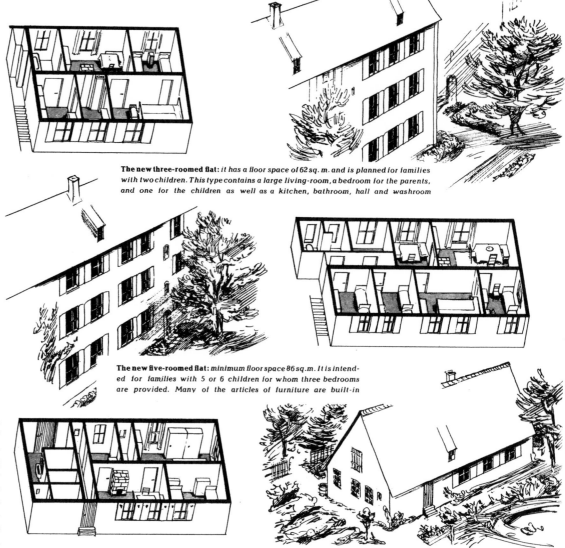

The new three-roomed flat: it has a floor space of 62 sq. m. and is planned for families with two children. This type contains a large living-room, a bedroom for the parents, and one for the children as well as a kitchen, bathroom, hall and washroom

The new five-roomed flat: minimum floor space 86 sq.m. It is intended for families with 5 or 6 children for whom three bedrooms are provided. Many of the articles of furniture are built-in

The settlement house: the smallest type as shown here contains, besides the living-rooms and offices, a pig-sty and a hen-house, a shed and a loft. In the next two pages you will find an account of the interior of the new people's dwellings

bound up with tradition. As the suggestions published by various German provinces and a number of successful exhibitions prove, the plans for the houses as well as those for the furniture and other equipment have taken into careful consideration the customs of the various regions. The results have fully justified this procedure: tradition, hygiene, technics, individuality and economy are harmoniously combined.

A close examination of the model furniture displayed in various German towns in recent months results in the surprising discovery of many forms which in their plain and simple style conform without exception to the laws of an ancient tradition which had been lost in the course of the 19th century. This fact considerably simplifies the endeavour to attain both a comprehensive and practical distribution of space by the arrangement of the furniture and healthy and sound working methods.

The living-room

The most important and at the same time the largest room in which the family life centres is the spacious living-room which, according to local customs, has been planned either as a kitchen-living-room or more usually as a living-dining-room with an adjacent independent little scullery. The combined living-room and kitchen not only saves the housewife from unnecessary waste of energy but also simplifies the supervision of the children.

A comparison of these plans with the solutions of former centuries emphasises the clear, comprehensive distribution of the furniture in accordance with the needs of the family. Formerly the table was placed in the middle of the room; nowadays modern experience has justified the revival of an ancient tradition and the table has been relegated to a corner. This does not in any way detract from the appearance of the room and the children have much more space to move about in. Besides the

seating accomodation—a corner bench or an upholstered settle which can be adapted as a kind of divan—this room usually contains a large sideboard for china, cutlery, table linen, books, and a smaller cabinet for the wireless set, sewing materials and other oddments. It is obvious that appearance is secondary to utility; all the furniture and equipment is carefully proportioned to suit the people who are to it. The elimination of everything but the essential and the simple arrangement of the furniture gives the living-room a certain unity and comfort that had disappeared from the overcrowded, pompous apartments of the 19th century. The parents' bedroom, the second largest room, contains besides the two beds and beside-tables twin wardrobes and a low chest of drawers which can be used as the baby's table. This versatile bedroom suite can easily be divided into two separate suites if the house is being rearranged. The children's bedrooms are similarly fitted up.

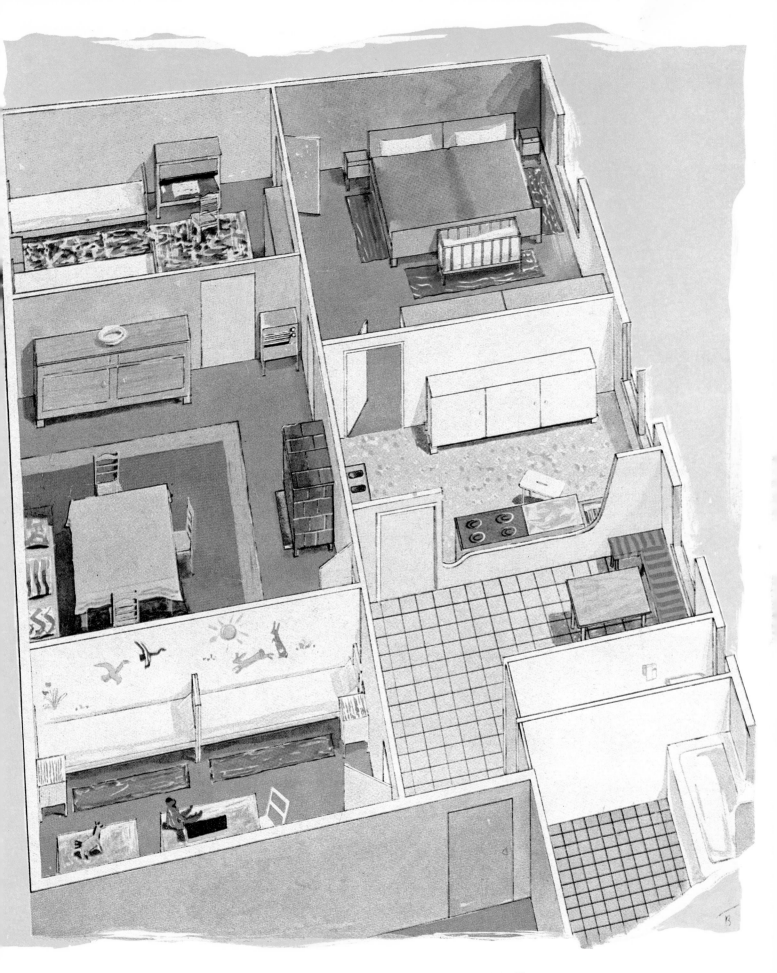

Dwellings for German workers and their families

A large scale social housing scheme was one of the first tasks which the young National Socialist state had to face—and work began on it very soon after the Party came to power. In 1932 only 159,000 houses were built in Germany, already in 1937, however, the number had risen to 340,000. In five short years 1,480,000 new dwellings had been built—an achievement surpassed over and over again until the outbreak of the war. But even the war did not bring the bricklayer's activity to a standstill let alone stop the comprehensive planning and experimenting on which "Signal" gives a short report in the following pages. Our colour picture shows a medium-sized worker's flat with a floor space of 74 sq. m. planned for a family with four children and rented at less than 50 R.M. a month. The children have been considered here first of all for they have been provided with a bright play-room, a living-room with soft carpets and a cheerful bedroom. The housewife will be delighted with the bath room and the kitchen fitted with all the latest gadgets invented by modern home planners

In the "House of German Art"

in Munich

On 27th July the Führer's deputy, Rudolf Hess, opened the fourth Great German Art Exhibition in Munich. At the opening ceremony the Minister for Propaganda Dr Goebbels, delivered a speech dealing with creative art during war time (below). A special room in the "House of German Art" was reserved this time for the works of artists, whose paintings reproduce what they have personally seen during their experiences at the front. Right, a picture in this room, "Soldier in Poland", by Franz Eichhorst. Below, on the right, the painter Paul Mathias Padua, who was wounded in Belgium, and his wife during a visit to the exhibition

Modern German plastic art

Works of modern German sculptors, who have made a name in plastic art, are being exhibited in the Artists House (Künstlerheim) in Berlin

Determination to fight *and inflexible strength are exemplified in Professor Arno Breker's work "In readiness"*

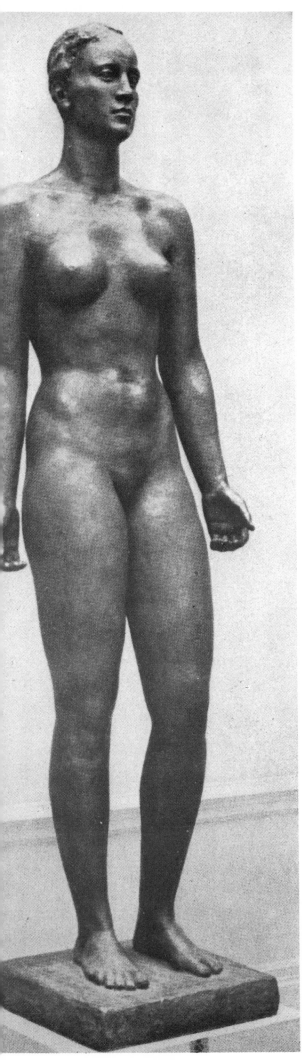

Arno Breker *has surprised us with a glorious "Amazon" in bronze*

"Olympia", *a bronze by Professor Fritz Klimsch*

One of the reliefs *by Professor Josef Wackerle for the Führer's tea-rooms on the Obersalzberg*

Professor Georg Kolbe *is also a master of wall friezes. "Starting for the fight" is the name of this large relief; it has not yet been decided where it is to be placed*

1940 European DECISION

Sept. 3
1939
England, F
ce and Po
are war a

Germany banished the war from the Continent

On the Sunday following Compiègne, at an early hour in the morning, the Führer arrived in Paris and visited Napoleon's tomb in Les Invalides. The man who had once and for all destroyed France's hostile power and initiated the German epoch in Europe stood plunged deep in thought in front of the red marble sarcophagus. Once more it had been necessary to conquer the Continent, because the nations yield only before the might of experience. In the eyes of the world, Adolf Hitler had now succeeded to Napoleon's position, and beyond this that process was in course of development which the Corsican had once foreseen while a prisoner in the hands of the British: the urge for unity, which in the long run no European nation could now escape, must be welded to a mighty will in order to appear immediately with the impetus of a natural phenomenon. It was a question of life and death whether in spite of all reactionary calculations the great simplification would succeed early enough for the good of Europe.

Even the most sober observer had been forced since the summer of 1940 to come to the conclusion that, with the German front along the Atlantic coast and Italy waging war in the Mediterranean, not only was France eliminated as a hostile power and England given the choice between renunciation and annihilation, but that the peoples of Europe did also in truth expect from the conqueror a complete reorganization of their own conditions and of conditions in general.

On the other side of the demarcation line, in the unoccupied part of France, the more or less honourable acknowledgement by the French, from the minister down to the lowliest reservist, that the collapse of the old world which had opposed Hitler and Mussolini was complete, corresponded to the completely natural transition which took place without any delay from the armistice with France to the total attack against England. With the Maginot Line there fell also the Chinese Wall which France had built between herself and the future of Europe.

The European Civil War

At that time a comparison involuntarily imposed itself with an upheaval on the American Continent which, however, from a military point of view took place in quite different circumstances. The secession of the Southern States which resulted in the American Civil War had not been merely a regrettable misunderstanding, but the avowed final struggle of an old civilisation which could brook no compromise with a young one. The future was with the Yankees. Their very real superiority corresponded to the inexorable path of America's destiny which was pushing forward towards a social break-through along the whole line. The Alliance of the Führer with the Duce resulted at the outbreak of war in a similar superiority in strength, for Germany and Italy who were forced to take up the struggle with the powers of European reaction, were able from the very commencement to act in the spirit and on behalf of the whole continent, the unification of which was to be the outcome of their victory. Hitler and Mussolini believed in this European solution because they were firmly convinced of the necessity of European reform by the process of the social rejuvenation of the German and Italian peoples. Herein lies the fundamental difference which distinguishes them from Napoleon who sought a solution of Europe's problems in half a dozen victorious campaigns and was not able to find it, because each time he merely conquered a further portion of Central Europe as a French glacis.

Adolf Hitler at Napoleon's tomb
Paris, June 1940

"I was forced to conquer Europe by arms.
Today Europe has to be convinced."

Napoleon in 1821 on the island of St. Helena

What Germany and Italy with their whole strength thought themselves capable of when the hour of the challenge came, what England and France feared, and yet would not recognize was regarded even before the outbreak of war as inevitable by the world beyond the boundaries of Europe in spite of all propaganda to the contrary. Even before England on September 3rd, 1939, took the step leading to armed conflict, Americans, Russians and Japanese all agreed in an impartial recognition of the fact that if war came, the Axis would revolutionize Europe. That is the chief reason why Stalin had no desire to pick the chestnuts out of the fire for the defunct Western Powers and why the Americans, in spite of their sympathies, judge the chances of European democracy in extremely sceptical fashion. It was for the same reason that the war in Europe accelerated the change in political structure aimed at in Japan and now realized by Prince Konoye: The final estrangement from England and the Three Power Pact between Japan and the Axis Powers. This time the last European civil war is being fought out before the eyes of the world and its outcome, by reason of its very finality, must appear to the powers outside Europe as the signal for an intercontinental reorganization. Whilst seeking to cover England's withdrawal from the Continent, the Americans believed they would be able to retard automatically the future course of events, whereas the Russians from the time of the pact with Germany until their occupation of Bessarabia established for themselves a new position based on facts.

No more war fronts on the Continent

The decision reached on the continent of Europe was the unprecedented result of one single year of war on European battle fields. Considering in retrospect the events of the year which began in the late summer months of 1939 and lead up to the siege of Great Britain, it becomes apparent that the German Command in collaboration with their Italian ally have systematically and step by step liberated Europe from war. The transference of the war from Poland via Norway to the Western front and later on its advance to the Western edge of the continent corresponded to the logical military conclusion that England's war had to be waged against England herself. Italy's entry into the war which was first directed against France, was accompanied by an essential feature of the war, the extension of the total anti-British front along the Southern border of Europe. An unprecedented application of military strength and a dogged consistency in the conduct of foreign policy during the war had been required in order to eliminate completely the military fronts within Europe during the course of a single year and to do away with the antiquated national ideals which have existed for centuries. It also becomes apparent, that the longest front against England stretching from the North Cape to the Bay of Biscay through the Mediterranean as far as the Indian Ocean and finally being completed by the Three Power Pact with Japan was at the same time the most economical and the shortest front possible.

Continental European Autarchy

The defeats suffered by the powers of the old Europe corresponded to the slogans of the re-

1940 : Successful conduct of war banishes war from the European Continent

volutionary propaganda in Germany and Italy. The English war itself provided the economic unification of Europe with a great impetus. There has never been any creative reorganization in the lives of nations which was not the result of exceptional circumstances. The misery during the great economic crisis had finally led Germany, then an impoverished State almost despairing of its own existence, to pursue a long-sighted policy of self-help. German autarchy as seen in the two Four Year Plans was neither a programme chosen at random nor an ideal condition. The same applied to Italian autarchy after the experiences of the British sanctions war during the Abyssinian campaign. The European autarchy which we are experiencing today could never have been carried through in peacetime even by the boldest pioneer of large-scale regional economics, although the victorious powers have made of it a vast act of peace in the midst of war. Necessity and discernment were on this occasion once more the teachers of the peoples. It was not the Nazis, but the English war which inflicted this necessity and this compulsion upon Europe. The blockade at sea, in contrast to the lack of effect which it had upon Germany in a state of war, did in fact economically sever Western Europe with the exception of France from England and oversea countries even before the German victory in the West. As a counter-measure the new powers in Central Europe extended at an accelerated pace due to war conditions the system of exchanging goods in German Central Europe and in the autarchic Italian Imperium which already existed against the background of the economic agreements with Russia and the free arrangement concerning export goods from the Danubian countries. When then first Scandinavia and very soon afterwards the whole of Western Europe came within the sphere of power of England's enemies, everything had already been prepared for the assimilation of the national economies of the countries concerned

into the new Continental System. Three necessary factors did the rest. They were :

1. The immediate use of all reserves in the occupied countries for increasing the war potential against England,

2. The reconstruction work in the elimination of the material damage during the war, and finally,

3. The creation of work and the maintainance of the millions of people belonging to those nations which had unwillingly crossed over to the camp of the victors.

Max Clauss, the author of

"EUROPEAN DECISION"

will discuss the reorganization of the world without England and the obstacles placed in the path of Pan-Europe in two further articles.

Every month of the war witnessed a further step towards the development and perfection of the German-Italian economic continental system. For now, in the compact region extending from Sweden to the North of Africa, the creative impulse of all the highly developed national economies which previously had not co-operated in a manner even remotely similar to this, took effect in accordance with a mutual project.

In the German Sphere of Power

During the autumn of 1940 Germany occupied as a result of the war approximately one million square kilometres of European soil with a total of approximately 66 million inhabitants. These figures included Norway, Denmark, Holland, and Belgium whose inhabitants with the exception of the Walloons in Belgium are of pure Germanic blood and a proportion of whom is racially closely

related to the German people. From the very outset Denmark occupied a special position, for her political independence was in no way influenced by the German troops which occupied the country to guarantee her defence and in order to protect German interests. There is no German military administration in Denmark and Danish agriculture, after the complete standstill of its oversea trade during 8 months of the war, adapted itself to the requirements of its German neighbour and took its place in the Continental System. The attitude of the German government towards relations with the Norwegians, the Dutch and the Belgians after the occupation of their respective countries was demonstrated by the release of the prisoners of war of all three countries soon after the conclusion of hostilities and whilst Germany was still waging war against England from their territories. Politically speaking there were on the one side the most unconditional respect for the closely related national characteristics and the no less unconditional determination not to tolerate any platforms hostile to Germany on the Western fringe of the continent and, on the other hand, the two poles between which the reorganization during the war would be carried out under the German occupation. This included the principle of not making any alteration in the sound institutions of the countries' administration as far as the necessities of war would allow and to leave the government of the respective nations in their own hands.

The broad basis of understanding was continually provided by the complete economic and social common destiny which was the result of the force of circumstances. The Danish and the Dutch peasant both enjoy the same advantage of the closest economic incorporation into Germany. The Belgian workman derives great profit from the reciprocal penetration of the heavy industries in his own country and those of Germany, all the more so since by Germany's incorporation of

Europe restored to peace: The protection and administration afforded by the victors replaces war

The decision in Europe

Luxemburg and Lorraine the most powerful centre of production in modern Europe has now been formed for the first time into one complete block. What had previously taken place in Silesia and Bohemia now also took place in the industrial area between the Rhine and the Meuse which suffered no damage when the German offensive broke through the Maginot Line and its extension towards the North. The war system of economy accelerated rationalisation and brought about that effective concentration of production with the technical pre-requisites of which the manufacturers had long been familiar before the customs barriers eventually fell. It would be a misrepresentation of methodical planning of the German government if the attempt were made to bring under the same category in the scheme of things the new relations with Germany which have been developed during the war in Holland, Belgium and in Scandinavia— for it is natural that Sweden also both politically and economically reorganized herself in accordance with the new continent. On the other hand it is immediately obvious that France in every way was a special case. France as a great power had wittingly sacrificed herself and accepted servitude to Britain. The German provinces of Alsace and Lorraine, in the same way as Luxemburg which is also German, were again incorporated into the German customs area. The political fact that the Gauleiters of Baden, Saarpfalz and Koblenz-Trier took over the civil administration of Strasburg, Metz and Luxemburg respectively emphasizes the definite reorganization in accordance with the homogeneity of neighbouring territories and ancient German tradition. The remainder of France was not merely divided into the occupied and unoccupied areas, but wide expanses of the occupied area continued to form part of the war zone facing England. There was, in addition, the special position of the French colonies. Although the victorious powers themselves had left the problem completely open during the Armistice, the brutal British attacks, the last of which took place against Dakar in West Africa, provided the French army, navy and air force

with the opportunity of proving to the British that France, although she had been vanquished, still had enough spirit to draw her own conclusions from these acts of British treachery.

The Axis System

The axis of the reorganization of Europe in wartime was that of the victorious nations themselves: The Berlin-Rome Axis. The real origin of the new Europe will always be that moment during the autumn of 1936 when the great national revolutions of National-Socialist Germany and Fascist Italy, each of which had until then marched along its own road, were brought together by what was politically and economically a senseless invention, Britain's war of sanctions against Italy. This was the classical example for the transformation of two national wills which had been developed to the highest degree, into one community which went beyond the barriers of nationality. The mystery of the quite open European conspiracy between the Führer and the Duce was as simple as it could be ; the elimination of any and every reason for friction between the two nations, the systematic removal of every harmful competition between the two Empires on either side of the Alps. And all this with the aim of immediately beginning to double German and Italian efforts in every sphere. Economically viewed, the agreement between Germany and Italy was the point where these two countries' autarchic systems which were of separate origin, by their systematic completion of one another rebutted the reproach made by the gold bloc of that time consisting of France, England and the United States of America, that autarchy was synonymous with isolation. In reality the determination of both countries to achieve economic independence as a pledge of political independence was directed towards the permanent establishment of a greater European sphere. The wholesome necessity of extracting the greatest advantage from a most restricted use of currency, even during the years before the European war, made the political experts in economics of the Axis Powers very inventive. There was scarcely a problem of organization in the whole range of the highly industrialised economic system to that of agricultural

or colonial raw materials which had not been jointly planned by Germany and Italy even before the victory of the Axis Powers had brought Europe under their influence.

As soon as the land communication across the Pyrenees had been re-established as a result of France's retiring from the war and the Italian control in the Mediterranean had been guaranteed, Spain was once more able to assume her national place in the system of the Axis which now comprised all the areas occupied by Germany north of the Alps as well as South Eastern Europe which had not become a theatre of war. The constructive policy of the Axis in the Danubian countries, the obvious success of which was the settlement of the territorial revision between Hungary, Rumania and Bulgaria, was, like the co-operation between Germany and Italy itself, based upon the principle that it was necessary to break down the internal fronts between the nations and systematically to organize the vast resources of the entire Danubian region for the benefit of Europe.

No blockades in the future

The reorganization of Europe in wartime had two precursors: Napoleon's Continental Blockade and the German Customs Union. The coercive method of the Continental Blockade was in accordance with Napoleon's purely military line of thought, whilst Prussia at a later date through the Customs Union laid the foundation stone of German industry and provided thereby the decisive impetus towards the unification of the Reich. Already in 1914 German production as well as that of North America had meanwhile surpassed that of England who now feared that the Central European Powers of those days might combine a repetition of the Napoleonic situation with the final establishment of an economic monopoly on the continent. These pre-requisites exist today and are, moreover, supported by a technical revolution in the entire economic system of supplies which in its turn has its origin in the years of misery and necessity through which Germany passed after the last war. A continent which supplements its own rich resources in natural products by products of colonies in Africa, can never again be blockaded.

At the window of the "New Palace" in Potsdam

The Japanese Minister for Foreign Affairs, Matsuoka, gained a true impression of the German soldier at historic spots in Potsdam. The visit, the purpose of which was that the statesmen of the friendly nations should become mutually acquainted, resulted in a particulary close contact being established between the Foreign Ministers of Germany and Japan. Illustrations on pages 6 and 7

Matsuoka in Berlin

Norwegian Girls in Berlin

The „Signal" pays a visit to a group of Norwegian girls. They came voluntarily to Germany and are following various professions here

Dinner in the canteen : *Eva and Evelyn are two Oslo girls belonging to a group of merry Norwegians who have been in Berlin for some months already. Eva was a companion-help and her friend a dental mechanic's assistant. Both wanted to get to know Germany and they could not find work in Norway they came to Berlin*

Neither Eva nor Evelyn had expected to see so much snow in Berlin! *But they had brought their skis from Noway in ease On Sunday they go to Grunewald, the ski paradise oi Berlin*

„Is that right?" *In the beginning the work was difficult, but her companion, a girl from Sudetenland, was always ready to help (Picture left)*

Fun in the snow — just like in Norway! *The snowball fight is over: Eva has won all along the line (Right)*

"BY THE FRENCH
FOR THE FRENCH"

*This is the slogan of a variety troupe from Paris which acts and sings
for their fellow-countrymen who have found good positions in offices and
factories in Berlin and other German towns. Aimée and Lucienne and
Marcel, too, who is serving with the volunteer legion, lose themselves in
rapturous enjoyment of the performances in their native style and language*

He knows they like his chanson. *Costume and pose
compel applause from every member of the audience*

A PARISIAN IN BERLIN

My first impression was that Berlin
is a city with electric tramways.
That is not especially interesting, you
object. But it is; for in the trams you
can see all kinds of things and acquire
there a preliminary vocabulary. After
ten stops you know the German for
wood, coal, butcher's shop, restaurant,
bakery, hairdresser and tobacconist's
shop. Such things are most important
today.

Living conditions here are more or
less the same as in Paris: the essential
food supplies are guaranteed by rationing. Tickets for everything, nothing
without tickets. But there are no
queues. There are no crowds in front
of the shops. There is no grumbling.
It · is unnecessary for policemen to
supervise women shoppers. On the
contrary, very few of the "arms of the
law" are to be seen. People maintain
order voluntarily so that policemen
are superfluous. They can still be seen,
however, at the busy crossings. There
they stand alert, their eyes watchful
under the patent leather helmets. If
you should dare to cross the street at
the wrong time they beckon to you
with a compelling gesture and you for-
feit a mark.

It is a fact that the French are popular in Berlin. They arouse people's
tolerance, curiosity, and sympathy. It
cannot be denied that we have all
kinds of peculiar habits. It is clear that
our manners are quite different from
those which prevail here. They call
forth surprise and do not always meet

with approval. For instance we like to
evade prohibitions; that offends the
disciplined German. But they forgive
us much and try to make things easy
for us. Tolerance.

Curiosity? Of course, but it is never
indiscreet. It is the kind of curiosity
that seems to say: "So you are a
Frenchman? How strange to meet you
here in wartime after all the ... But
now that you have come we are
glad ..."

And sympathy? Several thousand
French citizens are working in Berlin.
Not one of them has not encountered
the German's need to find common
ground, to make conversation about
the events of the past, conversations
full of compassion and hope for the
future. I have exchanged cordial hand-
shakes and a hearty "I hope we meet
again soon" with many a German.

In conclusion I should like to turn aside
from mere impressions. Berlin has two
French embassies: the one in Pariser
Platz, a dignified building in the most
beautiful quarter of a city which boasts
of much architectural splendour. The
shutters are closed. And then the other
embassy in the street, alive, full of
activity, consisting of those thousands
of ambassadors, consuls and chargés
d'affaires who are accredited to factories, landladies, families, business men,
and offices. Each one of them should
be conscious of his rank and fulfil his
diplomatic mission with devotion. That
is imperative and important for the
future.   M. B.

Soon the skies will open to them—*and the battle planes will have been released from the confines of the assembly shops and transferred to their real element, the spaces where military decisions are reached*

In the workshop of giants. *Guns of all calibres and constructions are standing and hanging next to and even on top of one another—only a few hours and they will be finished, only a few days and they will be ready for action*

THE STEEL STREAM

Unending rows. *Aeroplane engines and cylinder blocks, always alike yet never the same, move towards their destinations accompanied by the droning rhythm of work*

The Wilhelmstraße
from 7 o'clock in the morning . . .

The first visitor to the Foreign Office *is—the newspaper-boy with the morning papers*

On the stroke of 7 o'clock *the guards march down Wilhelmstrasse to relieve their comrades on duty before the new Reich's Chancellery in Vosstrasse*

Two minutes later *the night-watchman goes off to his well-earned rest, and*

. . . the cigarette seller *of Wilhelms Platz rolls his transportable kiosk into position to catch the buyers*

". . . it is now exactly three minutes past seven" *is heard from a window in the Reich's Chancellery—and the policeman regulates his watch*

The standard *flying from the Reich's Chancellery indicates that the Führer is in Berlin — and already...*

... visitors begin to collect. They kill the time as best they can and ...

... wait patiently in the hope that something will happen. It has been worth while for ...

...until midday...

5 minutes to 8. *The secretaries emerge from the Wilhelms Platz underground station*

In the drive before the Ministry for Propaganda *a car stops. Dr Goebbels gets out and goes to his day's work*

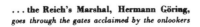

... **the Reich's Marshal, Hermann Göring,** *goes through the gates acclaimed by the onlookers*

A roll of drums! Words of command! *All watch through the railings of the old Reich's Chancellery where, on the stroke of 12, the assembly of the guard takes place—a ceremony which never loses its interest for the people of Berlin*

... 12 o'clock

Sightseeing tour through Berlin 1940: *Char-à-bancs, full of soldiers on leave, drive through Wilhelmstrasse*

The traffic swells — *The policemen on point duty at the different Wilhelmstrasse crossings set the traffic signals. It is exactly 12 o'clock*

THE WAR WITH BRITAIN

Signal had little to say about the Battle of Britain, which it scarcely acknowledged. Indeed, the Propaganda Company had a certain ambivalence about Britain which was not resolved until 1941. Hitler had always hoped to divide Eurasia between himself and the British, who would be allowed to retain their Empire if they acquiesced in the Nazi conquest of Europe. Britain presumably would have had to accede to Hitler's dreams of conquest in the East which included the overrunning of Russia. Hitler's Japanese ally was supposed to accept British rule in Hong Kong, Malaya and Burma as well, which in the event it was thoroughly unwilling to do. Once Churchill took power this hope of an all-Aryan, Anglo-German alliance was ill-founded and contradictory, a fact which the propagandists slowly accepted. Thus the British image in the pages of *Signal* changed by 1941 and vilification of the unconquered enemy continued unabated throughout the balance of the war. Assertions that the U-Boats were creating havoc with British trans-Atlantic shipping were, of course, true. Further assertions that the British blockade of the Continent was failing and that the Battle of the Atlantic was in the process of being lost to the Kriegsmarine were patently false.

Britain's support of Greece was particularly annoying to Hitler, since Mussolini had failed so completely in his attempt to crush the Greeks. As Bulgaria, Rumania and Yugoslavia joined the Tripartite Pact with varying degrees of reluctance in 1940–41, Hitler prepared his offensive against Greece and launched it in April 1941. The Greeks and their British allies fought vainly against the Wehrmacht, and the British withdrawal from Crete after General Kurt Student's paratroops proceeded to conquer it made it seem that the conquest of the Mediterranean might go as easily as the conquest of France. This proved not to be the case, even after the arrival of Rommel's Afrika Korps in Libya in 1941. British determination to hold the Suez Canal proved to be as frustrating to German ambitions in Africa as Britain's refusal to make peace after the fall of France had been in Europe. For a time Britain was the number one enemy of Germany, and indeed was the only viable one. But like the Battle of Britain, *Signal* downplayed the war in Africa when it became clear that no quick victory was in sight. From time to time stories appeared, but details of the fighting were never made clear in *Signal*. In any event once the titanic struggle against the Soviet Union began, the attentions of Nazi propagandists, like Germany itself, concentrated on the Soviet foe, and coverage of Britain on the high seas and in North Africa waned even further. *Signal* was created to cover Nazi victories. When none were in sight, *Signal* averted its eyes ... and its cameras. This was a sure sign to readers in Europe that the years of triumph were coming to an end.

"It's time now, Max..."

Before the night-raid on London

At a night-flying base somewhere on the coast. It is raining in torrents and the night is as black as pitch. The aerodrome is far away and in the distance green and red positional lights blink. Suddenly there is the flash of a torch-lamp. Dangerous reddish blue sparks are emitted out of the exhaust pipe of an aeroplane. Further off there is a jet of flame. There is everywhere the roaring of engines from different parts of the big aerodrome, it is a continuously vibrating noise; that is the music of the flying base. In the midst of all this can be heard the sound of hushed human voices, then the rattling of bombs and machines being handled, that is all.

"Be careful with the bomb. Push it and let us have a little more light. Now you can heave it up. Steady on. Come more this way."

"This one is also to go, but must first have the fuse put in. That's how it's done, do you see? Bring your torch-lamp nearer. Can you hear how the storm is beginning to rage out there? All the same it won't disturb us. What time is it? Almost midnight?"

"Well, gentlemen, it is now just 12 o'clock. Are there any more questions? There are not any? Very good, then be at your machines in ten minutes, please. Good luck."

The Squadron leader: "You're lucky boys, it's moonlight. Everyone get to his bus and start off. I'll follow you, and we'll meet over London. Get a move on, old chap"

"Get into the machine, Max. Have you got the log book and maps?" "Of course I've got them both, and also picture postcards, if that's what you mean." "Get a move on, Max, it's time"

"Is everything all correct, Max, and everyone at his post? You're doing the bombing, Max. Have you looked to see if the bombs have been attached?"

"Don't you worry. The bombs we've got with us are plenty. Well, what are we waiting for? Are we going to make a start or not?"

"Another minute and a half. It's time now, Max"

An old soldier of the ground personnel to a young one: — "Look
out, you're getting into the runway again. Just look at it, isn't
it like a huge and dangerous beast being hurled into the night?
Like a beast with flaming eyes? Look after your cap. You see,
it's been blown off, you must also beware of the wash from the
prop. Do you see how the machine is rising, it's now away from
the ground. Silence. Why are you stumbling? Can't you yet see
at night? You'll learn how to do so. Did you ask what kind of
wind that is? It's the storm, lad. the storm of the Atlantic. Did you
ask where the moon is? Well, it's disappeared again. old son."

Left:

The pilot: — "Do you see how they're searching for us, Max?
They've been waiting for us, Max, and now they're sending
their regards up to us. What they'd best like would be to burn
us up with their beams. What do you say? They're getting at
us? No, they're not, but we're getting at them. Are they still
disturbing you? I've already got used to them. And, even if
they find us, they can't hurt us. Why not? Because we're convinced
that they can't. They only give light, but they don't bite"

At the flying base: "Wireless message from the Squadron leader!"

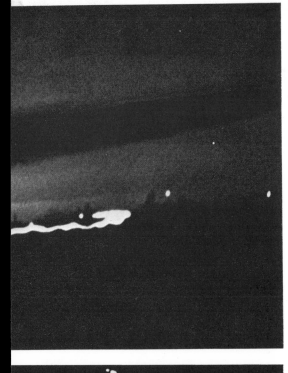

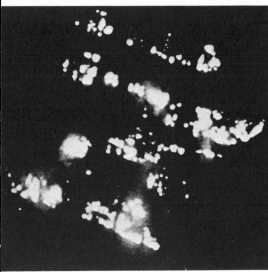

"Do you see London burning underneath us? I should hardly think the Englishmen are now singing their soldier song "The bells of hell go tingelingeling, for you and not for me". "Do you think they're singing that now?"

"Are you ready, Max? Have you got your finger on the button and the target sighted? You have, well drop the bombs":

Left:
"All machines on their way back from London undamaged, boys"

Right:
The soldier, showing the machine its place at the air base, shouts up to it as soon as the propellers stop: — "What's it look like in London?" A voice from the plane answers: — "In London did you say? Well, the bells of hell are tingelingeling-ing The bells of hell!"

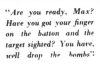

THE END

We are flying across the Channel in a formation of dive-bombers consisting of three machines. We are flying above the clouds. I photograph our two companions

The first dive-bomber in our formation, dips to the right and prepares to dive

And now the second

And now we too dip our wing

With the pilot's eyes...

and the long-distance camera in a dive-bomber

by PK. A. Grimm

I am a "Special Leader" in the Propaganda Company. But not in the Air Force. It is true I have often flown, but never in war time. But it is my great desire to take part in an attack on the enemy in a dive-bomber and at last I have received permission to do so. As far as cameras are concerned, I take my Leica with the long-distance lens with me.

I arrive about midday at the flying field from which we are to start. I immediately realize the difficulties of my whole situation: I cannot put on flying-kit, I cannot put on a parachute and above all, what is most important, I cannot be strapped in. I must be able to move, I must be able to stand and I must be able to take photographs across the pilot's shoulder. For this purpose the section between the two seats must be removed. This all comes to light whilst I am standing near a machine the engines of which are already warming up. The pilot, a lieutenant, smiles indulgently and says: "I don't think you will be successful in what you want to do. You see, you will no longer be able to tell what is above and what is below you and you will only have very vague ideas about your own person."

Of course, it is possible things will turn out that way. In any case, I climb up across the aeroplane wings to my seat behind the pilot. I am holding my camera, the best one I possess at the moment, tightly in my hand, and I am just about to arrange myself in my seat when the signal to start is given. We are off.

Everything now takes place incredibly quickly. In a very short time the aeroplane is flying at a height of 2500 metres. The Channel is already lying below us. We have penetrated a bank of clouds and climbed still higher. I now notice for the first time that we are not alone, but that we are flying in formation. Two dive-bombers are ahead of us. We are all at the same height. Beneath us, clouds. We sometimes catch a glimpse of the Channel through a gap in the clouds. Above us is the sun, below us snow white clouds and through the gaps patches of blue, the Channel. I know that our objective is a steamer which the reconnaissance planes have reported. The lieutenant flies on in silence. I hold my camera on my knees, consider my situation and come to the conclusion that at the moment, I am still in good form. I try myself out, I stand up and experiment to see in what attitude I shall best be able to take photographs during the dive which we are to make.

And now the moment has come when it seems that the adventure is to begin. I have as yet seen absolutely nothing on the surface of the Channel, but the lieutenant shouts through his microphone: "All clear for the attack!" I stand up.

I see the first machine in our formation plunge down to the left.

I see the second machine in our formation plunge down to the left.

Both machines are swallowed up by the clouds. Something is happening to my body. It changes place. Now I know what is happening to it. I am now really standing on my head, yet I do not fall. By a tremendous effort of will I hold my camera and like a flash of lightning the thought crosses my mind that I am after all able to hold it in such a way that at the critical moment I shall be able to take my photographs across the pilot's shoulder. I suddenly consider my position and discover that with a few fingers grasping some object or other I am in a position to steady my whole body and my camera. My will seems to triumph over the laws of gravity. Now, however, something happened which at the moment seemed so terrible to me that I shall never forget it. Until now it had naturally been light here. We are plunging in sunshine. All at once darkness surrounds me. Nothing is visible any longer. What has happened to me? Has some accident happened to us? — I must say that I find it very difficult to relate at all what occurred to me at this moment. A frightful depression swept over me which was all the more severe as I had previously been as it were in a state of happiness. I shouted aloud. I no longer have any idea of what I shouted. And the reason will also never be known. Or will it perhaps? The whole world beneath me had disappeared. It was completely erased. Nothing real existed any longer to form a hold for my sensations. We pierced the bank of clouds.

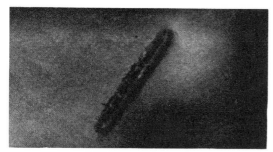

There is our objective: the ship

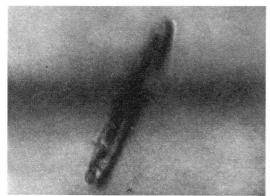

Fast as lightning we shoot towards the objective. The ship grows larger

And still larger. Another 1200 metres to the objective

Immediately a most extreme happiness overwhelms me: still hurtling downwards and as though liberated from my body and released from all material things I recognized the sunshine, the sea, the coast and also the objective. We have not flown straight down into hell, into grey oblivion, no, we are diving down to attack a ship. I have regained control over myself. Once more I am alive in the world of our war — and with a feeling of happiness I immediately realize that I have been successful in screwing up my concentration to the highest pitch. Below us is the steamer, our objective, my camera is in my hands and I am making one exposure after another. Uncanny, but very oppressive too; the ship continually grows bigger, it is rushing towards me.

Then — a wrench passes through the whole plane, my body is convulsed for

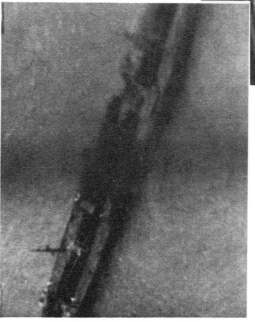

400 metres distance. Another photograph. The bomb will be released in another second

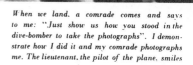

When we land, a comrade comes and says to me: "Just show us how you stood in the dive-bomber to take the photographs". I demonstrate how I did it and my comrade photographs me. The lieutenant, the pilot of the plane, smiles

the fraction of a second: the bomb has been released. I take another photograph, but a superhuman strength, an iron hand presses me downwards. I drop to my knees, I fall across the wireless apparatus, I am a worm, crushed and trampled upon, a being incapable of making the slightest movement and all my mental strength is just sufficient to enable me to realize that in this second the pilot arrested the dive.

I have already come to myself again. Below me lies our objective and I photograph the ship which has been struck and is belching forth a pillar of smoke.

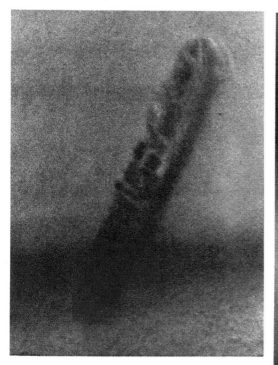

800 metres distance. The ship grows larger

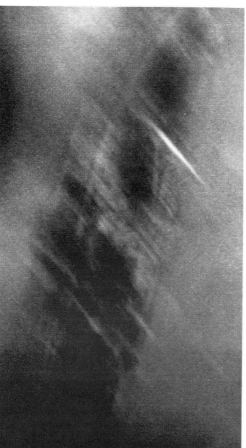

The plane is once more flying horizontally. I photograph the hit

The ship suddenly disappears from the view-finder. The plane has finished its dive

... and how it appears to his "victim"

I stand on the ship which the dive-bomber is going to approach.
A plane plunges out of the clouds at a height of 2500 metres

It hurtles towards me from a height of 1500 metres

The machine is only 400 metres distant now. It is plunging vertically at us. It is a terrible sight

Now the plane is only 200 metres above me. An infernal din. I would like to move my head away. A frightful sensation

800 metres! The sirens of the falling machine sound uncanny

A hundred metres above me the plane straightens out and flies away over my head

I turn and see a weird animal soaring upwards

I have also taken photographs from on board a ship of
what an attack by a dive-bomber on a ship looks like.
This was not during the course of a real engagement,
but I asked the pilot of a dive-bomber to fly down in
the direction of the ship on which I was. He did so.
What such an attack looks like when seen from the
ship is shown by the pictures on the following pages

*The dive-bomber is
moving away . . .*

*. . . and regains
the clouds*

The End

"I flew with them..."

Our photographer-correspondent, Hans Schaller, takes the first coloured photographs of an attack by German dive-bombers

Ready to start

Our fine planes, of the Ju 87 type, says Schaller, take their grim load on board from the long row of bombs (right)

Five hands grasp the crank

One engine after another begins to roar. In the meantime the commander has given ...

. . . his last instructions

to the crews. Two minutes later our flight begins. We speedily gain height and lay our course for X.

1

2

3

... flying towards the enemy

The first row of planes (left above) is flying next to my machine, our correspondent continues. I have been allowed to follow them with my camera until the bombs fall. We are already high above the clouds and "my" planes are below me. They are just changing their course. I cannot hear them above the noise of my own machine; they seem to be flying quietly and noiselessly above the landscape like sharp-eyed birds of prey, eager to claim their victim, thirsting to attack (above). We shall soon reach our objective — one of the dive-bombers is already leaving the formation! The machine tilts to one side (left), begins to dive ...

4

5

... plunges down through a milky wall of cloud towards the objective (left above), hurtles down steeper and steeper, stands on its head, dives almost perpendicularly and now the tension of the pilot has reached its climax. The machine has reached its objective, he releases the bombs (right above). Relieved of a weight of several hundredweights, the machine recovers and climbs above the clouds. The pilot has carried out his instructions and soon he is climbing out of his seat in order to make his report (right) ...

A second after the order to fire:

Thunder and lightning issue from the muzzle of the railway gun that has just been moved into position on the Channel coast. A huge projectile, aimed at one of the naval ports of the island fortress, screams through the air

Giant Guns—

along the Channel coast

A long-range gun belonging to the German Navy

raises its threatening barrel ready to open up devastating fire on an enemy convoy or dock yards

Seen with the hawk's eye of a modern telephoto-camera: **Dover**

Photographed from an aeroplane at a distance of 12½ miles
From Dover Castle (on the right) up to the entrance of the harbour (on the left), from the jetty to the highest barrage balloon
every detail of the British Channel port can be discerned. Th

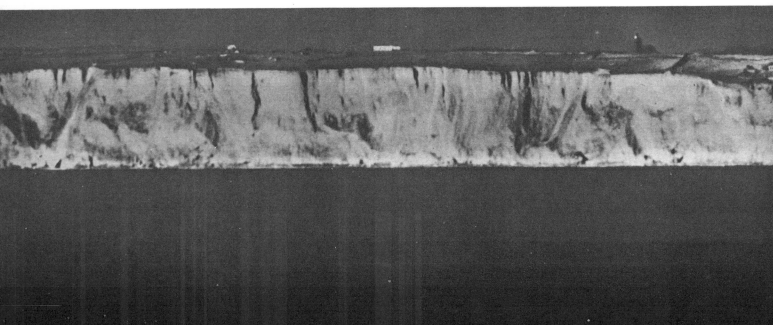

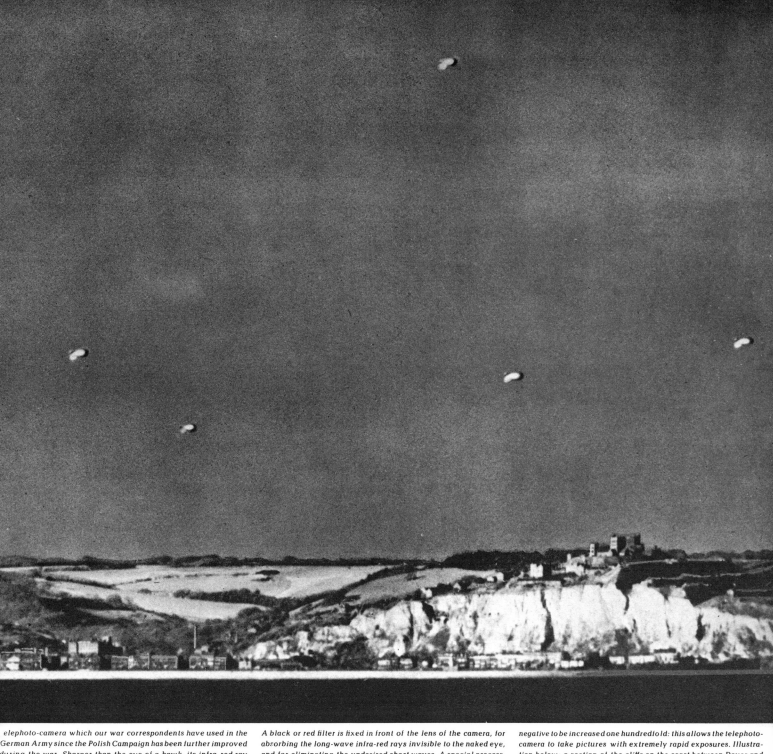

elephoto-camera which our war correspondents have used in the German Army since the Polish Campaign has been further improved during the war. Sharper than the eye of a hawk, its infra-red ray sensitive plates and films can pierce through miles of mist and fog.

A black or red filter is fixed in front of the lens of the camera, for absorbing the long-wave infra-red rays invisible to the naked eye, and for eliminating the undesired short waves. A special process, of German invention, enables the infra-red sensitiveness of the

negative to be increased one hundredfold: this allows the telephoto-camera to take pictures with extremely rapid exposures. Illustration below: a section of the cliffs on the coast between Dover and Deal north east of Dover. Every furrow and undulation is visible

Lieutenant Commander H. H. Ambrosius:

Maritime war against England – Not as in 1914-1918

The Battle of the Atlantic depends upon entirely new strategic conditions

Just as any war waged against England is bound to be primarily a naval war, so in the present conflict victory or defeat will depend on the outcome of the Battle of the Atlantic. This battle, which necessarily extends not only to the operations directed against the British Isles, but to all of Great Britain's oversea bases, is now in full swing. As soon as the campaign on the Eastern Front is over, this maritime struggle will completely determine the character of the war, for the decisive and historical war between England and Germany will be fought to a finish on the sea. Of all the battles of the war, this will be the greatest and the most important, and it will also be won by Germany — a fact which we can gather from a knowledge of the present strategic situation on the seas, as well as from a proper estimate of the present and future prospects of success as seen in the tactical difference between the naval strategy of England and that of Germany.

England's strategic position on the sea

In the first place, so far as England's position of strategic advantage on the sea is concerned, this has considerably changed for the worse in a war being waged against a continental power. If the English believe that they can carry on this war as they did the Great War, by means of a non-hazardous and comparatively bloodless blockade of enemy coasts, while at the same time safeguarding their own oversea lines of communication to as great an extent and as long as they pleased, they have become the victims of a false conclusion, which can only be accounted for by their inability to recognize the vast spiritual, political, and strategic changes which have since taken place all over the world. As a matter of fact, the strategic position on the seas of the British Isles has suffered greatly through the development of modern weapons. Whereas Britain formerly was able to confine herself to the establishment of a sea blockade and the dispatch of an expeditionary force to the Continent, so that the British Isles themselves would scarcely feel the effects of war, today England -- now geographically part of the Continent as far as her military position is concerned — has lost most of the advantages of being an island kingdom. The waters surrounding England have now become part of the coastal waters of continental Europe. English seaports and armament centres lie within the range of German air operations, while the island itself is in constant danger of invasion.

The strategic importance of the British Fleet has correspondingly diminished. All the island's naval bases are endangered by German air attacks. It is obliged to split up into a number of small units in order to protect England's overseas possessions and maritime routes, without being able to prevent the loss of tonnage continually suffered by the merchant fleet at the hands of German destroyers, planes, and submarines.

British plans to encircle Germany

In spite of their unfavourable strategic position on the seas, the British, true to their Great War traditions, are attempting to force Germany to the point of exhaustion by cutting off its entire supply of foreign raw materials. They hope to achieve this aim by a threefold plan of encirclement, which consists in enveloping Germany in a continental, an oceanic, and a world-wide ring. Each of these three encircling fronts was established too late for Britain to hope to force Germany to succumb by such means. For in the meantime Germany has made herself politically, economically, and militarily immune to any and every encircling plan.

Let us deal with the continental ring first. This was to be composed of a group of Continental European countries surrounding Germany, whereby England hoped to confine her own efforts to sending over small contingents of troops, closing all egress from the North Sea, and making air attacks against Germany's hinterland. What England accomplished by this encircling plan was quite the opposite of what she intended.

The German armies have defeated England's auxiliary nations one after another. England has not only lost her strategic bases on the coast of Continental Europe from which to organize an attack on Germany, but these very coastal countries now form part of the ring surrounding England so that she now finds herself blockaded by Germany from the sea.

Let us now turn to England's attempt to encircle Germany on the ocean. Here again the British have utterly failed to attain their object. The longer the war lasts, the less will Germany feel the effects of the cutting off her oversea import trade. The Four Year Plan, together with the economic reorganization of the countries occupied by Germany, has already progressed to a point where oversea communication is of no particular military importance to Germany. On the other hand, the longer the duration of the war the more will England be cut off from the supplies of raw material from the outside world, and in time will lose the greater part of her foreign markets. And lastly, let us now examine the encirclement of Germany by shutting her off from the rest of the world. This plan of England's consisted in enlisting the more remote continents of Asia, Africa and America in a united world-front against Germany. This plan, however, is also doomed to failure, because for the duration of the present war, Germany can do without her barter trade with these continents. Furthermore, Germany can never be overpowered either by a mobilization of the forces of these continents or by any attack which might be made by them. The more England avails herself of the help of these foreign powers, especially of that of the United States, the more she will become dependent upon them. The exclusion of Germany from these continents and the disposition of any forces which may be employed in these territories for the purpose of protecting British bases of operation and safeguarding her oversea connexions may possibly serve to prolong the war, but in the end can only weaken England's political prestige throughout the world.

How British naval and air power is employed

The operations of Great Britain's naval and air forces must be judged in the light of these encircling plans. These forces are putting up a stubborn fight which must, however, prove hopeless in the end. For if the strategic plans of the Government are based on an erroneous estimate of its own position and strength as well as that of the enemy, even the most advantageous use of their fighting forces will fail to achieve the strategic objects desired. A false political and strategic calculation cannot be made good by any amount of military efficiency.

"Maritime war against England"

So far as England's economic war against Germany is concerned, it is today fully apparent that England will never be able to achieve her goal, namely, that of breaking down Germany's powers of resistance by cutting her off from oversea communication, because of the autarchic character of the German-Continental war economy. Throughout the four years of the Great War, Germany waited in vain for a decisive naval battle which the British Fleet was able to avoid, as the strategic positions from which England made her long-distance sea blockade effective were never once the object of German attacks. In this war, through her measures of war economy and her campaigns on the Continent, Germany has rendered the British blockade ineffective, thereby winning an indirect victory over the British Navy.

As far as the strategy of defence is concerned, England's situation is also a hopeless one. She possesses no means whatever of permanently preventing the German counter-blockade from gradually destroying her oversea traffic. During the Great War, the British Fleet was able to keep open the vitally important oversea routes to and from the Mother Country, as the German Fleet had to confine itself to the limited area of operations along the coast of the North Sea, while the German Air Force was unable to take any effective part in the war being waged on the sea. Today, when the German air and naval forces can operate from the strategic bases along that part of the European coast which lies opposite England, and can strike at England's supply routes on the Atlantic, while in addition the seaports of England are within the zone of operations of Germany's superior air forces, the conditions are such that the British Navy is no longer able to perform its function of protecting and defending the British Isles or safeguarding the importation into England of raw materials and other vital necessities of life. British air operations must be judged in a like manner. The weak air attacks against Germany and the occupied countries are an attempted offensive to offset Britain's imperilled position in the Battle of the Atlantic. But England will not thereby succeed in effectively making up for the lack of success which has attended the conduct of her economic war, nor in detracting in any way from the increasing success of Germany's operations in this economic war. Where the Fleet as chief weapon has failed, the Air Force as an additional weapon cannot make good this failure. This is all the more true because the British air offensive is not being primarily directed against the German armament industry, but against the German civilian population. The employment of the British Air Force will, therefore, not be able to improve to any marked degree England's strategic position on the seas, nor her chances of success in the Battle of the Atlantic.

Germany's strategic position on the seas

Germany's strategic position on the seas presents a very different picture from that of England, inasmuch as it has vastly improved in comparison with 1918. To be sure, at the beginning of the present war the German Fleet was shut up in the "watery triangle" of the North Sea, whereas England controlled the gates of the Atlantic Ocean. But when the campaigns on the Continent led to the occupation of the entire coast of Norway and that of France on the Channel and the Atlantic, Germany came into possession of Atlantic bases and favourably situated strategic positions from which it could employ its naval and other forces in the Battle of the Atlantic. It is true that little advantage has yet been taken of these Atlantic coast bases on account of the comparatively small size of Germany's existing fleet, but their possession has greatly enhanced the value of such naval units as are available, as it has shortened the distance from the actual field of operations on the ocean. Furthermore, the strategic importance of these bases lies in the fact that they will to a large extent enable the German military authorities to take advantage of the increased effectiveness of the most modern weapons of naval warfare. Just as is already the case with respect to her warfare on land and in the air these improved modern weapons give Germany the advantage on the sea as she is on the offensive. This is especially true with respect to the power of the modern weapons of coast defence and coastal attack, which permits of a much more complete mastery and control over the waters surrounding the enemy coasts than was formerly possible. It also applies with respect to the increased speed and radius of operations obtained by the adaptation of ships to oil fuel, the use of which in this economic war has proved of the utmost value. In conclusion, mention must also be made of the importance of the employment of reconnaissance planes and fighters operating at distant points, which are equally useful in the conduct of the trade war at sea. These planes represent an especially decisive factor in the German operations. The main significance of the whole question is that the improved status of her strategic position on the seas has served to make Germany's naval fighting efficiency better than ever. The North Sea is today practically controlled by Germany, and almost entirely devoid of British naval forces. Along the German coast and those parts of the coast occupied by Germany a regular coastal shipping traffic is maintained under the protection of German convoy vessels, and includes all the German coast harbours, besides transporting the reserves required by the German fighting forces. From their bases on the Atlantic coast, the German naval and air forces operate against the transatlantic routes for the purpose of more and more effectively paralysing the maritime traffic to and from England, until it is eventually brought to a standstill. The achievement of this strategic object is bound to have a decisive effect on the outcome of the war, in contrast to the methods of commercial warfare employed against Germany by England. For England is not only not immune to the cutting of her oversea lines of communication, but is lost as soon as her imports from overseas are brought down below a certain minimum.

The tonnage problem

That notwithstanding Germany's comparatively small naval strength and in spite of the assistance given England by the U.S.A., Germany is on the way to achieving this result, is evidenced by the course which the war on the sea has hitherto taken. In its second August issue, in an article entitled, "If it goes on...", "Signal" described the way in which an American expert estimates England's chances in the Battle of the Atlantic.

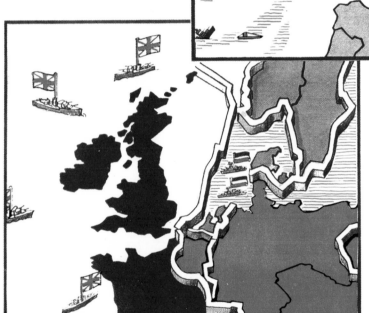

The new strategic conditions for the decision in the naval war against Britain. *The small map on the left shows the situation during the Great War of 1914-1918. The British Isles and the Atlantic lay outside the ring drawn round Germany on water and on land. The German Fleet was enclosed in the "moist triangle" of the North Sea whilst Britain held the key to the gates of the Atlantic. The situation is different today. The large map shows how completely different the position is. Germany's submarines, warships, planes and guns have at their disposal bases of operations which stretch without interruption from the most northerly point of Norway to France's Atlantic coast. The British Isles and the Atlantic thus lie completely within the range of Germany's weapons*
Maps: R. Heinisch

From his account it was evident that the race between British naval losses and the number of new vessels which can be built by England and America combined, will in the end be won by Germany. Even the American Secretary of the Navy, Knox, stated on 30th June 1941 that at present three times as much British tonnage is being sunk as England can build, and twice as much as the combined shipyards of England and America can produce.

British propaganda is now trying to take advantage of the lack of perception of the English masses by referring to the course of the naval war of 1914-1918, and by arguing that if the present war is prolonged, the situation will change in England's favour. But this speculative reliance on the element of time also lacks any sound basis in fact. The total additional tonnage which can be built in English and American shipyards, together with confiscated neutral vessels can be estimated at 2 million tons for 1941 and at 4 million, or at most, 5 million tons for 1942. When as against these figures it is reckoned that during the first six months of 1941 alone over 4 million tons of British shipping were sunk, that the United States, according to their own estimates, require an additional 2 ½ million tons of shipping, and that not only are new British and American merchant vessels being built, but also new German and Italian submarines, the only conclusion that can be arrived at is that in the future the number of vessels sunk will far exceed that of the new ships which can be built. It follows that the gradual shrinkage of England's available tonnage must inevitably reach the same catastrophic situation with which it was faced during the Great War under far more favourable conditions.

It may, therefore, be asserted that as compared with the years 1914-1918, the situation in regard to naval warfare has radically changed in Germany's favour. Whereas England, in view of the entire present strategic situation on the sea, has no longer the slightest chance of decisively weakening Germany's powers of resistance, and as this can never be effected solely by the operations of her Air Force, Germany, with her more favourable strategic bases for naval operations, is now in a position to employ her combined air and naval forces against Great Britain's oversea traffic, the complete interruption of which is bound to lead to a collapse of England's powers of resistance.

Against their better judgement, the warmongers in the United States are making quite the contrary assertion, as the political aim of America is to bleed the British Empire to the utmost extent, so that it can more easily inherit British world prestige, while at the same time preventing Germany from gaining complete victory. When on the other hand the British statesmen also make the contrary assertion, it is only because no other course is open to them, or because they are evidently still holding fast with remarkable obsinacy to the belief that in the end time will work in their favour, and that the outcome of the war will be as it was in 1918. Their present powers of resistance lie in the fact that they are unable to grasp the spiritual or political significance of the situation, or the change in the strategic possibilities resulting from this situation. In this lack of perception lies the tragic fate which awaits them. As Germany's repeated warnings have failed to convince them, they must now be taught their lesson by the German sword. No matter how often a prescribed formula of victory has proved efficacious, it cannot overcome an entirely changed set of conditions.

Meanwhile the Battle of the Atlantic will follow the course already indicated by the military events of the last two years, which in each and every respect show a tendency diametrically opposed to the events of 1914-1918. If today Germany has one powerful ally, that ally is time. British exertions and American aid may prolong the war, but they cannot halt the course of destiny, which in relentless succession is driving England in defeat from every part of the theatre of war where she attempts to make a stand and give battle, whether on the battlefields of the Continent or on the Atlantic Ocean.

Before sailing on high seas: —

tinned foodstuffs fly on board from the quay. At the same time the drinking-water tanks are filled, and the last dock hands leave the ship

After every trip in enemy waters

the submarines go into dock and are thoroughly overhauled. One can see the fins at the bow which belong to the diving gear. The water streams through the vent holes when ventilating the diving tanks

The most important cargo is taken over

A torpedo descends into the interior of the ship; before it disappears, it is smeared with grease. The coating of grease preserves it from the corrosive influence of the air saturated with moisture which is prevalent in the ship when in action

No Iementi from Reuter

The German battleship "Gneisenau" fires a salvo from all three heavily armed turrets at the British aircraft carrier "Glorious", a vessel of 22,500 tons displacement. Two flotillas of the German Navy under the command of Admiral Marschall were operating in the Arctic Ocean, in order to relieve the German troops fighting in Narvik (right)

British destroyers cover the aircraft carrier with a smoke-screen, she tries to escape behind a rain-storm, but in vain! She sinks under the heavy fire of the German naval guns. Reuter does not deny her loss. — Because of the great distances involved and large area in which the battle takes place, the eye perceives nothing but the far-off silhouettes of the fighting ships, the flashes of gun-fire, smoke, clouds, water and sky (Illustration below)

60%

British foodstuff is now to come from overseas

BRITAIN'S COWS....

The nation that possesses a large fleet needs no agriculture of its own. This election speech of British Free Traders resulted in such a decrease in British agriculture in the last decades, that before the war roughly 60% of the foodstuff requirements of Great Britain had to be imported from all over the world. One used to say not quite wrongly "Britain's cows are grazing on La Plata." The German Fleet — the Air Force excluded — has already reduced British shipping tonnage by 6.3 million tons and imports are becoming more and more difficult. The full force of submarine warfare will first be felt in spring.

British politicians have coined many slogans during this war. One of these which they are particularly fond of using just now is: "Britain's most important arm after the Navy and Air Force is agriculture." All interest is suddenly focussed on British agriculture. All at once, agriculture is extraordinarily important. It is a well known fact that during past years men of foresight have emphasized the coming importance of agriculture, but they were always looked on as cranks. Why further agriculture in one's own country when supplies can be bought so cheap from the Continent and from all over the world? As a result, at the outbreak of war, nearly 80 % of the British population were town-dwellers and arable land only occupied 6 % of the workers. There is no peasantry on the island in the continental meaning of the word. "Farming" on the other side is just as much a business as anything else. One just changes one's business if it is unprofitable.

Farming was unprofitable. During the last thirteen years land labour has decreased by a fifth, which resulted in Britain entering this war with 250.000 less farm hands than in 1914 and 1,980,000 acres less under the plough. Three-quarters of British farming country is today grazing land. Roughly 60 % of the peace-time foodstuff requirements had to be imported from all parts of the world. Britain could only supply about half its requirements in eggs, fish, potatoes and milk, providing, however, that the cattle were supplied with imported fodder. Independence from foreign sources only exists in Britain for very few foodstuffs.

The rapid occupation of the neighbouring countries by the German Army has been a very serious blow to British supplies. In peace-time Denmark

...are grazing on La Plata

Holland and the Baltic countries supplied the greater portion of Britain's butter. They also sent their early vegetables, cheese and butter, and especially bacon, across the Channel. In spring 1940 the British Food Ministry was deprived of all these resources, as then the barrels of butter and the bacon-sides now remained on the Continent. The basis of supply for the island has now been transferred to countries completely outside Europe.

On first glance this does not seem to present any particular disadvantage. Surely there is plenty of meat in the Argentine, New Zealand and Australia, and bacon can be bought in U.S.A., wheat in Canada. This is quite true but requires foreign exchange which is important for armaments. Then ships have to be sent half-way round the world to transport what formerly came across the Channel and the North Sea. The full use of the already restricted tonnage is diminished by the long journey, it was not without reason that the British Minister of Shipping, Mr. Cross, referred to the lack of shipping as the most dangerous of all Britain's predicaments. Then again butter and frozen meat can only be transported in special refrigerating ships across the Equator; the sinking of one of these ships is just as serious as the loss of a tanker or a battleship.

"Plough to victory" is one of the many British slogans of today; plough up the grazing land and sow potatoes and corn. Up to now, after one and a half years of war, only one twentieth portion of the grazing land has been ploughed up. The experiences of the Great War show clearly how limited these emergency measures really are, and how the conversion of land is hampered by the lack of labour and of tractors, which have to be imported from Canada. In fact, the whole of Britain's future foodstuff supply lies overseas and very soon the island will feel the full effect of the Führer's words: the submarine warfare will really start in spring.

The last day of sunshine. *The German army car is plough-ing its way through the deep snow on the road from Narvik to Kirkenes. Of late the days have become shorter and shorter, and the sun has been lower and lower on the horizon. Today, at midday, it was barely visible. For the last time the snow is dyed with brilliant colours, and the sky glows golden. Tomorrow thirty days and nights of darkness begin*

2.500 miles south. *The sun has already been burn-ing for seven hours. It is now directly overhead. The shadow of the rifles piled by the German guard outside the ancient temple of Apollonia does not even reach beyond the butts. The temperature has risen to 120 degrees Fahrenheit. In both places there are German soldiers station-ed 2,500 miles apart beneath the same heavenly bodies*

Snow and sand →

ut the same sun

The flags are waving in Bardia. German and Italian soldiers are on guard beneath them outside the gates of the city. They are wearing short trousers and their shirtsleeves are rolled up. The small town gleams white in the sun and the oleander by the side of the road is in blossom. The blue vault of the gleaming African sky covers everything

In Norway the Arctic circle cuts across the road, which crosses the mountains at an altitude of 3,000 feet. The lorry taking petrol northwards for the troops and the car coming from the north pull up at the highest point. Wrapped in warm coats, the men gaze at the sun. It has just appeared, yellow and cold, above the horizon. It looks as though there will be a fresh fall of snow   *Photographs: Wollschläger (2), PK. Kenneweg (2)*

The 61st Russian tank got through *but not far, for the gunners were soon upon it with their hand grenades and defeated the crew in a hand-to hand fight. After the battle they buried the dead tank gunners beside their shattered fortress. They could not, however, decide to erect crosses over the godless. But blood is thicker than water, and so they planted a piece of wood over the mounds and hung their caps on them. That's what mountain troops are like*

THE BRITISH OVER LÜBECK

A lorry rattles in the principal nave of the burnt out "Marienkirche" of Lübeck. Sappers and men belonging to the Emergency Service have dug a round bronze vessel out of the charred rafters and using their combined strength they push it into the lorry standing ready. "This is the only thing remaining over from all the treasures, pictures, carvings and works of art in this church," an elderly gentleman says to me. "This half melted bronze is a baptismal font dating from the 14th century and we are going to see if it can be restored." The old gentleman precedes me making his way across grating splinters of glass, ruined walls and smouldering pews. "This is where our famous organ stood. That, too, was devoured by the flames and is now buried under the ruins of the roof which caved in. The worst loss of all is probably that of a famous danse macabre by an unknown mediaeval master. But there are such a lot of things I could tell you. Not only this church is burnt out, but nearly all the churches, to which Lübeck owed its name the city of the golden towers, were destroyed during the night when the British attacked our town."

We leave the church and outside bright sunshine is streaming over the yellow ruins of the burnt down Old Town.

The streets of Old Lübeck have been turned into quarries. The market place is surrounded by ruins. The Town Hall is completely burnt out. The rich carving on the doors and panels, the magnificent tarsia work, the wonderful alabaster friezes and valuable treasures of the Renaissance were gutted in a single night. All the romantic alleys in the craftmen's quarter of the town no longer exist. In the air there is a penetrating odour of marzipan coming from what remains of the largest café in Lübeck which was famed for its marzipan... An inestimable number of art treasures, gathered together in the old patrician houses by generation after generation, were destroyed. There was the "Schifferhaus" with its magnificent wood carvings and iron work, models of mediaeval ships, there was the famous "Schabbelhaus" with its old museum... The Lübeck cathedral suffered severely. During the night a soldier penetrated into the burning interior of the church and out of the inferno of crashing rafters and caving in vaults saved the famous Memling Altar, a masterpiece of Flemish wall painting. The Cathedral Museum and Cathedral School were damaged by bombs, the Church of St Peter was burnt down as well as the Agidia Church and the "Katharineum," which housed the Municipal Library.

Blind destructive fury and murderous vandalism raged over the town and no attempt to alter the facts, however ingenious, will be able to make it appear credible that these were "military objectives." I flew over the town in the afternoon and convinced myself that the centre of the town, lying between broad stretches of water, cannot possibly be mistaken. There can be no question in this case of "bombs missing their mark" or "mistakes," particularly when it is taken into account that the moon was shining brightly over the town during the night of the attack. I am an airman myself and am able to judge.

PK. Front Correspondent Benno Wundshammer

THE ATTACK ON LÜBECK

This is what the propaganda attacks of the British Air Force on "military objectives" in Germany look like. This is what remained of one of the most venerable monuments of European culture, the Lübeck Cathedral, a masterpiece of early mediaeval church architecture. During the same night irreplaceable and world famous works of art were destroyed together with the old town of Lübeck

Photograph: PK. War Correspondent Benno Wundshamme

WHO DROPPED THE FIRST BOMBS?

by Hans Fritzsche

British propaganda maintains—it is remarkable of course that this has only been the case since January 1941—that it was the Germans who began dropping bombs in this war on towns and settlements. This statement was made in the House of Commons by Mr Butler, Under Secretary of State. This marks the end of a piece of propaganda which commenced immediately after the first German large-scale attack on military objectives in London and was still restricted at the time to the completely false allegation that the Germans had intentionally selected workmen's dwellings, churches or even the Royal Palace as the targets for their bombs. What, however, was the real truth?

But anyone who knows the facts is tempted silently to ignore the matter with a simple shrug of the shoulders and merely consider the whole affair, as it is in reality, a demonstration of weakness. Everyone knows what efforts the Führer made years before this war to limit modern armaments with their ever-increasing and immeasurable effect. Those who heard his proposals firstly for total disarmament and finally for the abolition of air-bombing warfare, provided of course that it was on a reciprocal basis, have not the slightest desire to resuscitate polemical arguments which already belong to past history. In addition, those Germans who remember those months in the past year during which the bulk of the population only heard, with increasing astonishment and anxiety, warnings given as a response to the British night bombing air-raids, must consider any further remark on the subject of "who started night air raid bombing" as entirely superfluous. But surely in such cases a reminder should be necessary that British propaganda always tries to make use of the superior indifference of an adversary, who underestimates the British agility in juggling with the meaning of bare facts within its grasp.

The first British bombs were dropped on 12th January 1940

The first German bomb dropped on British soil was on 16th March 1940, during an attack on British warships off the Orkney Islands when a coastal anti-air craft battery came into action and was then silenced by bombs.

Winston Churchill declared afterwards that a house had nearly been hit, but in reality it was only a dog.

As far back as two months previously, on 12th January 1940, British aeroplanes dropped bombs for the first time on country dwelling places in Germany. This was on the town of Westerland on Sylt. On the 20th March Sylt was raided again, the British maintained that they had bombed objects of military importance, but eyewitnesses of the foreign Press were able to see for themselves that only objects of a non-military nature had been damaged. As the British during these attacks scattered their bombs, destined, as they said, only for military objects, far and wide right up to Denmark, if sufficient allowance is made for incapability, the intention of hitting civilian objects can be contested.

On 12th April 1940 the British made a bombing raid on the small railway station of Heiligenhafen on the Schleswig-Holstein coast, which did but little damage, but represented the first British attack on a German railway of no military importance. Per-

haps if a broad view of matters is taken, this could still be considered as a case of over-estimation.

On 23rd April the residential quarter of Oslo was raided by British bombers, who had, having regard to the geographical and political situation, deliberately picked out these civilian objectives.

A few days later when the small bathing resort Wenningstedt and the town of Heide in Schleswig-Holstein were subjected to bombing, General Headquarters issued a statement: "The enemy has started air war on unfortified places of no military importance."

During the whole period from January to the end of April 1940 the German Air Force, in contrast to the British, only carried out reconnaissance flights and attacks on ships, the above-mentioned bombing of an anti-aircraft battery being the only exception.

From 10th to 13th May 71 enemy air raids on German territory

Perhaps it is possible to find some kind of excuse for the British behaviour during this period, but from the 10th of May onwards it became a very different matter. During the period from the 10th May up to 13th May no less than 71 air raids were made by enemy airmen on German territory, of which only 6 were directed against military objects, 14 against objects which might be considered to be of military importance, such as bridges, coal mines etc., but 51 took place on objects of a non-military nature.

On 10th May 57 civilians were killed in Freiburg im Breisgau, of which 13 were children between the age of 5 and 12. On 11th May the convent Marienburg near Boppard, used as a girls' boarding school was bombed. On the same day the hospital and several houses of the town of Emmerich were damaged. On 12th May bombs were dropped on Aix-la-Chapelle killing a child and wounding several people. On 13th May enemy bombs killed several persons in a home for old people in Düsseldorf, in a purely residential part of the town. On 15th May 3 were killed and 4 wounded in a house in Eschweiler. A peasant's farm buildings were blown to pieces in the district of München-Gladbach and on the following day a big raid was made on Hamburg, in which we mourned 43 dead and 110 wounded.

In all these cases there could be no question of a mistake or bad aiming. The number of enemy raids on German territory rose by the 22nd May to 228, of which 75 % had been made on non-military objects and had claimed as victims of the civil population, 136 dead, 305 wounded, amongst whom were very many women and children.

In June the raids on the civil population continued to be carried out systematically by the British. They never made the slightest attempt to deny these raids, but even referred to them with special pride, by stating that these "successful" raids would have a demoralizing effect on the German population and were the surest

means of breaking down the resistive power of the German nation. Winston Churchill himself made repeated statements on the radio and in the House of Commons of his faith in these British air raids.

On 20th June General Head Quarters stated, with reference to the British raids, that now the German Air Force had started reprisals on Britain. Today it is a definite fact that the German reprisals, which had only just started, were confined exclusively to military objects.

Curiously enough, the British still failed to comprehend what was in the wind and what fate awaited them. 48 hours after the important statement of General Headquarters, British aeroplanes reached the outskirts of Berlin for the first time and bombed the purely residential suburb of Babelsberg and amongst other things damaged a Post Office and a hospital. The British were proud of this exploit. The London Press was wild with joy that at last the capital of the Reich was "having its share." Incidentally a raid, with the clouds lying very low, killed children playing in the town of Herne, and on the following day the R. A. F. registered its first "success" with time-fuse bombs: 5 children were killed on their way to school near Allendorf, south of Arnsberg, as the German population had as yet not been instructed as to the effect of timefuse bombs.

As raids of this kind continued, for example, on the 3rd of July in Barmbeck, 22 children alone were killed, the Führer in his Peace speech on 19th July referring to these events warned Britain: "Until now I have ordered hardly any reprisals, but that does not mean that this is or will be my only reply." Even now, no attention was paid to this warning. On the contrary, new methods were invented for raiding the population such as incendiary strips, from the 26th August onwards Berlin's residential districts were systematically raided every night or every other night, so that the whole of the diplomatic corps and all the members of the foreign Press could repeatedly see for themselves that there was no question of mistake or bad aiming.

Great was the relief when the Führer declared in his speech on the 4th September: "For three months I have refrained from answering, in the hope that they would cease this stupidity. Mr. Churchill has taken this for a sign of weakness. You will understand that now we shall answer night for night and in an ever increasing degree." On 7th September G. H. Q. issued a communiqué: "The German Air Force has now started to undertake attacks on London with large forces."

On 8th November the Führer related how astonished he was that that "genius of a strategist" Winston Churchill should have picked out that weapon of attack which was Britain's weakest point in comparison to Germany. He declared that the man who could hatch such a scheme must be mad. After three months he had accepted the challenge and with the same determination as he had always shewn. He concluded with the words: The British people, for whom I am really sorry, will have to thank archcriminal Churchill for this.

From the very start of the German big offensive one was very careful in England to be silent about those attacks which had been boosted so much at the start, in order after a certain lapse of time to be able to say that it was the Germans who had started. But when the world remembered the real facts of the case, as recounted above, the London wireless pompously declared that these attacks had started with Warsaw. This argument, which had never even been considered, is false, as Warsaw was not bombarded until—due to British influence—the civil population had refused to evacuate the town and had determined to offer resistance as if it were a fortress. Incidentally this is exactly what occurred in Rotterdam.

England herself is to blame

The British themselves during the months in which they could bathe undisturbed in the glory of the success of their night raids, never once had occasion to refer to Warsaw or Rotterdam. The so-called Minister of Information Mr Duff Cooper, argued at that time from a different point of view by declaring in the "Daily Mail" that the expression "innocent civilian" belonged to the ideas of bygone centuries. In the epoch of totalitarian warfare limitations of war objectives were no longer possible. Finally we Germans have not forgotten that even the British Churches made efforts to justify the night raids of those months and that at that time statements were made in the pulpits breathing an unholy, unchristian will to radical destruction in reference to the German people.

Bombing raids are exactly the same as war itself; at the beginning of the war the British boasted: "You Germans never for a moment thought we would declare war on you!" Now when they are losing the war they squeal about the wicked Germans, who are supposed to be responsible for letting loose this war of theirs. A fraction of that humane feeling which Britain today pretends to possess, would, if it had been applied honestly and judiciously, have spared Britain the dire misery of her own making.

Hell in a Serbian village

"A short distance from a village," reports our correspondent, "we received the message that we were about to encounter the main body of the Morava Division. Immediately afterwards heavy enemy artillery fire rained down on our tanks. Enemy anti-tank guns were in position near the church. We had to break through. My tank rattled down the slightly curved street past the enemy gun emplacement. The shells burst right and left of the tank but the firing was very inaccurate. We stopped near the village school. Then suddenly we got a wireless message from the tank behind us: "Tank 'Schimmelmann to tank 'Erika'. Enemy artillery left is using your tank to get the range. Change your position at once and take cover." Without delay the tank turned on harshly grating tracks. A moment later a shell from the artillery transformed the spot where it had been stationed into a crater. At top speed we drove on. Our artillery and tank artillery prepared the next village for the approaching storm. We could observe the hits registered. Then our tanks attacked, every gun spat fire, but even before we reached the street barricade at the entrance to the village the resistance had been broken. Tanks and artillery lay shot to pieces, guns of the most modern pattern stood abandoned, and munition columns were on fire. The whole street was lost in haze and smoke. Suddenly a Serbian soldier, his face distorted with fright, ran up to our tank. He had left his post and had only one thought: to escape from this hell

ENGLAND

in the

Mediterranean

Political maps before the present war used to indicate the solidity of the British Empire by a broad firm line from the Atlantic Ocean through the Mediterranean, the Suez Canal and the Red Sea as far as India. This looked as if an iron chain had been forged between England and India, the links being welded together at Gibraltar, Malta, Port Said and Aden so that nothing could burst them asunder. The observer was naturally overwhelmed with a kind of admiration for the instinctive determination of the British statesmen who had systematically laid out this chain across the oceans. At the present time however the links seemed to be breaking, and the detour round the Cape which has to be made by English shipping is a sign of weakness. The Suez Canal is practically deserted, and the volume of traffic passing through it has sunk, with six ships daily, to a minimum. The iron chain has rusted through with surprising rapidity, for all that remains are the spots where the links were welded together, and they also are superfluous because they have nothing more to defend. They are merely lost "forlorn hopes" which are intended to save the "face" of the Empire, but it would be interesting to know how.

In view of this rapid collapse we must begin to doubt the pretended wisdom of those statesmen who took possession of the bases lying on this line. As a matter of fact if we do not allow ourselves to be blinded by old-fashioned prejudices, then we must regard England's intrusion into the Mediterranean as being a series of incidental and aimless encroachments upon foreign territory, these encroachments having indeed been dictated on each occasion by certain interests, but not being in reality the result of an imposing policy of expansion and security, unless, that is to say, we decide that taking is a greater blessing than giving and adopt this principle as the final aim of wise statesmanship.

I. The way in

Until the Suez Canal was built, Gibraltar was not on the route to India. For centuries people had thought it inconceivable that the enormous territories of the Turkish Empire would ever disintegrate, and this Empire was a barrier between Europe and the lands whence came spices, silk and cotton. The Ottoman Sultans like the mediaeval rulers of Islam did not allow European merchants to proceed through their territories nor to visit the markets within them. Any one wanting to go to India had to go round this barrier and to proceed by the northern route from Russia through Persia or by the sea route round Africa. English statesmen therefore, when they began to concern themselves with the Mediterranean and the countries on its shores, and so turned their attention to Gibraltar, were not led by any kind of clairvoyant foreboding of the future; they were merely thinking of trade with the Levant, and with the Greek, Syrian and Egyptian harbours of the Turkish Empire, that is to say of the export of wool and the import of currants, oils and medicaments.

Elizabeth, the "Virgin Queen", was the first to start English trade with this part of the world, and she herself contributed a sum, which would today be equivalent to ten million marks, to the Levant Company, which had been founded for this purpose; this capital she had acquired from her financial participation in Drake's famous cruise of piracy round the world. The booty brought home by Drake had been taken from Spanish ships, and it is therefore understandable that the people of Spain were not very edified at seeing how their English competitors were in a certain measure promoting their Levant trade with Spanish money, seeing that up to then this part of the world had been the reserve of Spanish merchants. On the other hand it could not fail to cause obvious discomfort in London, when it became known that negotiations were going on between Madrid and Venice, which had also suffered losses, for the purpose of closing the straits of Gibraltar to English ships.

As a matter of fact, this measure was at the time not resorted to, but English traders with the Levant had the sword of Damocles continually hanging over their heads. It is true that this trade amounted only to a comparatively small portion of the English trade budget, but on the other hand those engaging in it had influence enough in Parliament to be able to keep the continual attention of the rulers of England upon this menace in the Mediterranean. Also Cromwell, during his dictatorship, continued the expansion policy of Elizabeth in its entirety and by similar methods, and even contemplated securing an English base at the Columns of Hercules as a precaution against this threatened danger.

There was a further reason for this when England entered into the conflict against Louis XIV of France. For, as an English statesman once said, Gibraltar could be used "to separate France from France", that is to say to prevent the Atlantic and Mediterranean fleets of France from combining their operations. This strategic advantage also became evident during the war of the Spanish Succession to the Emperor, who was at that time an ally of England, and the moment thus came when England was able to realize her long cherished desire.

The joint purpose of England and her allies in entering the war was to take the Spanish crown from the grandson of Louis XIV and to give it to the son of the German Emperor in Vienna. The occupation of Gibraltar therefore should only have been a temporary military measure, and this was how Landgrave George of Hessen understood it when on the 1st August 1704, supported by English naval guns, he occupied the strip of land connecting the rock of Gibraltar with the Spanish mainland and after two days bombardment captured the harbour which was not strongly fortified. Landgrave George hoisted the Habsburg double eagle, which was the flag of the rightful King of Spain. After a short time however he took over another command and his successor, the English Admiral Rooke, amazed the Spanish population of Gibraltar by hauling down the flag of the Archduke and hoisting the English flag in its place. He thus demonstrated the fact that the Government in London was determined to treat Gibraltar, after the war as well, as English territory.

When the Spaniards and French tried to recover this place the English again required the Landgrave in order to secure their new possession for them, and established themselves there as masters. England was therefore only drawing the logical conclusion, when at the peace negotiations at Utrecht she stipulated for the permanent possession of Gibraltar.

II. The way to Egypt

During the whole of the 18th century England used Gibraltar and also Minorca as strategic bases against France and Spain; this however was not because of any tendency to extend her sphere of influence to the eastern Mediterranean or even to break through to India. For it was not England, but her sworn enemy Napoleon, who at the end of the century tried to force the first breach in the barrier of the Turks and thus to open up for the first time a new way to India.

Napoleon's expedition to Egypt has been rightly descrived as an historical event of primary importance;

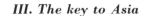

for owing to it the Turkish Empire became for the first time the victim of the European powers, and thus was established the connexion between Europe and India, which fact was of political importance for the whole world. The fact that the traditional politicians of England left these possibilities to be discovered by their gifted and clever enemy is hardly an indication of their far-sightedness, still less the fact that the failure of Napoleon's enterprise as a result of the naval superiority of England was of no avail to them. As in many other cases, it looks as if the statesmen in London were only interested in no one else undertaking anything which they had not the initiative to undertake themselves although they possessed the power to do so. Thus it was that they only took advantage of Napoleon's failure in one case, and even in this case their attention had to be drawn to the advantage by their enemy.

For Napoleon had chosen Malta as base of operations for his campaign against Egypt, and thus put an end to the sovereign state of the knights of St. John, who were ruling there as the liegemen of their feudal lord, the king of Sicily. Nelson was obviously acting in accordance with the demands of strategy when he tried to wrest from his great adversary this place, which had become all at once so important. The Bourbons in Palermo were allied with England and readily empowered Nelson to drive out the French, but of course this was done in the expectation that at the end of the war the old condition of affairs would be restored. Nelson thought the same. For it seemed to him that it would suffice if

the French disappeared from the place, and he therefore declared upon proclaiming the blockade of Valetta, that Malta would be returned to its rightful masters after the departure of the French.

This however did not happen, for it is true that, when the English forces had finally succeeded in seizing the island after two years blockade, London declared that it would only be occupied for the duration of the war, and that the sole desire was for a third power besides England and France to guarantee the independence of the state of Malta; but, after an agreement to this effect had been arrived at and it had been determined by the treaty of Amiens in March 1802 that the island should remain neutral and the English evacuate within three months, it transpired that London was not prepared to renounce this means of controlling the eastern Mediterranean, and the period of three months expired without any preparations at all being made to evacuate the island. The Sicilian flag, which had at first fluttered beside the English one, had long since been hauled down. The Pope sent warnings, and Paris pressed for fulfilment, but the English established themselves in Malta as if they were at home. A year and a quarter later, when France began to press categorically for fulfilment, the English Ambassador in Paris received instructions to ask for his passports. Malta had become all at once so important that a fresh war broke out on its account.

Malta had become important not as a base on the road to India but as an advanced base of the barrier which was intended to block the road to India to everyone. English policy was this time, just as in the case of Gibraltar, not a constructive policy, but was intended to form an obstacle to progress in this direction.

III. The key to Asia

This rare hesitation to strike out on new lines which was unworthy of a great empire manifested itself above all in England's attitude towards the decaying Ottoman Empire. Napoleon's expedition had proved that this decay had begun, for as a result of the shock caused by it, Egypt and Syria commenced to free themselves from the suzerainty of the Sultan. But all the same England chose this moment to establish it as a leading principle of her eastern policy that the Turkish Empire must remain intact, and obstinately opposed any territorial changes, whether in the Balkans, in Africa or in Asia, because these territories helped to constitute the barrier she desired; she was indeed acting more like a Sultan than the Sultan himself and was prepared at the worst to close this road to India to everyone and even to herself.

However, in spite of England, history went its way in the Mediterranean. The Suez Canal was built without English capital, for the Foreign Office had declared the project of Lesseps to be absolutely dangerous for the interests of England. But that followed which London had not expected, for with Egypt the cornerstone was broken of the Turkish Empire and thus Disraeli's famous *coup*, which brought the Suez Canal shares owned by the Khedive into the possession of England, was not able to secure her control over the road to India. Thus there remained nothing for it but to do as the others were doing, that is to say, England must secure for herselfe share in the property of the Turkish Empire, which

she had previously wanted to be regarded as sacrosanct.

Many Englishmen listened in astonishment when Disraeli declared in the House of Commons that the Isle of Cyprus constituted "the key to Western Asia". This was in the year 1878 just after he had offered the Sultan a guarantee for the latter's possessions against Russian attacks in return for the cession of Cyprus. As a matter of fact this Russian attack was not carried out, and English experts declared this island to be strategically valueless, Lord Derby, the Secretary for Foreign Affairs, actually resigning because he did not want to condone the departure from this principle of English policy. All the same Disraeli gained the majority in Parliament for his policy.

It was only the assent of the Sultan which had to be awaited. This delay was so long that the English Ambassador in Constantinople made preparations for getting the obstinate fellow out of the way by means of a palace revolution, this he did of course "for the sake of the safety of the state and of our own vital interests" (as he wrote to London). Hereupon Abdul Hamid thought it better to give his signature. All the same the evacuation of Cyprus by the Turkish troops could only be brought about afterwards by means of a threatening telegram, in which Disraeli reproached the Sultan with "breach of faith and ingratitude", telling him that at the pending Berlin congress he would support a further cession of Turkish territory to Greece. The English historian Seton-Watson is of the opinion that this had the desired effect but sounded too much like blackmail.

Here again we see that British policy in the Mediterranean lacked a broad basis, and amounted to nothing other than a roundabout way of proceeding, which was not in the least calculated to increase the prosperity of the countries there. Dr. Ernst Lewalter

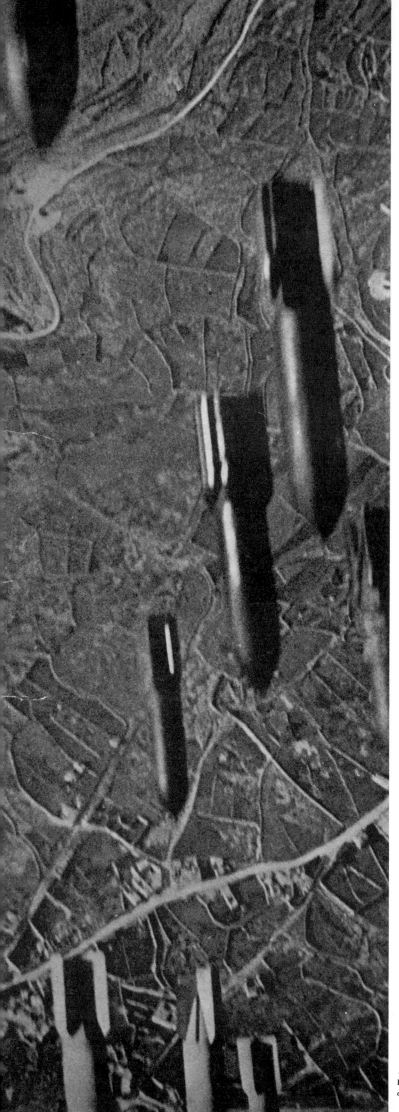

The rocky promontory before **La Valetta** *where the British coastal fortifications and A. A. positions are particularly concentrated is a favourite objective*

BESIE

Italian

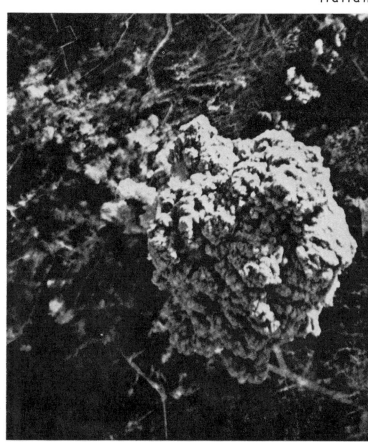

An unusually luxuriant "cauliflower." *After breaking through the murderous barrage of light and heavy A. A. fire by diving low, the dive-bomber picked out an ammunition dump. He must have aimed well, for a few seconds later this gigantic cloud rose over the explosion . . .*

←

Bombs on Malta—*day after day, almost without a break, they are dropped on the numerous military objectives on the rocky island*

The old and new fortifications of the "Cottonera Lines" as well as docks, workshops, and harbour facilities are the objectives of these bombing attacks

Storehouses are blown into the air—on Fort Tigné close to the big parade ground

ED FROM THE AIR

erman airmen destroy Britain's barrier to Africa

... that is lit up again and again by flashes from new explosions which can be seen by the crew of the dive-bomber whose bomb traps are still open

The bomber has already reached the sea. And from the fiery crater the clouds from the explosion, like the powerless fist of a threatening giant, continue to rise into the air   PK. Photographs: Front Correspondent Billhardt

Thermo-pylæ

During the hard fighting in the Greek mountains, heavy German artillery continually had to be employed in order to force a breakthrough by the Germans. Above the flash of the guns and the smoke, the white peaks of Olympus rise in eternal peace

The main resistance of the enemy has been broken at Thermopylæ. Mechanized columns follow the rapid advance of the tanks. Enemy fire is still occasionally directed against the line of advance. The crew leap from the lorry and take cover. But the advance can no longer be held up

After days of fighting and marching: the warm springs of Thermopylæ! Uniforms are stripped off in a moment, and the marching troops have soon become a jolly group of bathers
Photographs:
P.K. Müller

This is how the German troops were greeted in most places in Greece

At the head of the population, the Greek Orthodox Archbishop and the Mayor of a small town greet the commander of the troops just marching in

A memorable sight:
The flag of the young and victorious German Army waves above the centuries old pillars of the Acropolis

To the Führer of the German people

The entry of the German troops has once more brought law and order to Greece. A letter addressed to the Führer by the People's Commission of Alexandropolis (formerly Dedeagach), the capital of the Greek district of Ebros, provides especial confirmation of this fact:

"The population of Alexandropolis, who for three days have now lived in the territory occupied by the glorious German troops, have today voluntarily gathered together in order to express their heartfelt thanks to Your Excellency as Supreme Commander of the glorious German army. They promise always to give testimony to their unalterable gratitude for the great civility and true chivalry shown by the courageous troops of occupation to the population. Life, honour, property as well as customs and national tradition have remained untouched. This is already demonstrated by the fact that life is continuing just as before along the same paths."

Alexandropolis, 10th April 1941
The People's Commission of Alexandropolis wishes to convey to your Excellency its gratitude and admiration.

Bishop   President
Pataron Heletios   Anas. Pentzos
Members
Nic. Stiropoulos   Konst. Saridis
General Secretary Manganaris

The capitulation

The agreements are signed. Left: General Jodl from the Führer's Headquarters; behind (standing): The Chief of Staff of the South-East Army, General Greiffenberg; in the middle (seated): The representative of the Greek Army. General Tsolacoglu who later formed the new Greek Government
Photograph: Schlickum (P. Com.)

SUCCESSFUL STRATEGY

The author provides what is in view of the vast material a concise account of the preliminary history of this war and then descr:bes in clear outline the events which have taken place during the first three years of its duration. The abundance of news every day and the increase in the amount of work each individual has to perform make it difficult for those participating in the actual experiences and events to survey the development of the war and thus create a foundation on which to base their judgment. They will find both in the following article.

by Colonel Max Baron von Pitreich

Versailles was an injustice, and even Lloyd George, the then Prime Minister of Great Britain, was of the opinion that nothing good could come of it. Contrary to the assurances of the United States President, Wilson, in acceptance of which Germany had laid down her arms, a heavy dictate was inflicted on the Reich. It was an injustice that the German town of Danzig was severed from the Reich and that the German territories of West Prussia, Poznań and East Upper Silesia were transferred to Poland, and it was intolerable that East Prussia was separated from the mother country by the "Corridor." The overwhelming burden of debt laid upon the Reich increased the danger of Bolshevism. It was on this foundation that National Socialism developed in Germany under Adolf Hitler's leadership.

Germany's disarmament did not suffice for the French, and at Geneva they launched a campaign using the catchwords of collective security and indivisible peace as a cloak for the strategy of encirclement which they were planning against Germany. The Soviet Russians for the time being made no alliances but continually increased their armaments.

Encirclement as in 1914—but . . .

Wedged in between military states, the German Reich had to be armed for every eventuality. The many disarmament proposals made by Hitler brought no result at Geneva. Lloyd George, however, subsequently regretted that none of the German proposals had been adopted during these negotiations. Mussolini's assertion that it was a "pure illusion" to believe that the German people could be kept unarmed for ever, also had no effect. Germany withdrew from the League of Nations, proclaimed her sovereign right to arm and occupied the demilitarized Rhineland.

In 1935, the Conservatives were in office in Britain and Baldwin was Prime Minister. They were faced with an election and did not wish its result to be influenced by unpopular armament questions. There were many indications that a fresh counterpoise to France was not unwelcome. As in former times, Britain again pursued her policy of a balance of power in which the comfortable part of umpire was to be played by the British. Then came the war in Abyssinia and the conflagration in Spain where Britain quite obviously was on the side of the Reds. Germany was in the opposite camp and

"Fatal accidents during the blackout! Life over there seems to be very dangerous, Billy!"—That was in the Maginot Line a long time before the campaign in France

the antagonism between Great Britain and the Reich, which had so far existed behind the scenes, now manifested itself openly.

France had meanwhile concluded an alliance with the Soviet Union, and the Comintern once again began to become more active. Threats against Germany were uttered in Moscow and Stalin declared that the Soviet Union was on the eve of great events and that the call might come to the Red Army at any moment. The Minister of War, Voroshilov, was even more drastic in his utterances and said: "We shall defeat the enemy on his own territory."

An agreement directed against the activities of the Comintern had been concluded in 1936 between Germany and Japan. Churchill spoke at that time of the "enemies of liberty and peace who are very loud, well organized and powerful."

Roosevelt, too, was beginning to make his voice heard. Clearly referring to the Axis Powers, he spoke of "nations responsible for the madness of autarchies and armaments," which were striving to obtain a settlement by the sword and not by common sense, which wished to obtain new markets by conquest and treated the sacred character of treaties with contempt.

That so-called "treaty," the Dictate of Versailles, had been extorted by the French Premier, Clemenceau, and the promises made by President Wilson had been broken. President Wilson had meanwhile fallen ill and died, the United States had withdrawn from Europe and one of Wilson's successors, Roosevelt, was now trying to declare that the Dictate of Versailles was a sacred treaty. He was encouraged by Litvinov, the Soviet Russian Commissar for Foreign Affairs, who opposed those governments which were supposed to base their foreign policy on "contempt of peace and on aggression."

The circle of Germany's enemies was already complete by 1936. The Führer's attitude nevertheless remained consistently directed towards peace. The constraint of her position compelled Germany to arm. British statesmen were soon to provide the objective justification of the step she had taken. Britain suddenly began to emphasize the fact "that unarmed nations can neither hold back other armed states from war nor protect their own liberty or soil."

These words were not pronounced in Germany's favour but in Britain's own interests, and after his trip to Germany in 1936, Lloyd George wrote that the Germans would resist to the death if war were forced upon them, but that they themselves had no aggressive intentions. He added that they were just as little prepared to invade Soviet Russia as they were for a military expedition to the moon.

In the meantime, Britain had begun to arm, and Anthony Eden, temporarily Minister of War, declared that there could be no disarmament unless Britain's armaments were taken as the basis. As at all naval conferences, Britain was here, too, to take first place. Even at that time Churchill's opinion was that Germany was becoming too strong and must be annihilated, and he said that in a new war Britain would tear the Huns to pieces so as not to have any more trouble from them for at least a century. Britain's attitude during the next few years was determined by this aim. Confirmation of this was given not long ago by a British journalist when reporting an interview with the British Minister of War, Anthony Eden, in which the latter stated that Britain's attempts to come to an agreement with Germany were intended exclusively to gain time in order to enable Great Britain to complete her armaments.

Austria and the Sudeten German territory were incorporated in the Reich in 1938 and the occupation of Czechoslovakia occurred a few months later. Documentary proof is available which shows that the war against Germany had already been decided upon previously Even at that time, as is proved

by documents later discovered in Warsaw. Roosevelt also had his finger in the pie. Neither the discussions at Godesberg and Munich in 1938 nor the sincere enthusiasm with which Neville Chamberlain and Daladier were greeted on their return by their countrymen had done anything to alter the Allies' desire for war. Britain and France increased their armaments and conscription was introduced in Britain in April 1939.

On 23rd August 1939 Germany had concluded with the Soviet Union a non-aggression and consultation pact which united the two Powers in the determination never to let their peoples fight against one another again.—Germany did not intend to export her doctrines, the Führer declared, and if the Russians had no intention of exporting their doctrines to Germany, there was no longer any reason for ever opposing one another again.

An agreement had already been reached in the west by the German-French declaration of 6th December 1938, and Germany was now looking for a satisfactory settlement for her eastern frontier. The Reich could not relinquish its claim to Danzig. Germany merely demanded the return of that German city, which did not even belong to Poland, and an exterritorial road through the Corridor, in return for which the Führer was prepared to guarantee Poland's western frontier for a full quarter of a century. Today, after the full unfolding of Germany's military strength, after the great victories commencing with the "campaign of 18 days" against Poland, the world will scarcely understand that Germany's enemies began the war so rashly. How different, on the other hand, was the desire for peace of the Führer who, in spite of knowing Germany's strength, made such moderate conditions. But the Poles, who had already been given a blank cheque by London and Paris, turned them down. The terrorization of people of German blood and other Polish acts of aggression started the conflagration. On 1st September 1939 the Führer was obliged to order the German Army to march into Poland. Britain and France declared war on Germany on 3rd September.

The first laurels

Feeling had been stirred up in Poland by the use of the slogan "the march on Berlin," whereby a considerable part had been played by mistaken conceptions of military ideas. Mobile warfare was being demanded in many places as a reaction to the wearisome trench fighting during the Great War. Far too much one-sidedness led people to overlook the fact that the four years of trench fighting during the World War were nothing but a mobile war which had got stuck from a lack of means. The eternal truth was not recognized that every mobile war is the outcome of the victorious operations preceding it and that every army, which is being defeated in the fight-

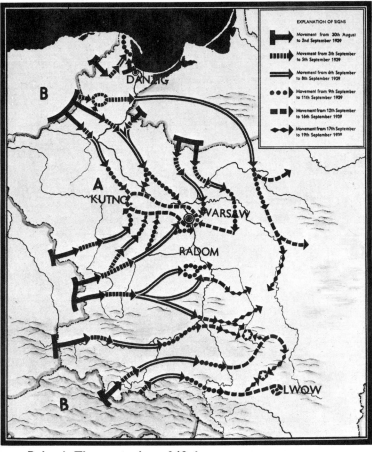

Poland: The campaign of 18 days

*In order to put a stop to Polish violence, the troops of the German Army, supported by strong
squadrons of the Air Force, marched to the counter-attack across all the German-Polish
frontiers on 1st September 1939. The intention was to liberate Danzig and to encircle and
annihilate by means of a large-scale outflanking movement the Polish army (A) concentrated in the bend of the Vistula. This plan was carried out in a connected series of battles
of annihilation the most decisive of which was at Kutno and on the Bzura. Not one of
the Polish divisions and independent brigades escaped being either completely destroyed or
taken prisoner. The help promised by the British did not arrive. Whilst the battle in
the bend of the Vistula sealed the fate of the Polish army, two other great German
outflanking armies coming from East Prussia and Galicia (B) established contact east
of the Vistula. Warsaw was simultaneously encircled and capitulated on 27th September.
The campaign in Poland had thus been brought to a close for all practical purposes and the enemy's plan of encirclement shattered by Germany's bold operations*

For the first time in the history of warfare

*One of the most exciting questions on the outbreak of war was that concerning new weapons and new
methods of fighting. The whole world had continued arming for 20 years. Only Germany, after complete
disarmament, had had the short space of 5 years in which to build up her Armed Forces anew. It was
one of the biggest surprises experienced by her enemies that she had employed that time and her opportunities better than had ever been suspected. The heroic march of the tanks began in the Polish campaign
and already in France became a triumphal procession. In conjunction with them the tank grenadiers,
the tank infantrymen, who later were to win such renown, and the assault guns made their début. Airborne
troops and parachutists (picture on right) were used in the extreme north of Norway in large-scale
operations for the first time. These were followed by the bold attacks on Eben Emael and Rotterdam.
The leap on to the Peloponnese and across to Crete were particulary successful and glorious achieve-
ments by these newly created units. In the technique and organization of new weapons as well
as in their strategic and tactical development, Germany had everywhere outstripped her opponents*

PK. Photograph: Front Correspondent Trapp

ing, very soon sees its advantage in
clinging to the ground and holding up
the enemy's superior attacks by positional warfare.

Overestimating their own strength
and expecting rapid help from the
Allies, believing probably also that
strong German forces would be tied
down in the west, the Polish Supreme
Command intended to adopt the offensive "at least to a certain degree," occupy Danzig and attack East Prussia
from three sides. The strongest Polish
army was concentrated in the Poznan
area. It was to launch a flank attack
against any German offensive aimed
at the Corridor or coming from Silesia.
This, too, was a plan of offensive warfare although based upon a defensive
idea.

It was the Führer's aim "to encircle,
attack and annihilate the vast Polish
army concentrated in the bend of the

Vistula." In a series of connected
battles the fate of the Polish army,
and consequently also of the whole
campaign, was sealed for all practical
purposes after only 8 days.

The defeat of the Polish army in the
Corridor was followed a few days later
by the encirclement of retreating Polish troops at Radom. In the meantime,
a German tank spearhead had pushed
forward as far as the gates of Warsaw
thus cutting off the retreat across the
Vistula of the enemy forces falling back
from Poznań and the Corridor. In
many places the Polish troops had believed that the British were coming to
their aid, yet it had always been German troops who had already penetrated
into their rear. The Polish divisions,
continually more and more hemmed in
by incessant attacks, attempted, by
launching desperate counter-attacks
at various places, to break the ring sur-

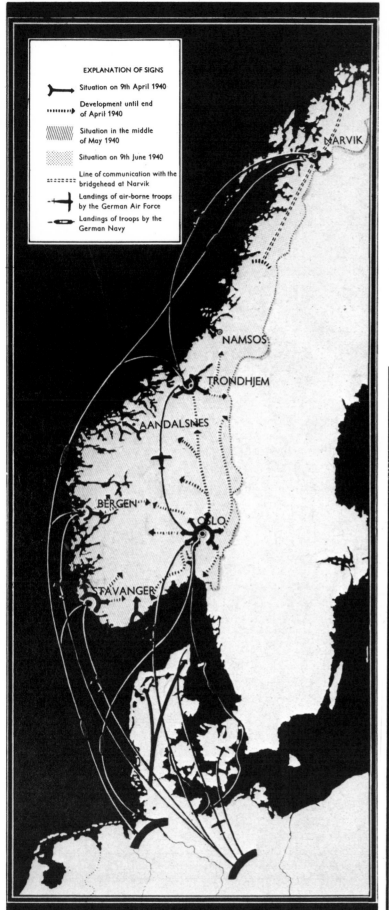

Norway: The protection of the northern flank

The projected occupation of Norway by an Anglo-French Expeditionary Corps was opposed by the German Armed Forces at the very last moment. The operations were carried out by the land, sea and air arms in unique co-operation. The brunt of the first landing was borne by the German Navy which carried out the transport of the troops and together with the Air Force provided protection against an enemy far superior at sea. Whilst in the fighting on land the enemy's resistance was everywhere broken in a short time and the British troops landed at Namsos and Aandalsnes were either forced to flee or were captured, the German Navy and Air Force inflicted very heavy losses on the enemy fleet. By 6th May Southern and Central Norway were in the firm hold of the Germans. The fight for Narvik, which after some time was also concluded victoriously, can never be forgotten. — The flank was protected, the fighting in the west began

SUCCESSFUL STRATEGY

rounding them at Kutno and on the Bzura. But the steadfastness of the German divisions now stood up to the test just as successfully as their attacking powers had previously answered every call made upon them. A five or sixfold numerically superior force consisting of four Polish divisions and a number of cavalry units attacked a single German division holding a line nearly 20 miles long. In spite of the excessive fatigue of the troops, this division held up the attack, threw back the enemy, in some places in severe hand-to-hand fighting, and neither wavered nor withdrew until the necessary reinforcements had been brought up. In the meantime, two other armies executing large-scale enveloping movements from East Prussia and Galicia had established contact, thereby completing the final encircle-

France: Attaque brusquée

Whilst the Polish nation was shedding its blood, France, heavily armed and placing her confidence in the Maginot Line, was standing ready. The plan of attacking the Ruhr district, to which Holland and Belgium opened their frontiers, came too late. On 10th May the northern wing of the German Army launched its attack, captured the key position of Eben Emael, penetrated the Dyle position south of Louvain on 16th May and, taking the enemy completely by surprise, broke through the extension of the Maginot Line on a front 60 miles wide, the main thrust being directed through the Ardennes. In a bold manœuvre and in entire disregard of the flank, the Channel coast was reached at Abbeville on 21st May. The enemy forces were thus split into two parts. Belgium capitulated on 27th May. Dunkirk meant the end of the British and French troops in Flanders. (Map on right.) The second phase of the operations began on 5th June. The Weygand Line collapsed. Paris was occupied on 14th June and Verdun, where both sides suffered heavy losses in the Great War, fell on the 15th. Whilst the thrust towards the south was carried across the Loire and towards the southeast was pushed as far as the Swiss frontier, the Maginot Line in the east was carried by storm. The armies in Alsace and Lorraine were forced to capitulate. The pursuit was concluded by the armistice of 21st June. The conditions on which the enemy's war plan depended were no longer present, the ring round Germany had also been broken in the west. (Map below)

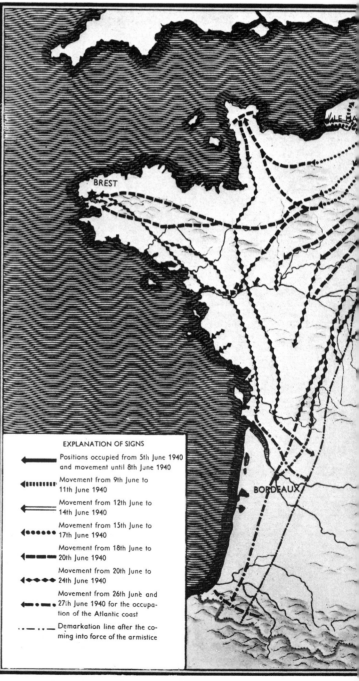

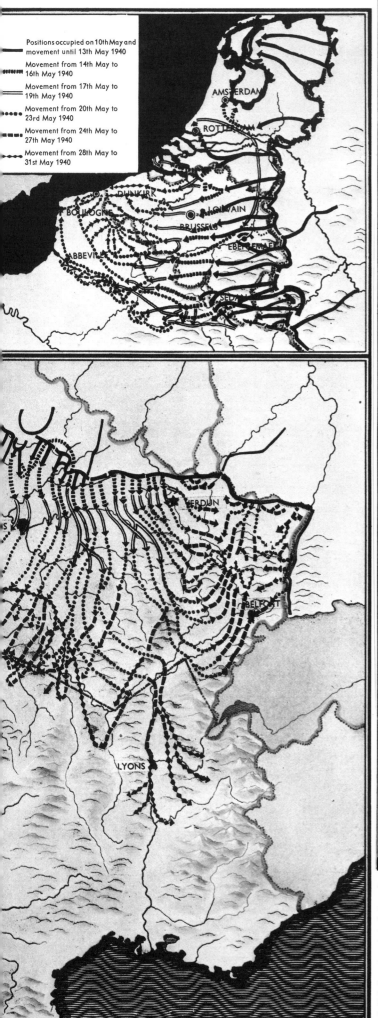

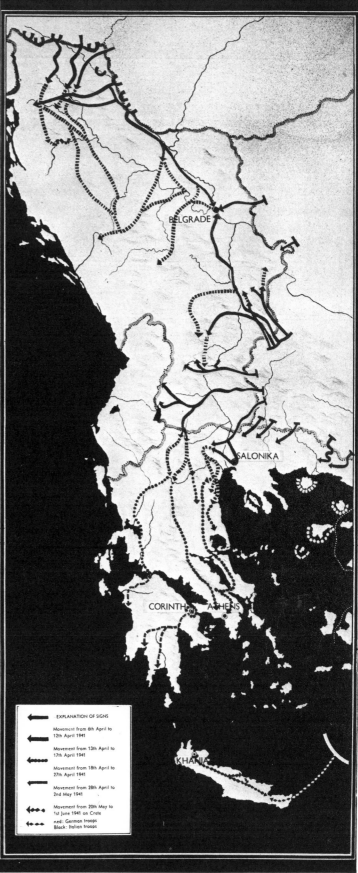

The Balkans: The British flee for the third time

Almost exactly a year after the campaign in Norway, the German Armed Forces also anticipated the enemy in the southeast in order to protect the threatened flank. On 6th April 1941, side by side with Italian troops who had already demonstrated their comradeship in France, German troops crossed the frontiers of the states which had been driven into the war by Britain and some of which were also supported by the Soviet Union. The Greek Eastern Army capitulated after three days. Belgrade was taken on 13th April 1941. On the 17th Yugoslavia had ceased to exist. Australians and New Zealanders were forced to maintain a pretence of help in Greece. They fled when the situation became dangerous. Athens was occupied on 27th April, the operations on the Peloponnese were concluded by 2nd May by the impetuously attacking German and Italian soldiers. German parachutists and airborne troops supported by Italian formations occupied Greece. Germany and her allies now had a free hand against the danger increasingly threatening them from the east

ment of the Poles in the area east of the Vistula and isolating Warsaw. The attack on the fortified city commenced on 25th September and ended with its surrender on the 27th. With 120,000 men the Poles had not dared to make a bold sortie as the German General Litzmann had done in the Great War with far inferior forces at Brzeziny. The Allies had lost fifty divisions. 720,000 Poles were taken prisoner, the remainder had either fled or run straight into the arms of the Russians who by agreement had occupied Poland as far as the Bug. At the conclusion of the campaign, the Führer affirmed that "the German soldier has again placed securely on his brow the crown of laurels of which he was cheated in 1918."

The boldest deed in history

It was a typical British statement that was made by the Minister of Information, Duff Cooper, when he said that Britain must tell the neutrals what she demanded and what part each of them had to play in the alliance aiming at Germany's annihilation. If one of the neutral states should show any signs of hesitation, he continued, the British should take steps to ensure that it was immediately overcome. When these words were pronounced, Great Britain had already shown her preparedness for action, in the case of the "Altmark," by laying mines in Norwegian territorial waters, and on 6th April, by embarking an expeditionary force of British and French troops for the occupation of Norway. But it was already too late.

The German Government, which had got to know of the attack planned by the British, anticipated them by eight hours in order to protect Norway against Britain's coup de main. Denmark, too, had to be protected and occupied. A foothold was established from the sea at six points on the 2,125 mile long, rugged, Norwegian coast. These landings were supplemented at some places by airborne troops. Although Britain had already incited the Norwegian troops, the local resistance was quickly overcome and a stream of German reinforcements was soon flowing through Oslo.

When London received news of Germany's counter-action, the convoys were recalled, the intention being that the battle fleet should deal the German operations a decisive blow. As early as the afternoon of 9th April, four British battleships and five cruisers were seriously damaged by the German Air Force and the fleet forced to withdraw. Churchill spoke to his countrymen of a continuous day and night naval battle in the Kattegat and Skagerrak, but the truth soon became known. "Britain is faced with a difficult task if she is to throw the Germans out again. Hitler's tactics have worked according to plan," was the commentary of a London newspaper. The British nevertheless landed troops on Norwegian soil on both sides of Trondhjem, at Namsos and Aandalsnes.

From the "Daily Herald" of 9th April 1940

"Hand across the sea"—published the day on which the German Armed Forces landed in Norway

But that, too, was soon to prove a failure.

The Oslo region first had to be mopped up before the Germans proceeded to the attack against the Norwegians assembling north of Oslo and the British who had meanwhile appeared at Aandalsnes.

Mountain operations more than any others are centred round important places. The great valley connexions Hamar-Stören (Østerdal), Lillehammer-Dombaas (Gudbrandsdal), and Drammen-Bergen (Hallingdal) now played the most important part. Whilst the first two of these mountain valleys run almost parallel in a northerly and northwesterly direction respectively, thus enabling a uniform plan of operations to be carried out, a special force had to be diverted along the Hallingdal.

North of Hamar and near Lillehammer, the enemy was thrown back from 22nd to 25th April. It was here, too, that the first British prisoners were made and important documents found on them which provided an abundance of information regarding the British plans. The retreating enemy was pursued without pause and only a few days later the fighting in the Röros-Dombaas sector and at Stören was brought to a victorious conclusion by the German troops. The actual course taken by the operations and the localities in which the fighting chanced to occur were of less importance than the determination of the German Command to establish contact with the enemy, particularly the British, and deal him a decisive blow. These efforts were crowned with success. In their hasty retreat, the British were obliged to abandon Stören and Dombaas, and subsequently also Aandalsnes and Namsos.

Particularly the German Alpine troops, which fought out the heroic struggle at Narvik, covered themselves with glory. Shoulder to shoulder with them fought the marines belonging to a squadron of destroyers which had been put out of action by enemy shell fire.

The extremely bold attacks of the German Air Force had inflicted heavy losses on the enemy fleet. Britain lost more than 60 warships, whilst twice as many other war units and 7 battleships were damaged. For the first time she had suffered a considerable defeat at sea and a permanent disadvantage for her naval supremacy had been revealed in the fact that battleships no longer have to fight only against battleships but also against the enemy Air Force which, particularly in narrow seas, sometimes plays a decisive part.

A factor typical for the further course of the war was that the Führer had introduced a new element into naval strategy. It was certainly unprecedented for the side which was weaker at sea to carry out a landing operation literally under the very nose of an enemy at least six times superior in naval strength. The Norwegian Campaign was justifiably called the "boldest deed in history."

Contrary to the Schlieffen plan

As long as France could speak to disarmed Germany in a tone of superiority, her governments had found everything quite easy. As soon as the Führer called upon the German people to reassert themselves and broke the shackles of Versailles, the whole structure of France's power began to sway. The French Government could not lay any very great military burden on the country, for the people did not want a second war against Germany.

In the declaration of war on Germany of 3rd September 1939 France had said that she "feels herself obliged to support Poland." The necessary consequence would presumably have been an offensive blow by the French armies, but France had no war aim to justify decisions of any great boldness. The many urgent peace proposals made by the Führer had not remained unheard on the other side of the frontier and the desire to overthrow Germany did not spring from the French people. And then—after all, France had her Maginot Line. Its importance for the country's security, in view of the vast expenditure it had involved, had been continually drummed into the broad masses.

A particularly vulnerable factor was that Britain had sent only 10 divisions to the Continent, just enough to cheer the French up. Plans for an offensive were nevertheless ventilated. The first plan was for an attack on Germany from the southeast to be carried out with troops from Syria and Egypt together with the hoped for 60 Balkan divisions. But the example of Poland had frightened all the small states. Finally it was thought that an attack on the Ruhr would be best after all. Germany had to anticipate this danger on 10th May 1940.

Only now, at the beginning of the 9th month of war, did that already legendary "attaque brusquée" take place which Weygand, Debeney and many other French generals had expected Germany to make on the outbreak of war. In an amazingly original manner it was directed against the individual fortresses forming the frontier fortifications of Holland and Belgium, who had both opened their countries to French and British forces.

The Belgian fortresses on the Albert Canal and the strongest fort of the fortress of Liége, Eben-Emael, were at once taken and the line held by the Dutch penetrated. French mechanized and motorized divisions were already approaching but were only able to attack the German tanks on the Gette to the southeast of Louvain. Remembering the words of a Prussian Chief of the General Staff, Count Schlieffen: "Make the right wing as strong as you can," the Allied High Command concentrated their forces on the Dyle. In the meantime, the Dutch had been cut off and capitulated on 15th May. Already on the following day the German attack penetrated the Dyle position south of Louvain making a further retreat necessary.

As surprise is always the greatest factor in strategy, the Führer had directed the powerful tank thrust through the Ardennes contrary to the Schlieffen Plan. That was what the enemy were least expecting. The French 9th Army, which consisted entirely of old troops, held a widely spread out position at Sedan on the Meuse. "The Germans are heading straight for destruction," was the opinion held in Paris, but already the French front had begun to waver. On the 16th, the prolonged Maginot Line was penetrated along a front 60 miles wide.

"The flood of mechanized and motorized German divisions must be held up," Gamelin ordered, but his last hour had already struck. His place was taken by Weygand, of whom Foch had said: "If France is in need, take him." Paris issued instructions that "the method of trench warfare is to be abandoned and replaced by mobile warfare in the open field." This mobile warfare had spelt disaster to Poland and the French General Staff was not going to be able to master it.

Everybody was convinced that Germany, being financially poor, could not fight a modern war: "The mechanical war of 1940 differs from that of 1914 by reason of the fact that it is much more costly and that Germany is much poorer than she was 26 years ago."

By 21st May the German Tank Corps had completely torn open the enemy front and reached the Channel coast near Abbeville. British, Belgians and a part of the French were encircled in Flanders all round Dunkirk. On the 22nd, Churchill and the British General Dill arrived at the French H. Q. Weygand demanded of the British a decisive breakthrough attack via Cambrai, whilst he offered to send a French army from the south to attack the German offensive position at Amiens. Both operations were carried out, but were unsuccessful. Suddenly the British Commander-in-Chief in Flanders, General Gort, declared that he had run out of ammunition and withdrew his tanks on Dunkirk. French objections were in vain, all Churchill's promises, as so often, had faded into nothing and even the last urgent appeal made by the French for aeroplanes fell on deaf ears in London. The military connexion between the British and the French had been broken. That was the great success of the German victory in Flanders.

The Belgians capitulated on 27th May, the British fled from Dunkirk to escape from the clutches of the Germans. On 4th June the greatest battle of annihilation of all time was over. It ended with the capture of 1.2 million prisoners and inestimable quantities of war material including almost all the equipment of the British. Its second great effect, the capitulation of the French, who had been left in the lurch by their British allies, occurred soon after.

On 5th June, the German troops

From the "News Chronicle" of 7th May 1940

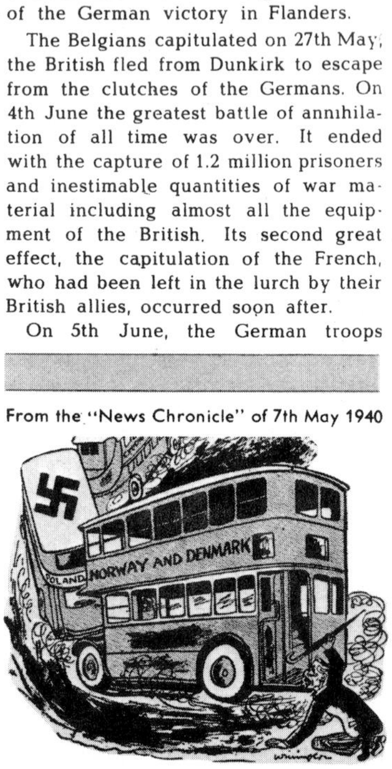

"Whatever may be the reason—whether it was that Hitler thought he might get away with what he had got without fighting for it, or whether it was that after all the preparations were not sufficiently complete—however, one thing is certain: he missed the 'bus."—Mr. Chamberlain, addressing the Central Council of the National Union of Conservative and Unionist Associations on 4th April 1940. This appeared four weeks later, after the campaign in Norway

An unforgettable picture symbolic of this war:

A bridge of lorries made by the British to their ships at Dunkirk, the bridge of their great flight from Europe where one after another they left their allies and mercenaries in the lurch—Poland, Norway, Holland, Belgium, France, Yugoslavia, Greece and, finally, the Soviet Union   PK. Photograph: Front Correspondent Schmidt

launched the attack on the "Weygand Line" on the Somme and the Aisne. Even on the following day the French thought they could report a successful resistance, but their front had again been penetrated by 7th June. The battle now quickly extended to a breadth of over 200 miles from the Channel coast to the Meuse. The German troops marched into Paris on the morning of 14th June and Verdun fell the next day.

In 1916, German guns had rained down 1,350,000 tons of steel on Verdun. The laborious storming of 3 outlying forts and the gain of a few miles of ground, of which a part immediately had to be abandoned again, was the result of one of the most terrible battles of material of the first World War. This time, however, thanks to the superior strategy and excellent equipment of the German Army, this extremely strong French fortress, which had been thoroughly modernized, was taken in a very short time.

From Paris the German wedges were pushed forward in a south and southeasterly direction towards the Loire and through Burgundy to the Swiss frontier. But the Maginot Line, which was considered by the French to be impregnable was also captured as well as all the big fortresses behind it. Three French armies, which had fought in Alsace and Lorraine, were encircled and forced to capitulate. Whilst in the rest of France the dispersed masses of the enemy were fleeing towards the south and south-west, the French requested an armistice on 17th June. It came into force on 21st June in Compiègne, the place where the armistice had also been concluded in 1918. On that occasion, however, the United States President, Wilson made promises which were later ruthlessly pushed on one side by the French.

A vital artery severed

It had always been Adolf Hitler's great strategic aim to prevent Germany from being encircled. Poland no longer existed, the Maginot Line had been broken, and now Britain's naval supremacy was to be restricted. The military occupation of the European coastline from the North Cape to the Bay of Biscay had created the conditions necessary for a large-scale U-boat war against Britain. As early as the end of 1940 there could scarcely be any more doubt on the subject and the United States, too, were of the opinion that Britain could no longer hold out alone.

The Campaign in France had brought the young Italian Imperium into the war. Its active participation on Ger-

many's side meant a considerable step forward on the road to the unification of Europe in the struggle against Britain and later, too, against Bolshevism. On entering the war, however, Italy had to reckon with the temporary loss of her possessions in East Africa which in spite of an extremely courageous defence could not be held against the superior British forces there. Libya too, was seriously threatened at times, but the British were finally driven far back towards Egypt by the combined forces of the allied powers.

The fact that the Mediterranean had ceased to serve as an unobstructed transit road for Great Britain was of the greatest importance, for the enemies of

the Axis now had to split up their naval strength. At the same time, the detour round Africa which had become necessary placed extra demands on their merchant shipping equivalent to one third.

Churchill looks for helpers

In the struggle against Italy and for the protection of the Eastern Mediterranean, Churchill required the Greek peninsula. He reduced Greece to a state of dependence at the end of 1940. The British Prime Minister now matured the plan, which had already so often been discussed, of carrying out an attack against Germany from the Balkans, at the same time looking out for prospects of Russian help. He, too, counted on at least 60 Balkan divisions as Gamelin had done in his project early in 1940, which Roosevelt had warmly commended through Colonel Donovan.

The Greeks demanded Yugoslavia's participation. A military pyramid was to be built having its base on the Aegean Sea and in Greece and its apex in the Yugoslav capital. The weakness of this initial position was revealed when the German attack suddenly and irresistibly bored into the base of this strategic structure from the flank in spite of the great difficulties of the terrain.

Before the commencement of the operations Belgrade had been very thoughtful, for the strategic calculations also had to take account of political factors. Germany was fighting along the interior line and could concentrate her strength. In opposition to the Reich, Yugoslavia held one of the exterior lines, which might easily result in her finding herself alone. Yet the French influence exercised for many years won the day, and perhaps the memory of the Salonika offensive in 1918 also played a part, for to it the Serbs owed the re-establishment and extension of their State. The feelings of the incited population could not be kept within predetermined limits as British emissa-

ries and Russian influences swayed the masses. General Simović, who was prepared to resort to extreme measures, took over the Government, yet the German Army once more acted quicker than its opponents.

The German operations began on 6th April. Only three days later Kosovo Polje had been reached, Salonika taken and the Greek Eastern Army cut off in Thrace. Belgrade was reached on the 14th and Croatia's independence proclaimed in Zagreb. The whole of the Serbian Army capitulated on 17th April. Churchill reproached the Serbs for having asked for help too late. But he had driven them into the war. Just as in Poland, Britain was to a very great extent responsible for Serbia's defeat, for without Britain's promises of help this Balkan war would never have broken out.

In the meantime Australians and New Zealanders, who everywhere bore the heaviest burden of the fighting for Britain had been sent to Greece from Africa, because after a few transitory successes in Libya it was thought they were no longer required there. The German Africa Corps, however, together with the Italians, soon dealt a counterblow in the Cyrenaica taking Derna on 7th April and Bardia and Sollum on the 14th.

When the German advance against Greece commenced shortly after, the British fled and the main body of the Greeks soon capitulated. The German troops entered Athens on 27th April and the peninsula was occupied as far as its southern extremity Italian troops played a successful part in the operations. Beaten and shipwrecked, a number of the British had returned to Alexandria, others together with some

Greek troops they had dragged off with them, established themselves on Crete. But even this 60 miles of sea offered the defeated enemy no protection, although nature, as in Norway, favoured the island's defence. German parachutists and airborne troops here carried out an achievement unparalleled up to then. The greater part of the enemy was annihilated after embittered fighting and the remainder again forced to flee. The losses of the Australians and New Zealanders amounted to 64 %, those of the British to only 25 %. The British Eastern Mediterranean Fleet had also been dealt heavy blows. The assurance given by Churchill on 7th May that Britain would defend Crete without thought of retreating had again proved to be empty bombast.

The Bolshevist danger

The eastern soul of the Soviet Russians proved as unfathomable as the wide spaces in the east and found its chief expression in a lack of sincerity.

The Soviet Russians had concluded pacts with the Reich in 1939, yet immediately afterwards the Komintern began a campaign of agitation directed against Germany. This was followed shortly afterwards by the attack on Finland, the occupation of the Baltic States, the Bukovina and Bessarabia. What had been said in 1936 was now repeated in 1941—the Army was prepared to fall upon the enemy on his own territory. Remarks passed shortly before by the Russian Commissar for Foreign Affairs, Molotov, on the occasion of his visit to Berlin, had revealed the Bolshevists' designs on the Balkans. On 5th April 1941, the Russians even concluded a pact of friendship with the Simovic Government in Belgrade, whose anti-German sentiments were well known, an agreement which was greeted with enthusiasm by Britain and the United States.

The massing of 150 Russian divisions at this time on the frontier of German territory spoke very plain language. No country has ever yet been able to ignore such a concentration of strength on its frontiers and the Führer could not do so either. Documents discovered soon afterwards revealed the aggressive intentions of the Russians. The arrows of Soviet Russian General Staff maps are illustrative of the tentacles of Bolshevism stretching out to clutch at Central Europe.

The Führer made his biggest and most difficult decision when he gave orders to begin the counterblow to the Soviet Russian menace on 22nd June 1941. Not until after comparison with the many lost opportunities in history does it stand out in powerful relief. A decision of such proportions could only be assumed by a statesman, who was able to foresee clearly the consequences it would have on events throughout the world, a statesman who was also the creator of his armed forces and knew exactly what he could expect of that unique instrument.

Strategy and battle tactics melted into one on the Eastern Front. From the very beginning the Russians had established a 950 mile long front extending from the Black Sea to the Gulf of Finland. One stone after another had to be broken out of the enemy's front, and thanks to the tremendous attacking power of the German thrusts, which continually bored deep into the enemy's flesh and encircled large sectors of the Soviet front, great successes were gained among which the victory at Bialystok and Minsk was especially prominent. The second phase of the hostilities was accompanied by the breach made in the Stalin Line and a number of other great battle victories, in August the great victories at Smolensk and Uman and then at Gomel and Velikie Luki, in September the vast battle at Kiev. But important successes were also gained in South Ukraine and on the Sea of Azov as well as on the northern sector of the Eastern Front, on Lake Ilmen, in the Baltic region and on the Volchov. The early and particularly severe winter brought to a standstill the victorious operations carried out with the co-operation of Germany's allies. Already in October 1941, the result of the four months' campaign amounted to 2½ million prisoners, 17,500 tanks, 21,600 guns and 14,200 planes.

The names and areas mentioned are those of battles unprecedented in history for their nature and their extent, each one of them a larger scale Tannenberg, but quite different from their predecessor in the Great War by reason of the shaping of the operations from which they proceeded. It must also be remembered that these battles were fought simultaneously in very different latitudes and often under extremely difficult conditions as far as space and distances were concerned. Together they form an unbroken series of victories won by the German Army.

The course of the war on the Eastern Front was different from the preceding campaign against France. It was necessary to become accustomed to that fact. The Soviets had created out of the 180 millions of their united republics an instrument which, as the fighting has since shown, could have endangered the whole of Europe, if the Führer had not recognized this menace in time.

The defeats suffered by the Russians were also inflicted on Churchill. He and his agent, Cripps, had contributed a great deal towards bringing the Bolshevists into the war. The German Foreign Office had obtained irrefutable proof of the intrigues of the British in Moscow. Now, too, on the Eastern Front, failure dogged the British Prime Minister. Churchill had predicted "blood and tears," when he, the warmonger par excellence, had taken office in May 1940. Since that time he had been compelled to add "mistakes and insufficiencies" in order to explain his failures. The alliance he concluded with the Russians on 12th July 1941 had not eased the pressure on them, Churchill was unable to establish the second front desired by Moscow. The German U-boat war waged against Britain's supply lines continued to take disastrous toll on the ships and already in the summer of 1941, Churchill found himself obliged to surrender himself body and soul to the President of the United States of America.

The prelude

Whilst the German Armed Forces put Poland out of action, protected the northern flank of the Reich by the operations in Norway and broke the ring in the west by overwhelming France, the Soviet Union slowly advanced against Europe by means of malicious separate actions and the exploitation of the various military crises. The first step was taken already during the last phase of the campaign in Poland. Soviet Russian troops marched into Poland and a demarcation line between the German and Soviet Russian spheres of interest was laid down on 22nd September 1939 (I). In the winter of 1939 to 1940 the Bolshevists invaded Finland and after a bitter struggle annexed Finnish territory (II). Coerced by Soviet Russian threats, Rumania was obliged to cede Bessarabia and North Bukovina on 28th June 1940 (III). Lithuania was incorporated into the U.S.S.R. on 3rd August (IV). Latvia and Estonia followed on 5th and 6th August respectively (V and VI). The huge assembly base for the march against Europe had been created. The attempt to incite Southeast Europe against Germany now followed, but was soon crushed by the Balkan campaign. The time was now ripe for Germany's counterblow which was to save Europe from the Bolshevist invasion

The struggle on the eastern front

On 22nd June 1941 the German Armed Forces together with their allies launched a counter-attack against Bolshevism. Three German thrusts penetrated deep into the massed enemy armies winning their first successes above all in the battle of Bialystok (A) and Minsk (B). The second phase began with the breach of the Stalin Line (C), which was followed by a series of battles of annihilation. This fighting was crowned by the number of prisoner taken at Kiev (665,000), a figure unique in history, whilst on 8th September the encirclement of Leningrad was completed by the fall of Schlüsselburg. On 2nd October the German Supreme Command dealt the third great blow of the year which was concluded in the main with the twin battles of Viasma (D) and Briansk (E) and the battle on the sea of Azov (F) as well as with the capture of Kharkov (G) on 24th October. In the meantime the brave Finnish people had liberated Karelia, which they had lost during the Winter War, and established a firm front on the Svir after embittered fighting. The early approach and the exceptional severity of the winter brought operations to a temporary standstill. The Bolshevists failed during the winter to smash the German front, the great German offensive of the year 1942 was prepared with the battles of Kerch (H) and Sevastopol (I). The Soviet Russian armies concentrated in the Ukraine for an offensive were meanwhile encircled and annihilated at Kharkov (G). The German and allied armies thereupon launched their attack, pushed forward to the Don and the Volga (in the direction of Stalingrad) and at the end of the third year of the war had reached the northern part of the Caucasus. The colours of the Reich were hoisted on the Elbrus (K) on 21st August. Side by side with Germany her allies are fighting: Italy, Rumania, Finland, Hungary, Slovakia and Croatia, together with volunteer units composed of Spaniards, Frenchmen, Danes, Norwegians, Dutchmen and Belgians. Recently volunteer formations of liberated Lithuanians, Letts, Estonians, Ukrainians and Tartars have joined in the common European defensive front

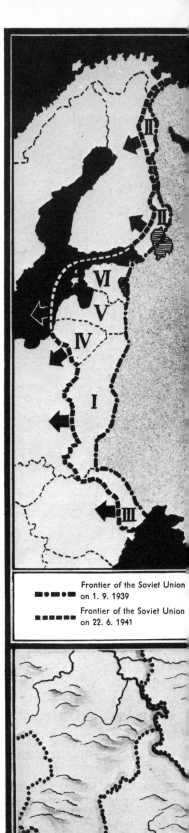

Frontier of the Soviet Union on 1. 9. 1939

Frontier of the Soviet Union on 22. 6. 1941

EXPLANATION OF SIGNS

Situation until the commencement of July 19

Situation until the end of September 1941

Situation until April 1942

Situation until the end of August 1942

Stalin-Line

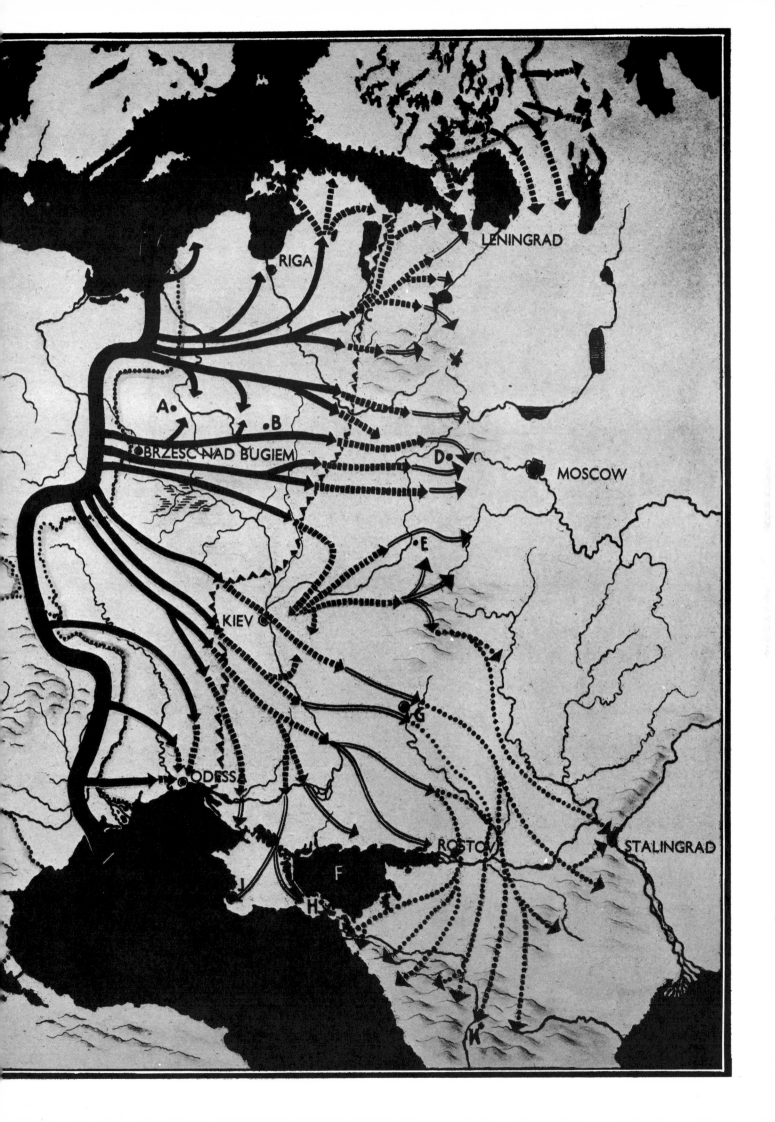

THE WAR WITH RUSSIA

Operation Barbarossa, the German attack on the Soviet Union, was the most ambitious assault ever planned by the High Command. It was to be the ultimate in blitzkrieg warfare, designed to last three to four months at most. It was Hitler's final blitzkrieg. Neither short nor ultimately victorious, the campaign in Russia broke the power of Nazi Germany and destroyed it. Nevertheless, the first months of the campaign which began in the early morning hours of 22 June 1941 seemed to go well, and *Signal*'s reporters and cameramen were there to publicize it. The Wehrmacht encountered little opposition initially, and what appeared to be a walk-over ground to a halt after the Ukraine was largely overrun and Nazi troops stood before the gates of Moscow and Leningrad. Many Soviet citizens in the first days of the fighting, particularly in the Ukraine, greeted the Nazis as liberators from the Communist yoke, but their cheers quickly died away as Hitler's dreams of an Aryan Empire in the East were put into practice. The euphoria created by the Soviet withdrawal was obvious, and *Signal* captured the mood perfectly, but as the advance slowed, stories and photographs of the first weeks continued to re-appear, and the Soviet counteroffensive before Moscow as well as the failure of the Wehrmacht to take Leningrad were not reported. By 1942 the difficulty in defeating Russia was acknowledged, but the international aspect of the Nazi fighting on behalf of Europe against a cruel and semi-barbaric foe was stressed. The Waffen SS, which took an increasingly important role in 1942 and after, was actually an international army which drew much of its strength from foreign volunteers which eventually numbered more than one million. The Spanish Blue Division, though perhaps the most famous of the foreign legions, was not actually part of the Waffen SS, but the Charlemagne Division from France and the relatively large contingents from Flanders, Holland, Wallonia, Finland and virtually every Eastern European state certainly were. The Wehrmacht, which was the publisher of *Signal* under the auspices of the PK, was not enthusiastic about the manner in which the Waffen SS usurped the role of the Army, but the presence of foreigners in the Waffen SS, unlike the Army itself, was an extremely useful propaganda tool which *Signal* put to increasingly good use once the victories in the East became fewer and more disparate. Nevertheless, the German advance in the late spring and summer of 1942, particularly in the Ukraine and the Caucasus, gave *Signal* something to shout about once more. In many respects it was *Signal*'s, and Nazi Germany's last hurrah. *Signal* began to publicize the expected victory at Stalingrad in the October and November issues of the magazine in 1942, but again, as in the Western Desert or over Britain, the stories ceased to appear. Goebbels made the decision, after a long silence, to admit openly that Germany had suffered a monumental defeat at Stalingrad months after the battle was over, and from then on *Signal*'s 'victories' were imaginary, and the subtle mixture of truth and fantasy gave way to a presentation of a coarse blend of wishful thinking and outright lie. *Signal*'s years of triumphs were over, once Germany went on the permanent defensive. Hitler's years of retreat and disaster had begun.

The Capture of Kishinev by Assault

PK. Hubmann reports for the "Signal" the German-Rumanian assault on the burning capital of Bessarabia

Our correspondent writes: "We were fiv miles from Kishinev. A menacing black colum of smoke rises from the burning capita as the vanguard of the Rumanian troops, wit whom I am, drives into a village which had jus been evacuated by the Russians. We were gree ed with enthusiastic shouts of 'Heil Hitler' the inhabitants kiss our hands and embrace us

"I am a German airman!"

"A young peasant hurries out towards us from a farmyard shouting: 'Hallo comrades, here you are at last!' . . . and turns out to be not a farmer, but a German sergeant-major who four days previously had had to make a forced landing on Russian territory, 50 miles from the German lines, while flying a dive bomber. He set his plane on fire and fled into the woods. After three days of strenuous walking in the direction of the German lines, he met a Rumanian farmer and his wife. The farmer was able to speak a little German which he had learned during the Great War. The farmer's wife brought clothing, food and drink to the German airman in his place of hiding in the woods."

"While smoking his first cigarette he relates his adventures. Seated beside him is the captain of a Rumanian propaganda company"

"The men of the vanguard of the Rumanian tanks impatiently await the order to attack"

Two and one half miles from the capital

"The major in command of the advance guard (in the command car) is being informed of the position of the Soviet troops. He decides to send motorcycle riflemen and tanks to reconnoitre. I am permitted to accompany them in the foremost tank.

"As dusk was falling the Rumanian infantry combed the fields on both sides of the road"

"With the burning city in front of us, we lay down with our Rumanian comrades at a well for a short night's rest"

"In front of us are a few motorcycle riflemen, behind us follows another tank and some additional motorcycle riflemen. In this order we drove up the hill. Shortly before reaching the top we were greeted by murderous enemy fire. The Soviet artillery had previously got the range of the road we were on. In addition, anti-tank guns raked our tanks, and machine-guns took the riflemen under fire. Like a flash our riflemen dismounted and returned the fire. Our tank drove forward at top speed continually stopping to fire at the anti-tank guns. The latter's fire missed us, usually by a narrow margin, but a few times we were severely hit. After a hundred yards our tank was brought to a halt by a direct hit more serious than the others. We made preparations for close combat fighting and held our hand grenades ready for use. The Soviet artillery withdrew, however, because they believed there were many more tanks advancing behind us"

At 50. m.p.h. the car crosses the vast plain stretching beyond the south-eastern frontier of the Government General. The roads here, re-paired by the Germans, are in perfect condition. We started out on our journey through the barren wastes into the unknown from Luck on the Styr

The road to the front

The tour we made of the eastern front with PK. Artur Grimm, "Signal's" front correspondent, began at the frontiers of the Government General. Leaving these peaceful districts behind them, the foremost German lines have advanced hundreds of miles during the weeks of bitter fighting. In the short space of three days we were able to take a number of unique pictures

In conversatio

When, after his work is completed, the Führer gives free rein to his thoughts and talks, these are the most beautiful hours for his closest collaborators. Drawing upon his limitless store of recollections, he tells the merriest anecdotes and the most delightful stories. Whenever he touches on a subject, which seems to him worth dwelling upon, he sketches his ideas in a lively manner, delves deeply into the past and develops his creative and far-reaching ideas for the future

with the German Minister for Foreign Affairs

A series of photographs from Headquarters

German
infantry on the march

The marvellous marching feats of the German infantry — as much as 45 miles on some days — have brought London's optimistic hopes crashing to the ground. The endless Russian landscape is not beyond the powers of the German soldier. The melancholy of the apparently interminable plains, the oppressive expanse of the Russian sky, fatigue and heavy fighting, nothing can break the determination with which the German soldier forces his way forward   Photograph: PK. Bauer

In the granary of the Soviet Union

Infantry combing a field of maize, a type of terrain just as treacherous as woodland

PK. Photographs: Front Correspondent A. Grimm

We capture a bridge

A two day tank battle for a railway bridge

REPORTED BY PK. ARTHUR GRIMM

The double track railway line from Przemysl to Kiev via Lwów crosses the River Goryn at Brodov 10 miles north of Ostrog. Our tank division had been ordered to capture this bridge intact and to form a bridge-head. The execution of this order took 2 days of incessant and heavy fighting. The whole region to the north of Ostrog was occupied by strong enemy forces. On the morning of the appointed day, our tank division went forward to the attack at 3 a.m. This surprise was successful. The greatly superior enemy was unable to cope with the combination of tanks, infantry, and A.A. artillery. After 2 days of hard fighting we had carried out our task, and the German advance moved forward irresistibly across the captured bridge.

He thinks for all of us. *On his maps our commander marks in the order to storm the railway bridge. Speaking through the microphone hanging round his neck, he issues his orders by means of a short-wave transmitter. The action begins.*

The first day

The Soviets know what they are up against. *Our advance has scarcely begun when a Soviet reconnaissance plane appears over our heads. He gives warning that we are on the move*

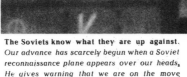

The enemy opens fire immediately. *The infantrymen we are taking forward with us are perched on our tanks. The enemy tries to hold up our advance with harrassing fire, but irresistibly we tear along with our unusual passengers*

A rocket: the enemy attacks. *Our advance guard and scouts send up rockets. They tell us the enemy tanks are coming now. We have already captured a defended village . . .*

. . . and now we attack in various directions! *Whilst our A. A. artillery takes under fire the tanks, which are still about a mile in front of us, our own tanks make wide detours to attack from the flank and fall upon the Soviet tanks which are already near. The foremost Soviet tank twice covers us with showers of earth. Our third shell is fatal*

Calmness personified — the gunner. *During this engagement I succeeded in taking an unusual photograph; I snapped our observer and the gunner during the engagement. With a calm hand he transfers the ranges given to him on to the aiming apparatus*

Two worlds

The Soviet troops set the houses of their "comrades" on fire before they abandon the towns and villages to the advancing German troops

Immediately after the occupation of a town, the German soldiers set about saving the dwellings of the population from the flames
Photographs: PK. Göhring

Vitebsk, just one example

Always when the Soviets have finally lost a position, the sign of their defeat is that they set the place on fire. The fugitives enter the burning towns with the German soldiers and wander among the ruins seeking to save what is still left
Photograph: PK. Wundshammer

The end of Smolensk

A German car equipped with a loud speaker drives into the blazing city. The last Soviet soldiers hiding in the cellars of the burning houses are called upon to surrender by means of the loudspeaker. Not until the car has finished its patrol does the work of clearing the town of the enemy begin
Photograph: PK. Bohnes

KHARKOV

In the sector under the command of General Field Marshal von Bock, it was the armies under Colonel-General von Kleist and General Paulus of the Tank Corps and the Rumanian divisions commanded by General Corneliu Dragalina which, together with Hungarian, Italian, Croatian and Slovakian units, held up the desperate large scale attacks of the Soviets, smashed them and then themselves launched counter-attacks. An offensive with very ambitious aims had ended not only in defeat, but in an annihilating collapse of all the Soviet armies engaged. The victorious conclusion of the Battle of Kharkov wrecked the great hopes of the Bolshevists of finally being able to take the initiative after ten months of fighting. The second spring battle of the year also revealed to the world the unbroken strength of the German Fighting Forces and their Allies.

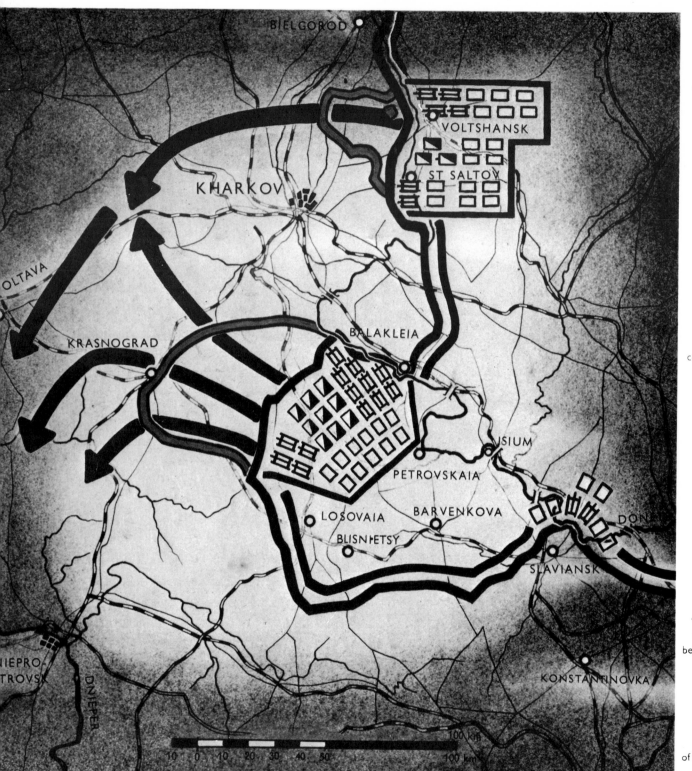

The Soviet plan
of offence

Soviet
tank brigade

Soviet
cavalry division

Soviet
rifle division

Position
of the Germans
and their Allies
before the offensive

Position
at the collapse
of the Soviet offensi

The aim of the great Soviet offensive in May 1942 was the annihilation of the German forces in the Kharkov area by encircling them from both sides. After capturing the most important industrial areas round Kharkov, the enemy intended, by pushing forward to the Dnieper, to bring about a collapse of the southern part of the Eastern Front. For that purpose, Timoshenko had concentrated the main part of his forces with numerous tank brigades and cavalry divisions in the sector of the front to the west of Isium. A further strong attacking group with mobile units was being held ready in the area round St Saltov and Voltshansk. On 12th May the large scale attack of the Soviets to the south and to the north-east of Kharkov began simultaneously. After intensive artillery bombardment, hundreds of enemy tanks in the front line advanced towards the German positions. The mass attacks lasted for five days. The fortunes of battle favoured now the one side, now the other. At terribly heavy loss, the enemy was able to penetrate into the positions at various places, in other sectors the German troops were systematically withdrawn to more favourable defensive positions. By 16th May already, it was clear that Timoshenko could not gain any operational success. By that date he had already lost more than 250 tanks, many of which were of British construction. The attacks were continued for a few days, it is true, but they diminished in vigour and began to be carried out increasingly without method. The German command had meanwhile completed all necessary counter-measures. The Führer's plan of operations did not provide for a strengthening of the defence, but by a bold counter-offensive aimed at annihilating the mass of the enemy's forces

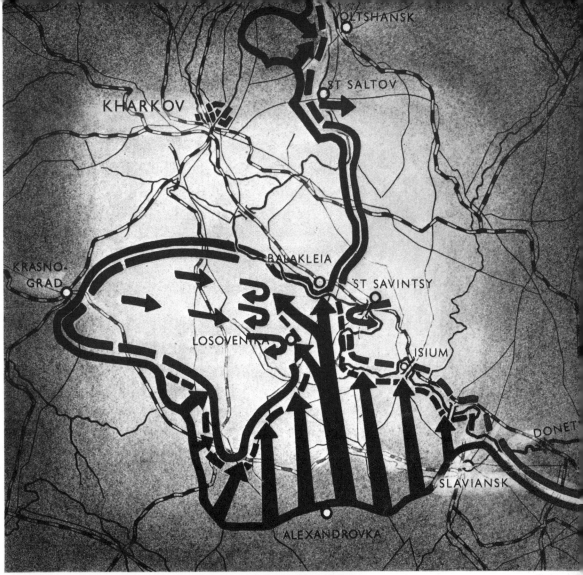

The German counter-offensive was launched as early as the sixth day of the enemy's big offensive. The rapid concentration of the attacking forces, the determining of the objectives and the co-operation between the Army and the Air Force represent a masterly achievement of the German Command. The collaboration with the Rumanian commanders and those of the other allies was also perfectly smooth in every way. On 17th May mobile units pushed forward towards the north from the Slaviansk-Alexandrovka area. On the second day of the attack, tank units had already thrust 40 kilometres deep into the enemy. The Donets was reached between the area north of Slaviansk and south of Isium. The most important decision in the battle came on 22nd May. On that day tank units pushed forward to a point south of Balakleia and joined up with the German troops there. Three Soviet armies were thus encircled. The attempts to break out of the pocket, launched for the most part at Losovenika, were embittered and desperate. Rifle divisions and tank units vainly attacked from the east in the Savintsy sector with the object of breaking through the German barrier. But it came too late to save them. For not until 21st May, that is to say one day before the circle was closed, did Timoshenko discontinue his offensive. The main part of his forces was still on the front to the south of Kharkov at that time and attempting in vain to escape across the Donets towards the south-east. In the sector to the north-east of Kharkov, the enemy was also repulsed and the old front re-established by the attack of German tank and infantry units. Here Slovakian troops also successfully drove back Soviet counter-attacks

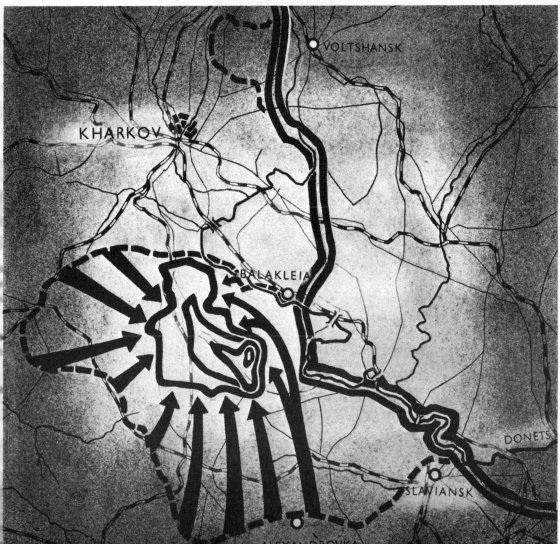

⭕ The narrowing of the pocket between 24th and 27th May

▪▪▪ Position before the beginning of the attack

▬▬ Position after the battle

On 23rd May the concentric attacks of German and Rumanian divisions began with the object of narrowing the pocket and annihilating the encircled enemy. Hungarian, Italian and Croatian units also participated in the fighting. Every gain in ground made the attacking line of the divisions shorter and increased the power of their thrust. On 26th May the Soviet units were completely mixed up together and no longer under the control of their commanders, a last big attempt to break out having failed on the previous day. The Commander-in-Chief of the 57th Army shot himself to avoid being taken prisoner and the Commander-in-Chief of the 6th Army was killed in battle. The fighting with detached remnants and the combing of the battlefield lasted only a few days longer, and then the annihilation of 20 rifle divisions, 7 cavalry divisions and 14 tank brigades was over. The enemy's casualties were again extremely heavy as a result of his desperate attempts to break out and the waves of German attacks from the air. 240,000 prisoners were taken, 2,026 guns, 1,249 tanks and 538 planes were destroyed or captured

How an attempt at flight ended

The drivers of the Soviet tanks had maps of Germany with them, but they were not familiar with their own country. Near Tolotshin on the Drut, these gigantic Soviet tanks, each weighing 42 tons, in attempting to break through the enveloping German forces, ran into the marshy land near the river where they finished wretchedly by sticking in the mud. Whilst the Soviet soldiers thus fall into the natural traps of their own country, the German advance continues past all obstacles according to plan.
Photograph: PK. Huschke

Flight
and
advance

A bridge is thrown across the Velikaia. *Near Opotshka, on the other side of the Latvian frontier, the retreating Soviet soldiers attempted to hold up the German advance by blowing up the large bridge. Covered by the artillery, a unit of the SS on active service quickly throws a makeshift bridge across the river and the advance continues. The German soldier remains at the heels of the fleeing enemy and forces him to the decisive struggle*   *Photograph: PK. SS Baumann*

Farther and farther into the land of the Soviets

The great battle of Bialystok and Minsk has been brought to a victorious conclusion — the cavalry vanguards of the German armies are now pushing forward far ahead of the infantry in pursuit of the enemy.   Photograph: PK. Gronefeld

In the early hours of the morning, *the General can be found bending over his maps on his observation post in the Russian forest. Yet a "map general" is the last thing he is, for this commander can be seen almost everywhere and his face is quite familiar to all his men*

Guderian everywhere

A "Signal" report by PK. Hanns Hubmann

Not only in the vast regions where German arms are supreme but throughout the whole world General Guderian, the "father of the German tanks," the "steel Ziethen," has become an almost legendary figure. In all the theatres of war and now also on the Eastern Front, the feared and admired sign "G" on thousands of tanks and war vehicles is surrounded by undying fame. Wherever this undaunted soldier, to whom the Führer recently awarded the Oak Leaves to the Knight's Cross, appears among his soldiers, he is greeted by an enthusiasm which is ready even to face the jaws of Hell

He has put in a sudden appearance. *The General's rapid comings and goings in the various sectors of his extensive command have long since become proverbial. He is here seen discussing the situation with the Tank Corps General Geyr von Schweppenburg (left) and a few minutes later...*

Strategy by the side of the road. *In Roslav, which has been captured by his tank divisions, the General discusses the operations of large units with one of his generals*

... **Guderian's light car once more provides the well-known spectacle** *of the "father of the tanks" darting through the teeming activity on the line of advance past his troops' vehicles towards the front*

General Guderian's car *followed by the commander's tank has cautiously picked its way across the wreckage of an emergency bridge which the heavy tanks cannot yet pass. The journey continues through country where the enemy are still lurking*

With the tank vanguard. *The General has reached the foremost tank column which is very close to the enemy. The Tank Corps men of the light advance guard are reporting to him. Reinforcements are urgently required in order to close the ring round the Soviets, and the General...*

... **gives the necessary orders** *to the wireless operator in the accompanying tank. They are immediately transferred into code and are soon on their way through the ether*

The reinforcements have arrived, *the attack can commence. The tanks spread out fanwise across the country and may come up against the enemy at any moment. The "steel Ziethen" will then climb into his car and, as always, will be found there where the battle rages at its fiercest*

Wedding ceremony without the bride—6 miles from the enemy

A short ceremony behind the lines. The battery's heavy guns point their silent barrels towards the sky. A young corporal steps forward from among his comrades. The divisional commander officiates at the ceremony and confirms the solemn act by shaking hands

Photograph: PK. front correspondent Artur **Grimm**

The male population of Pavlovsk, has assembled in front of the former summer residence of the Czar Paul I order to register under the German administration. All available workers are required to repair the worst damage done during the war and to bring in the harvest

In front of the old palaces in Soviet Russia

A Soviet engineer and a farm labourer show their papers to the German interpreter when they come to register

The Alexander Palace in Dietskoie Selo (formerly Zarskoie Selo), the summer palace of the last Czar, fell undamaged into German hands but was later senselessly bombarded and damaged by Soviet long-range artillery Photographs: PK. front correspondent Hanns Hubmann

The great silence is broken

In and around Smolensk the comrades relate . . .

Special report for the "Signal" by PK Hanns Hubmann

"Signal's" special correspondent writes: "The people in Smolensk gain confidence when they see my camera. It is a rare event for them to be photographed and they get a lot of fun from it. I come across most of them in the neighbourhood of the German field kitchen. I like the old man with the beard. He immediately comes up to me and says: 'I am not a Bolshevik!' And to prove it he pulls out a small crucifix from beneath his ragged shirt. Ivan Rosanov is 75 years old. In order not to starve, this former builder's labourer had to work as a night watchmann and earned 100 roubles a month at the job. Konstantin Vusum, a labourer working on the railway, his friend, is 47 years old, married, with two children. 'I earn 172 roubles a month,' he relates. 'My family lived in one room and we ate groats, potatoes and bread, but had not sufficient for the whole month. We were always hungry for the last four or five days!'"

"Ivan Ivanovitch Tchimskov smiles at me when he realizes that I have no intention of taking the treasures away from him which he is carrying in a sack on his shoulder—potatoes and bread which he begged from the German soldiers for himself and his parents. He is 23 years old, a 'tcherno rabotchi' or unskilled labourer, a 'black workman' is the term used in the Soviet State, and was employed as an extra hand on building work earning 120 roubles a month. He lives with his parents and owns a pair of patched trousers as well as a ragged jacket which was given to him. His best article of clothing is his shirt, but he has only one. His friend comes from Tula and was condemned to do forced labour on an aerodrome in Smolensk, because in Tula he had twice arrived late for work"

"I particulary noticed these two young girls on account of their good clothes and the way their hair was done. Kira Safkina (left), who is 19 years old and a medical student, even speaks a little German. She has relatives in Cologne and is probably of German origin. She asks me if it would be possible for her to continue her studies in Germany after the war. Her father was a surveyor in Smolensk but fell into disfavour in 1937. The O.G.P.U. fetched him away and his family has not heard of him since. The mother goes to work in order to enable her daughter to study"

"The lad with the cap decorated with beads is a schoolboy, Basil Popokov. He is 13 years old and the son of a workman in a weaving factory. He lives with his parents and six brothers and sisters in two rooms. He is in a hurry to get home as the German soldiers have given him some bread. I let him run off, but he comes back again and asks if it is true that the boys in Germany have a fine uniform and their own leather belt with their own dagger, that they are allowed to wander throughout Germany and to sleep in their own tents on the way. Yes, it is true. 'Their own leather belt with their own dagger?' he asks several times in surprise.

"The 'specialist' Szepan Sverlotch together with his wife earns 900 roubles a month. "You can see by our clothes how far it went. I was able to take my wife to the pictures once a month. We technicians were always afraid of being condemned for sabotage, for whenever anything went wrong with a machine, we were responsible. It is a good thing that you have come. Of course, we have to suffer from the war, but we hope that you will soon have smashed Bolshevism"

Across the river. *Pioneers have thrown a bridge across the river, and the first companies advance into enemy territory*

A young lieutenant
snaps his own baptism of fire

A young lieutenant is leading his platoon into action for the first time. It is his baptism of fire, and his whole attention is concentrated on the engagement. He is cool enough, however, to take his colour camera with him. "Signal" here publishes a report of the encounter the various phases of which the young lieutenant photographed

The distant thunder of the guns has been going on for seven hours—and still we have to wait. The pioneers have not yet finished the bridge across the river somewhere on the Eastern Front. At last everything is ready. The two companies to attack before us begin to advance and we follow some distance behind. The bridge made of newly sawn timber stands out white against the green of the bank beyond. With almost exaggerated care the pioneers nail on the railing ... As we march through the meadows by the riverside, I compose a better melody for our new company song.

Suddenly we are met by several bursts of M.G. fire. It has begun! We throw ourselves flat on the grass with our eyes on the companies in front of us. The

Under fire! *We have only gone a few hundred yards when we receive our baptism of fire. My platoon takes cover and waits for further orders*

The huts on the edge of the wood are our objective. *Scattered over a wide front, the companies get ready to attack*

Soviet barrage. *The camera caught the moment when
a ricocheting grenade exploded in the air (yellow smudge)*

meadows slope gently upwards towards a wood in front of which the farmhouses are scattered. The company commander's order is: The farmhouses at the edge of the wood, rapid fire! I look round me: my platoon has extended to right and left, the other platoons are advancing rapidly — a thrilling picture!

The enemy M.G. fire becomes sharper. Then suddenly the air is full of the screaming, howling and exploding of shells: fountains of earth are thrown up into the air and splinters hiss around us. It is Soviet artillery barrage. We

dash through just as coolly as on the parade ground. Strange how often I have imagined what my baptism of fire would be like and what my feelings would be — and now that the moment has come I scarcely realize it, for every nerve and fibre is concentrated on the development of the action . . .

We reach the "village" and see Soviet steel helmets moving about on the grey thatched roofs. "Set fire to the house to the left," I shout. A few bursts of M.G. fire are enough. The flames rise from the roof and the shooting stops. "They're running away!" my M. G. gunner ex-

claims with a beaming face. Now I see them too: greenish yellow figures making for the wood. "After them!" In less than no time we storm up the little hill and, keeping an eye on the wood, search the bushes behind the houses. We are interrupted by a strange droning—a formation of Soviet planes appears over the wood. Are they looking for us? No, they are moving west. The company sends a strong reconnaissance party into the wood, while we surround the houses on all sides. We see something moving on one of the roofs. There is no time for a search, so we throw hand

Led by the N.C.O., *the reconnaissance
party hurries through the "village."
They are covered by the M.G. on the right*

Smoking out the first islet of resistance. *The Soviets
have a great preference for farmhouses as battery positions, but
a few bursts of fire from the M.Gs. are enough to silence the guns*

The drone of Soviet planes is heard from behind the wall of smoke rising from the burning hut. The N. C. O. keeps watch and the soldier on the left takes cover

grenades through the windows. After the explosion, thick clouds of black smoke issue from the windows; there will be no more sniping from there ...

The reconnaissance troop returns. It reports the discovery of abandoned mortar positions and brings back a few prisoners. Towards evening the companies comb the whole wood and the next day we leave it far behind as we continue our irresistible advance.

After the attack. In the background, the company reserves are occupying the positions that have just been stormed, while in the foreground, the "souvenir snap" is being taken
Photographs: Lt. Brendel

"In this village, as in many others," relates the "Signal" reporter, "the men had heard that the retreating Soviet Russians were compelling all the male inhabitants to go with them. They therefore hid themselves in the dense forests in the vicinity, and reappeared after having heard that the Germans had occupied their village. They still stand about uncertain what to do, as they do not know what is to become of them . . ."

Peace has returned once more…

In a little Ukrainian village not far behind the battle-front, the peasants are resuming their peaceful occupations, although their village has been taken by the Germans

Pictorial report by PK. Arthur Grimm

"Everywhere are scattered the wrecks of farming implements and machinery wantonly destroyed by the Soviet Russians . . ."

". . . but it is not long before here and there the men begin to busy themselves repairing what they can. For instance, I saw how a threshing machine was put in order under the direction of a German technician"

"Then came the big surprise of the day. A German officer suddenly appeared who not only spoke perfect Ukrainian, but also designated the former deputy Kolchose leader as head of the village administration. The former leader of the Kolchose, a Soviet official, had fled. The printed paper, with the name of the new leader written in with pen and ink, and the official German seal made a deep impression on the peasants"

"The village seemed to a-wake to new life after a long illness. I saw one woman giving the outer walls of her house a new coat of paint..."

"... scarcely an hour later I saw the men of the village starting to cut the corn, not with reaping machines and tractors, but with scythes and even sickles, just as their fore-fathers had done more than a generation ago"

"... And as if to complete the picture, on the evening of the day on which I took these pictures, the cattle of the village, which had vanished as if by magic, began to put in an appearance. The peasants had driven them into the forest to prevent their falling into the hands of the Soviets. The young village lads were bringing these animals back to their stables. Far in the distance could still be heard the thunder of cannon, but into this little Ukrainian village peace had come once more . . ."

Tanks
in the
steppes

The tank advance guard halts somewhere in the wide Caucasian steppes. The close range reconnaissance plane transmits the enemy's position to them. (Picture on right). The tanks immediately move forward against the enemy who is well hidden in the tall steppe grass. As contact with the enemy may come unexpectedly at any moment, the tank grenadiers advance with them keeping well under cover out of the way of the defensive fire from the Russians. Exploding shells have set the dry steppe grass on fire at a number of places.

Tank No. 633 soon encounters a Russian anti-tank gun and puts it out of action. Whilst the tank grenadiers make prisoners of the survivors of the gun crew, the tank turns off to the left towards a new enemy

PK. Photographs:
Front Correspondent Artur Grimm

The great counter-attack. *Massed in hundreds of thousands, Timoshenko's armies, supported by swarms of tanks and heavy artillery, pressed against the German line to the south of Kharkov with the object of winning back that large industrial city. The Germans answered with a counter-attack by the infantry on a wide front which very soon repulsed the attacking lines and forward tanks of the Soviets throwing them back on to the main body*

How German infantry won the Battle of Kharkov

The ring round three Soviet armies is closed. *The hedged-in enemy is no longer able to carry out any strategical movements—all that can be expected is desperate attempts to escape from the hell in the pocket, which is exposed to a rain of bombs and shells. The German infantry bring their guns into position in rapidly constructed trenches, anti-tank guns are brought forward: now they can come . . .*

PK. Photographs: Front Correspondent Hähle

The mountain troops with the range-finder. *The soldier using the machine-gun in rugged and difficult terrain in mountain warfare requires an incomparably more all-round training than the machine-gunner fighting on normal terrain. Work with a range-finder in the steppes of Russia is, therefore, child's play for the mountain gunner, and his shots always hit their mark. "Wherever Hans measures, no grass can grow," say his comrades. In addition, Hans has the experience gathered in three campaigns behind him*

No. 1 gunner at the light grenade thrower. *He too has gone through a special course of training and is an expert on indirect fire. Light and medium artillery are much more important to the mountain troops than to the infantry. for mountain troops cannot always count on support from heavy artillery because of the terrain. Trained in sport like all mountain troops, No. 1 gunner carries his gun through Russia. A 25 mile march in the plains is, according to him, nothing in comparison with a climb with a heavy load such as he has exercised over and over again in his native mountains*

IN THE RIGHT PLACE
IN SPITE OF ALL

Mountain troops in the steppes

of Russia

60 Russian tanks in two days. *That is the record of a single division of mountain troops in one battle during the eastern campaign. Such a result is only possible if the fuses are adjusted with the painstaking exactitude of the mountain artillerymen who have studied in the school of indirect and high-angle firing*

Company sergeant-major Haslberger acts the madman. *Among the special qualities required of mountain troops even during their training are sharp intelligence and the power to make rapid decisions. Company sergeant-major Haslberger displayed both these faculties in a very special way on one occasion during this campaign. While reconnoitring the enemy line of dug-outs, he was surprised by Bolshevists. The situation seemed hopeless but he had an idea. Screaming wildly he danced towards the Bolshevists and before they could recover from their surprise he had discovered a trench in which he was able to escape from capture and bullets*

The pack animal driver. *Mountain troops have not only special equipment, they have also special animals for the transport of weapons and ammunition. These animals—either horses or a special breed of mule—must be hardy and satisfied with little. They must be able to endure snow and cold, rain, wind and sun. These are all qualities which can prove their worth in the Russian campaign even where there are no mountains. The pack animal drivers have learnt to take care of animals even before they became soldiers since they are, for the most part, mountain farmers from Styria, Carinthia, the Tyrol or Upper Bavaria*

PK. Photograph:
Front Correspondent Kempter

''When building up an army, the soldier's stomach comes first,'' *wrote Frederick the Great. The commander of the mountain troops division follows this maxim by inspecting the field kitchen before the day of battle has drawn to a close. And later, when the food is being distributed and the men say: "The soup tastes good, General!" the day is well and truly ended. The mountain troops have still something to do, it is true, that speaks just as highly for them as their soldierly deeds...*

The sixth meeting during this war between the Führer and the Duce took place on the Eastern Front. The invincible will of the German and Italian peoples to continue the struggle until victory is won and to give Europe a new and just order after this victory found its expression in these discussions

The Duce in the Führer's Headquarters

Mussolini greets the Commander-in-Chief of the Army, *General Field Marshal von Brauchitsch. The Duce also visited the Headquarters of Reich Marshal Göring and inspected one of the Italian divisons which are taking part in the struggle against Bolshevism*

Military discussions *took place as well as political. The Duce's suite included General Cavallero, the Chief of the Italian Army General Staff. This picture shows him (behind the two Heads of State) conversing with the Chief of the Supreme Army Command, General Field Marshal Keitel*

Photographs: PK. Middendorf (2), Presse Hoffmann

The Soviet Army Communiqué of 24th May: "Our troops have evacuated the Kerch Peninsula in perfect order and with their material intact..."

↑ Demolished by artillery and dive-bombers, *large masses of military vehicles are strewn over the marshy land on the Donets Front. They include tanks of British manufacture—a long journey to their destruction!*

A chaos of dead bodies and smashed material: *that is the picture provided by the beach at Kerch from where the remnants of the Bolshevist armies sought to save themselves by crossing the straits*

↓ PK. Photographs: Front Correspondent Wett

Priest and President

"Signal" visits the President of Slovakia, Dr. Tiso

A priest makes a tour of his parish — *the President of the Republic, Dr. Tiso. For the last 20 years he has known every house and every family in the little town of Banovce. Here he has remained in close contact with the people*

peasant's son at the head of a peasant state, a priest for whom a whole nation is his parish — that is Dr. Josef Tiso, the first President of the young Slovakian Republic. At the end of the Great War, he had just been appointed Professor of Catholic Theology at the University of Vienna. After a few months, however, he left the seclusion of his study for the political arena. While the revolution was in progress, he established in his native country the Slovakian National Council. Later, he was associated with the foundation of the Slovakian People's Party. When his comrade, Pater Hlinka, died, he succeeded him at its leader. While he was a member of the Parliament of the former Czechoslovakia, Tiso had ample opportunity to study the monstrosities of the Versailles system. The more political experience he gathered, the more energetically he fought for the independence of his people and for a reconstruction of Europe in accordance with its own laws

An austerehouse beside the grammar school in Banovce *is the home of the Slovakian President. Almost every Sunday he returns here from the capital. In Banovce Tiso founded a boys' school of which he has retained the headship even today*

Tiso's writing-desk *Many a sermon and many a political speech were written here before the dean left it in 1939 to go to Bratislava to take over the heavy responsibilities of the President of the young Slovakian state*

The President visits his grey-haired mother, *who lives in a village in the valley of the Waag, as often as his governmental duties permit. He was born in 1887, and from the very beginning, his mother has followed his career with maternal anxiety and pride*

The hospitable President *often gives receptions where his colleagues and friends can mingle freely with foreign visitors. At these reunions one can see guests in clerical attire, in peasant costume, lounge suits and in political uniforms. Right: the Leader of the Slovakian Youth, Aloyz Macek*

Right: This political veteran, formerly an uncompromising antagonist of the Czechs, today shows his people the only way which can lead to a happy future

The priest and the soldiers. *They are inspired by the common resolve to fight for the freedom of their nation and the integrity of their state. Twice already the Slovakian Army has fought side by side with the German forces: in 1939 against Poland and to-uay against Bolschevism*

Peasant girls welcome the President *and in accordance with the old custom offer him bread and salt. The white-haired man on the left is Dr Tuka, the Prime Minister, an old comrade of Tiso´s and a national martyr whom the Czechs once condemned to fifteen years' imprisonment*
Photographs: Bernd Lohse

THE FRONT AGAINST BOLSHEVISM

The significance of the campaign against Bolshevism quite clear: it does not aim at the protection of individual countries, for the existence of the whole of Europe s at stake. Men from almost every country on the Continent have recognized the stern necessity of the hour and been ready to act. They are fighting with Germany

Allies, Legionaries and Volunteer Corps of the Fighting S.S. in the struggle against Bolshevism

I. Allies on the Eastern Front

"It is not a problem of power politics which is being decided on this front, but the fate of 3,000 years of Western culture."
Count Ciano

ITALIANS

When the Bolshevists concentrated their armies on the German frontier, Italy declared her readiness to fight shoulder to shoulder with Germany in that struggle also. Her part in the successes on the southern sector of the Eastern Front will for ever be inscribed in the history of this campaign

FINNS The small, courageous, Finnish nation has been engaged for 25 years in an unceasing struggle against an enemy of superior strength who has menaced her liberty with espionage, sabotage, agitation, threats of force and finally by force itself. Finland has now recovered Karelia, which she had lost in the winter of 1939 to 1940, and now occupies strategically important points on Soviet Russian territory

HUNGARIANS

Hungary, like Finland, is one of those European states which long ago made bloody acquaintance with Bolshevism. Béla Kun's ConfederateGovernment in 1919 will never be forgotten. By joining in the struggle against the Soviet Union, Hungary has kept to her traditional policy of the preservation of European culture

RUMANIANS Under coercion from the Soviet Union, Rumania in June 1940 was forced to cede Bessarabia and North Bukovina. The Soviet Union was about to spread its tentacles over the whole of the Balkans. After outstanding deeds of valour at Odessa and Sevastopol, Rumania's troops are now fighting on the southern sector of the Eastern Front as far as the Caucasus

PK. Photographs: Front Correspondents Adendorf, Leher, Rauchwetter, Springmann, Gebauer, Volkmann, Schürer, Pfitzner, Brantsen

SLOVAKS

Slovakia's Army is fighting as an ally of the Axis Powers. In the battles on the Eastern Front it is defending the liberty recently gained by Slovakia and is fighting for its preservation in the first bloody encounter

II. Legionaries

and Eastern Legionaries

SPANIARDS

Shortly after the outbreak of the war against Bolshevism, Spain established a Volunteer Legion under the command of General Munoz Grande. As the "Blue Division" it took up arms on the Eastern Front against the old enemy, which shortly before had driven their homeland to the brink of destruction

WALLOONS

The Walloon Volunteer Corps, with which the leader of the Rexists, Léon Degrelle, (right) is fighting, took a decisive part after the Winter Campaign of 1941—1942 in the Battle of Kharkov, the crossing of the Don, the storming of Rostov and in the hostilities in the Kuban region

FRENCHMEN

The first French Legion was established at Versailles in 1941. Its numbers increased from month to month. Its operations on the Eastern Front, which have called for almost superhuman exertions, have been rewarded by glorious victories

CROATS

Apart from the Croat volunteers serving in the Army, members of the Air Force have also joined in the struggle. Many thousands of flights against the enemy and a large number of air victories are the result of their determination to contribute to the safeguarding of Europe

COSSACKS

This world-famous people of horsemen from the Lower Caucasus once more gives proof of its hereditary military virtues in the struggle against Red oppression

FROM TURKESTAN

The men of Turkestan are less famous for bold horsemanship than the Cossacks. Nevertheless these descendants of Genghis Khan belong to the best riders of the Asiatic steppes. Today they are riding against Moscow

VOLGA TATARS

From time immemorial the Volga Tatars have been renowned as daring warriors. Their volunteer legion, equipped with German arms, is now fighting for the liberation of their people

ASERBAIDJANS

The Aserbaidjans from the Eastern Caucasus were given military training by German soldiers and are now fighting as volunteers against the Soviet enemies of their nation

ARMENIANS

The Armenians, ancient inhabitants of the Caucasus, have preserved their national character in the face of all tyranny. The volunteers in the picture alongside are receiving military instruction

GEORGIANS

The history of the Georgians goes back over two thousand years. This ancient, freedom loving people, too, is taking part in the struggle against the former despots

NORTH CAUCASIANS

In the North Caucasian Legion volunteers from all the North Caucasian peoples have enlisted. They, too, are now fighting in German uniforms and with German weapons

III. Volunteers in the Fighting S.S.

"Norway would be degraded as a nation if she were not present where Europe's fate is being decided."
Quisling

DANES *Denmark's volunteers have been fighting on the northern sector since 20th July 1941. The spirit of these men is expressed by the words of one of their leaders: "Europe is at stake—it is impossible for us to stand aside inactive"*

NORWEGIANS *During the first three weeks of Europe's defensive struggle against Bolshevism, more Norwegians volunteered than during the first three months of the Finnish War of 1939 to 1940. Many more thousands of young Norwegians are today serving on the northern and central sectors of the Eastern Front. Some ski battalions are composed entirely of Norwegians*

FLEMINGS *When the leader of the Flemish National Association, Staf de Clerq, called upon the Flemings to take up the fight against Bolshevism, his appeal met with an enthusiastic response. Today the Flemings are serving at the front in their own legion and in the units of the Fighting S.S.*

NETHER-LANDERS *Many young Netherlanders had already joined the S.S. standards "Westland" and "Nordwest" when the special Volunteer Legion "Niederland" was formed. Their commander is the former Chief of the General Staff of the Netherlandish Army, Lieutenant-General Seyffardt. On the southern sector of the Eastern Front, two companies of this legion captured a whole Soviet regiment*

After two years of Soviet rule: the first divine service!

In Ptycza near Dubno, in one of the districts occupied by the Soviets after the war in Poland and now liberated by the German troops, the population has once more been able to assist at a divine service . . .

Photograph :
PK. - front - correspondent Wagner

Everyone came to have the fruits of the fields blessed as in olden times. Bolshevism, which took everything else from them, was not able to kill their faith. At last the hour for which they had waited so confidently has come: they can thank God for their delivery from the Bolshevist yoke

One of the few priests who managed to escape from the Soviets holds the service before a holy picture, an oleograph which was sent specially from Warsaw. The vestments worn were buried secretly when the Soviets came. The church itself suffered badly during the big tank battles, but the faithful see nothing of all this wretchedness

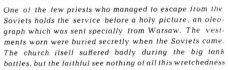

Only the bare walls of the church remain standing. It is open to the sky, and wind and rain come in through the broken windows

That was the first service! Many came with their simple vessels to get holy water. Everybody knows that the church will be rebuilt more splendid than it was before

A section of the 35 kilometres long "Stalingrad Inferno"

The extensive factories of Stalingrad stretch along the bank of the Volga to a distance of 35 kilometres, for they all seek the proximity of the river. The Russians had converted this town of more than a million inhabitants into a fortress and defended it factory by factory, street by street, house by house. The German Army has systematically attacked and captured one pill-box after another. Our photograph shows a dive-bomber attack on a Stalingrad factory. The plane is just pulling out of the dive, the falling bomb can be seen obliquely under it. "Signal's" special account of the fight for Stalingrad begins on page 11 of this number   PK. Photograph: Front Correspondent Benno Wundshammer

That was
GENERAL WINTER

How they bore it and overcame it

'Signal' here publishes the description by a front correspondent of the winter campaign in the East, which is unique, because it summarizes all the courage and endurance demanded of the soldiers during these six month. It was written in February, at a time, therefore, when the severest winter in the East for more than 100 years still prevailed in its full intensity. Today, when the reader has this description in his hands, the thought with which it concludes has been fulfilled: "When the gleaming ice of the Donets thaws, when the river once more flows to the sea, the signal for the new advance will resound. And the knowledge that the ice will thaw inspires and supports us during these weeks, wherever we are, in villages or towns, on the hills or in the plain." ... General Winter has been borne and overcome.

The roads over which we have passed have changed as many times as the number of months the campaign has lasted. Their aspect has altered in the same way as scenery changes the stage. An idyll lying picturesquely at rest among broad fields of maize and groves of overripe sunflowers would suddenly become angry and challenge to open battle. Who can count the men on whom it inflicted physical agony, or the vehicles which came to grief through the impassability of its roads, or the draught animals which died under its onslaught? No soldier any longer speaks of what it was like in the dry dust of summer swarming with myriads of insects or in the grim and boundless mud of autumn, for the snow lying yards deep, beneath which the remains of the victims of that time sleep, the skeletons of dead horses and the scrap metal of wrecked lorries provides sufficient new cares for topics of conversation in the evenings in the Soviet billets.

The yarns exchanged by the comrades in the flickering light of the 'lampa for kerosene,' as the primitive paraffin lamps are called in the gibberish forming the soldiers' usual attempt at Russian, continue uninterruptedly like the apparently endless thread of the distaff. The icy wind rattles the doors, dogs pass whining beneath the windows, the cocks in the neighbouring stable quarrel restlessly. The words come slowly, and experiences form the background of every sentence spoken. Not all of these men have looked into the white of the enemy's eye, but every one of them, riflemen and gunners, anti-tank gunners and sappers, wireless signallers and riders, but above all the drivers of the waggons and lorries have fought against the country s neglected roads as though they were dangerous enemy weapons. On days when the sticky mud oozed over the top of the long boots without its being allowed to hold up the advance, during hours of bitterest cold and at times when the tyres burst, the respect for every separate mile was born. What meant little in France or even in Serbia and Greece is now remembered with the clarity of deep-rooted experience—that a mile has 1760 yards and that 1760 yards mean more than 1760 paces.

You have to talk of the roads when you talk of this war. And when those who have covered these roads hesitate in the telling of their experiences, and become silent thinking over the events in that chapter of their life, you need only look at their weatherbeaten faces. Their eyes reflect their sufferings, and he who has eyes to see discovers that these sufferings were very great. And he knows, therefore, that the stories would have not been related to the end even by morning when the brightly twinkling stars fade.

Six hundred and fifty miles separate us from the frontier of Germany. Six hundred and fifty miles of road in the Soviet Union.

The river

The Donets is not a really tremendous river. We have never learnt how long its course is or how broad it is at its widest point, because the small books of reference from which we obtain our knowledge of the geographical data of the Soviet Union deal with it only summarily. As far as we are able to judge for ourselves, we can only say that where we have seen it, it is unimpressive when compared with the Dnieper.

And yet we experienced a certain feeling of relief when we penetrated into the region of the Donets, without realizing, however, that it was the river which gave us this feeling of content-ment. At first we thought that the road wished to propitiate us. It was firm and dry at that time, and described a sudden curve as though it were just as tired of the oppressively monotonous plain as our eyes. We glanced up and saw villages which no longer rose out of the flat ground, but crept and strayed over the slopes of the hills rising from the plain. And then we smiled at one another without any particular reason. Or was that a reason for smiling because over yonder, on the further bank, there was a wood? A mighty ribbon of luxurious trees, mostly ash, ran along by the water flowing calmly and power-fully towards the south. We followed it, for it led to the industrial region with its cities.

That was before the snow came down from the clouds throwing a mantle over the plain and the gentle slopes. Since then the hoar frost has hidden the dark green shimmer of the woods. The river no longer moves, the ice goes right down to the river bed. If the name of the river is mentioned, we see a map of the front in our mind's eye. The Donets has become its symbol, even although it does not follow its course. If you wanted to keep an exact record of the swings of the pendulum by which the front approaches or withdraws from the river, it would be necessary to go to our Army Staff H.Q. every evening when the Intelligence Officer and the Staff Officer mark the foremost lines on the map. But it would not be worth while, for the night can bring a change in what was true in the morning.

Villages

The front touches and embraces many villages. Every single house is occupied by soldiers. What was instinctively avoided during the Great War and what has since been taught as a tactical law cannot be applied in the present phase of the campaign: the principle that villages and towns should be avoided during war. From 1914 to 1918 the outskirts of inhabited places were feared because they provided the enemy artillery with good targets and thus increased the casualties. Our troops were faced with the choice between

Relief forward! *All through the long Russian winter the relieving infantry fought their way forward to the front lines through the blinding snowstorm*

Photographs: PK. Front Correspondents Hanns Hubmann and Captain Puschner

being exposed to the fire of Soviet guns on the one hand and the cold on the other. This winter the cold was the greater danger.

The villages have thus become the

On to the front! *All through the long winter supply columns advanced through the deep snow along the never ending roads leading to the Eastern Front*

objectives of the fighting. They consist of wretched peasant dwellings made of clay, but the same soldiers who until the beginning of the winter had entered them only with feelings of disgust, now

defend these clay hovels like a costly possession. It is no longer important whether they consist of only one room, and it does not matter if every corner is full of vermin, the stove and the roof are all-important, they provide the warmth. To be able to sit among the ragged peasants from the co-operative farms, whose only possessions are a little cracked crockery and a few dilapidated articles of furniture, even although the mice scamper across the clay floor in swarms, is a real blessing when you have lain in a trench for hours or been out on patrol. In the steam which rises from the sourish smelling pumpkin soup simmering on the grate, you feel that the blood is still flowing in your veins and there is still life in your limbs. Hundreds and thousands of companies have great difficulty in keeping these wretched quarters habitable. Wood and coal are necessary for that purpose. The mines, however, are concentrated in restricted areas. If you leave the river, the trees disappear. What is more than about a mile away is unreachable. The garden fences can be burnt, but they are soon used up. Often the only remaining possibility is indefatigably to feed the jaws of the stove with straw in order to prevent the fire from going out. The troops in the villages are cut off from the others. A telephone wire connects them with the organization of the division — it brings the orders. Everything beyond that is in the realm of uncertainty. When the wind whirls up the snow so that the drifts lie across

the roads like white table-topped mountains, no supply column arrives punctually and the supply line may be cut for several days. The men are always prepared for that, as such situations have already arisen more than once. Then they bake their own bread. I shall never forget seeing two infantrymen, already getting on in years, sitting in a peasant's kitchen turning the handle of an old coffee grinder in order to grind flour for themselves.

It is particularly bad when for a whole day or more there is no tobacco. How often our soldiers have smoked the dried stalks of sunflowers can be estimated only with difficulty, but in any case, it was very often.

Towns

Their names are familiar to us as though we had always known them. And we find our way about these towns as though things had never been different. During the last few months, it is true, we have been now in this town, now in that town, but that we can move about in them so confidently is explained chiefly by the fact that any two of them are as like as two peas. That one town, for example, has a grotesque cubist monument and that another has a miserable tramway which runs along one straight stretch for ten minutes and nothing else, these features are soon forgotten. But the impression of swollen villages crowded together round slag heaps, hoisting towers and blast furnaces remains. Low, jerry-built houses, all herded together, extend confusedly into the country. They are inhabited by the workers in the mines and iron works, the majority of the population which has been attracted by the prospect of employment. It is only in the vicinity of the stations that buildings of more than one storey are encountered, two, three or even half a dozen concrete boxes in which the administration was housed.

It seems incredible at first that there are more than 100,000 souls in each of these towns. In the end you discover that this fact is not so fantastic after all, for each of the little houses contains about ten people, that is to say two or even three families. The housing shortage has assumed proportions which to us appear tremendous. The result is that billets in towns are usually no better than those in the villages. The restricted space at the disposal of the working families now has to suffice for two or three soldiers as well. To find a bed or a suitable bench is a great stroke of fortune, usually the men have to sleep on the floor. The greatcoats and tunics are hung up on nails driven into the wall with great pains. They are always covered with the bluish-white dust from the whitewash, for it comes off wherever you go.

Indomitable! *He braved storm, Siberian cold, and heavy snow drifts — for he knew that spring would come again*

With the exception of the asphalted main road connecting these towns, all the streets are unpaved. There are no shops, no restaurants, no public houses. It is impossible to buy anything anywhere. Wherever possible, the Soviets took away with them or destroyed all supplies and all industrial plant. Many buildings are burnt out and the forlorn bare walls gape disconsolately to the sky. We move through the streets from one office to another on army duty only with feelings of aversion. The inhabitants stand around in gloomy silence killing time. They offer to do every conceivable kind of job in exchange for a piece of bread or a few shreds of tobacco.

Sometimes a film is shown or a news reel. The news reel is usually too old to satisfy our hunger for news, but for us it is an experience to see well dressed people in the background or somewhere on the scene who laugh or move about quietly, women such as we know and love, but have not met since we marched across Germany's frontiers. In the films, too, it is not only the story which is full of interest, but it is also derived from the spectacle of familiar things, of that which everybody in the field-grey audience used to accept as something obvious, from the pictures of civilization. After such

hours as these, conversation is more alive and the soldiers again feel more consciously the contrasts of their present surroundings.

The wireless is the other connecting link. When we unexpectedly hear a few bars of Schubert or Mozart, we involuntarily hold our breath. It lasts quite a long time before we forget them again. Others are moved when they hear one of the latest song hits. But often enough the sets are silent. It is difficult to obtain the current, because our technical units have first had to get the electricity works going again and do their best to repair the long-distance cables. No wonder that the current then often only suffices to light the army offices. That imposes a rigid economy. The radio may only be switched on for a short time and at certain hours.

And light is indispensable, because it is needed for the writing of letters; candles and paraffin lamps are scarce even if they are at all obtainable.

Attacks

About 13th January the New Year's Day of the Orthodox Church, the Ukrainian who had learnt a little German as a prisoner during the Great War, said that the worst of the winter was now over. The temperature would soon begin to rise again and there would be no more severe frosts. At that time the thermometer registered exactly 68⁰ Fahrenheit of frost. The next morning the street door seemed to have been frozen up, it had grown another 28⁰ colder and during the course of the next few hours the mercury fell another 9⁰.

Simultaneously the Soviet attacks increased in intensity. The hardest part of this campaign now began for the troops in the front line. The enemy stormed our positions with increasingly larger forces, and never before had the Bolshevists deliberately sacrificed men to such an extent, in order to gain possession of the smallest tactical positions. When one battalion had been annihilated in an attack on the sector held by one company, it lasted only a few hours before a second wave, just as strong as the first, dashed forwards. This was repeated three and four times, and it happened not only at one spot, but on our right and left flanks as well. It continually became more evident that Timoshenko saw a hope dawn in the ice and snow of winning back what had been lost of the Donets Basin, the most important industrial area in the Soviet Union. He knew that at this time we could not oppose him with the entire superiority of our mechanization. He set his hopes on the dourness of the masses at his disposal and on his cavalry.

Here and there our troops were obliged to withdraw in the face of superior numbers. When the last German bullet had been fired, the Bolshevists were able to gain ground. But they had to pay an unusually high price for every square yard. It is not possible to establish a normal standard of comparison, but the proportion of 1:10 in the casualties was rather the average than the exception. The difficulties experienced by the other side were shown by the fact that these offensives could often be carried out only with regiments which had been hurriedly formed and sometimes were inadequately trained. Machine gunners have often witnessed horrible scenes. Particularly during the night fighting, the Soviets often ran into their field of fire drunk, throwing their arms round one another and yelling, waving their weapons wildly in the air. The dead were afterwards strewn over the fields of snow like limestones. Their swollen, expressionless faces stared

out from beneath their white painted steel helmets. The statements made by prisoners showed that the casualties with which we reckoned had to be even further increased, as the cold put a proportion of the Soviet troops out of action even before the first shot was fired. They were forced to form up in the open for the attack and to move forward slowly towards our lines in the open. They literally froze to the ground, for the villages were in our possession.

Naturally our losses were also bitter. But the superiority of our fighting troops, based upon their thorough training is beyond description.

The spirit

What is the spirit like, is a question often asked in the letters sent to the front. The soldiers read this sentence which recurs in an innumerable variety of forms and when they try to give a satisfying answer, they wonder what is really meant by it. They would prefer to answer: "We have no spirit." But that might be misunderstood. And so they merely say: "We are in good spirits," knowing full well that they are leaving much unsaid which ought to be said in this connexion.

Not only do nearly 1,250 miles separate them from home, but also many months. They have changed whilst they have been mastering the roads and surviving time. Their uniforms are patched and the field-grey, which was originally deep in colour, has faded in the dust, rain, mud and snow. No quartermaster in a barracks at home would issue them again. Their underwear is torn, but they manage as best they can, for it does not matter what it looks like. This campaign is not a kit inspection.

They have learnt a great deal on the march and during the journey to the Donets. What once seemed to them to be of importance no longer affects them and that to which they formerly scarcely paid attention has become important. They now cling only to what has stood the test of this life, to what appeared to them just as certain yesterday as it does today. This first manifests itself in their everyday actions, but it also affects their opinions, feelings, and intentions. Regarded in this way, their spirits seem to them to be something unstable, something without substance. They realize that in circumstances which do not penetrate so far under the surface of existence, they can have a favourable or unfavourable effect on their state of well-being. For a long time they have been incapable of reacting in such a manner. They are on familiar terms with the inexorableness of this war, and there is no interruption in this feeling as there was perhaps in France where hours were sometimes spent in cosy quarters with a bottle of exquisite wine. They are satisfied now if their most elementary needs are met, if they have something to eat, something to smoke and a roof over their heads. If the post arrives now and then, they are grateful, and when they read what their wives, mothers and friends wrote several weeks before, they experience something in the nature of a holiday.

But we cannot speak of good or low spirits. The certainty has become ingrained in every one of them, from private to general, that we must stay in this country until the enemy has been finally conquered. Until then there will not be much leave, if there is any at all. For here, there is only one railway connexion, and that they know is fully taken up with transports of wounded and ammunition trains. They have the preference. The soldiers' wishes are of secondary importance.

They do not grow sentimental when they consider that fact and even those who used to like high-sounding phrases are now silent. They are faced by a grim alternative. They have to master it alone and in the squad, in the platoon and in the company. Every one has to identify himself with the historical task, and not one fails to do so, because his own destiny is also embraced by it.

Such convictions are not formed in a day. They develop gradually, but they take possession of a person in the same way as the eyes become accustomed to a light. For they alone hold what is most important. Everything else is secondary to them, and everything else will be solved when the armies reach their objectives. That will be a hard job of work. And he who works hard will primarily feel the earnestness of work and will be obliged to keep his high spirits within bounds.

The signal

For days past the sky has been as grey as water colour. It has ceased snowing, but the thermometer has stuck at minus 36⁰ Fahrenheit. The fighting continues with undiminished intensity. But there is also good news. At L., where there were only supply columns, transports that is to say, the Soviets were repulsed. A company which had been completely encircled annihilated a battalion attacking it and then fought its way out through the ring of Bolshevists suffering only few casualties. Above all, however, fresh tanks are arriving and today assault guns set out for the front. The Soviet air attacks, which were repeated almost every hour, have become less frequent since our bombers and chasers have made their appearance.

The soldier sees the front only in the sector with which he is concerned. He knows only about the enemy facing him. He has to fight out the battle with them and has no time to pay any attention to anything beyond that. And we notice and feel that our counterattack is growing stronger. The pocket in which the Soviets were attempting to encircle the industrial region has a number of large holes in it. The ring will not be closed, it will be broken. Hard days are still ahead of us, but the winter will not last for ever.

In the meantime supplies are ceaselessly being moved up to the front. Small shaggy horses are straining in the harness as they drag the sledges laden with ammunition and provisions. These columns used to be motorized. Now, however, the lorries lie behind the lines, the engines have been taken down, pistons are being ground, and spare parts fitted. The soldiers, who are now cracking the whips in order to urge on the horses, will again be sitting at the wheel . . . For the days are falling like drops into the great urn of time. Some of them pass quickly, others seem to be never-ending. But the wheel keeps on turning. This winter is a season of our life through which we must pass in the same way as we must pass through the other difficult times with which we are burdened as individuals.

When the gleaming ice of the Donets thaws, when the river once more flows to the sea, the signal for the new advance will resound. And the knowledge that the ice will thaw inspires and supports us during these weeks, wherever we are, in villages or towns, on the hills or in the plain.

On the Eastern Front, February 1942.

Front Correspondent Hubert Neun